FIRST
GENERATIONS

WOMEN
IN
COLONIAL
AMERICA

FIRST GENERATIONS

WOMEN
IN
COLONIAL
AMERICA

CAROL BERKIN

CONSULTING EDITOR: ERIC FONER

HILL AND WANG

A DIVISION OF FARRAR, STRAUS AND GIROUX

NEW YORK

Hill and Wang
A division of Farrar, Straus and Giroux
18 West 18th Street, New York 10011

Copyright © 1996 by Carol Berkin

Published in 1996 by Hill and Wang
First paperback edition, 1997

The Library of Congress has cataloged the hardcover edition as follows:
Berkin, Carol.
    First generations : women in colonial America / Carol Berkin ;
consulting editor, Eric Foner.
        p. cm.
    Includes bibliographical references and index.
    ISBN 0-8090-4561-3
    1. Women—United States—History—17th century. 2. Women—
United States—History—18th century. I. Foner, Eric. II. Title.
HQ1416.B43   1996
305.42'0973'09032—dc20   96-11686

Paperback ISBN-13: 978-0-8090-1606-8
Paperback ISBN-10: 0-8090-1606-0

Designed by Abby Kagan

www.fsgbooks.com

P1

TO HANNAH AND MATTHEW

PREFACE

THIS BOOK, like those old Hollywood epics, has been over ten years in the making. While it may have been an editor's nightmare, it has proven to be a scholar's dream, for the field of early American women's history has flourished during my decade of work on *First Generations*. Had this study been speedily completed in 1985, it would have been based on books and articles that could fit into a commodious briefcase—with room left over for a set of freshman exams. Fortunately, life intervened with such diversions as babies, family crises, stints in college administration, and assorted writing projects—delays which allowed me time to observe and to relish a growing literature on colonial women that has added new pieces to the puzzle of our past each day. The long delay certainly made the task of writing this book more difficult, but it made it more interesting as well.

Over the past few years I have asked my students to serve as guinea pigs for this project—assigning them to read Xeroxes of chapters as soon as they came off my printer. Their critiques have been instructive, not the least because in their responses two aspects of the same issue emerged. On one hand, many students were concerned about the tentative voice in which I often speak in this book. They told me that I should not qualify my interpretation with "perhaps" and "it is possible that." They urged me to speak with authority, if not for my own sake, then for the sake of the discipline whose reputation I put at risk by admitting that we do not know the answers to critical questions, that scholars often disagree, that we have failed to consider important factors, or that we have let subjectivity and presentist concerns influence our reading of the past. On the other hand, an equal number of students expressed concern that the whole did not emerge from its parts, that there was no closure to the topic; in short, that the book was not a synthesis.

These concerns, no matter how delicately phrased by students who were both politic and polite, deserve to be addressed. I will offer here a few observations that may also serve as explanations. First, historians are perhaps the last of the independent artisans. They write about what interests them and employ the methods and theories they know best or that seem most appropriate. They firmly reject collective agendas no matter what group suggests them and no matter what pressing problems those agendas might promise to resolve. While these are perhaps endearing qualities, fierce individualism does have certain consequences. The literature upon which *First Generations* is based has not produced a body of knowledge that is equitably distributed across time or space. For example, the role of white women in the American Revolution has been the topic of countless books, producing anecdotes and accounts so extensive that it occasionally seems every woman of the era can enjoy that "fifteen minutes of fame" Andy Warhol once promised. Women of the first half of the eighteenth century, however, have failed to capture scholars' fancies, just as women of the middle colonies are virtual historical orphans when compared to their New England neighbors. Similarly, many studies on the same issue or topic rely on such differing sources that a generalization is often problematic and sometimes downright foolhardy. In scholarship, as in fruit bowls, pears and apples sit side by side: studies of New England marriage patterns based on diaries and letters and studies of Chesapeake marriage patterns drawn

from demographic data are equally valid, but they do not allow
for a conclusive comparison. Finally, no collective portrait of colonial women can emerge as long as our knowledge of European
women in the colonial period remains so much deeper, broader,
and more particular than our knowledge of Indian or African-
American women. What we know cannot be placed with enough
precision upon the grid of race, class, and gender for an appropriately complex picture to emerge. Of course, a sensible scholar
trembles when she announces an absence of sources. No matter
how diligent she has been, no matter how dogged her investi-
gation of journals and books, she is certain to have overlooked
important new works or significant older ones. Indeed, just as
I completed this manuscript, word came that Mary Beth Norton had finished what promises to be a monumental work on
seventeenth-century women and a publisher forwarded a dissertation to me that makes subtle but important revisions in our
knowledge of inheritance laws. The field keeps moving, yet the
scholar must produce a freeze frame when she sits down to write.
For these reasons, I have retained the tentative voice with which
I began this project. And for these reasons, I have not tried to
force pattern or order on a field when it does not yet exist.

Women's history has come a long way since the days when
scholars were expected to teach courses that ran, roughly, from
"Eve to Gloria Steinem." Still, we colonial historians continue to
be asked to cover almost two hundred years of women's experience in about fourteen weeks. I kept this in mind as I organized
this book. Whenever possible, I ordered the chapters chronolog-
ically, and structured the narrative to move across time from contact and colonization, to what scholars call the maturation of
colonial society, through protest and revolution, and, finally, to
the decades of the early republic.

Although chronology might be said to be the frame for *First
Generations*, the book also reflects a commitment to locate women
along the axes of race, region, and social class. Where it seems
appropriate and useful, therefore, I have written a chapter along
the lines of one of these categories. Thus, seventeenth-century

white women's experiences are divided by region in several chapters and the lives of Native American and African-American women are explored in separate chapters. Within each chapter on European women, I have tried to refract women's lives through the prism of class, and I have attended to life-cycle issues as well.

The resulting volume is divided into seven chapters and an epilogue. In Chapter 1, "Immigrants to Paradise: White Women in the Seventeenth-Century Chesapeake," I portray immigrant and creole white women in Virginia and Maryland, and describe the adaptations their society made in family structures and inheritance patterns in response to two unusual conditions: the demographic disasters of the seventeenth century and the skewed sex ratio produced by an overwhelmingly male labor force. I also analyze the extent to which married women and widows enjoyed greater authority within the family and greater control of its economic resources than the women in the more stable patriarchal white families of New England.

Chapter 2, "Goodwives and Bad: New England Women in the Seventeenth Century," explores the daily life of New England women as wives, mothers, and household producers in a colonial setting. Here, I examine the multiple roles married women played as "notable housewives," and the separate and overlapping spheres of women and men. This chapter looks closely at women's role within the church, in the Salem witch-hunts, and in struggles between white colonists and Indians for control of New England.

In Chapter 3, "The Sisters of Pocahontas: Native American Women in the Centuries of Colonization," I examine women's economic and political roles in East Coast Indian societies. I look at the variations in Indian women's childhood, rites of passage, marital relationships, and mothering practices. This portrait draws on anthropological studies and accounts by European observers.

In Chapter 4, "In a 'Babel of Confusion': Women in the Middle Colonies," my focus returns to European-American women, including the women of the Dutch, German, and English Quaker communities of New York and Pennsylvania. I compare Dutch marital relationships and inheritance patterns with English ones, and look at family strategies to sustain and increase wealth. I also examine the active role women took within the Quaker community and its institutions. Finally, I demonstrate that social class is a critical factor in shaping the experiences of these middle-colony women.

Chapter 5, "The Rhythms of Labor: African-American Women in Colonial Society," explores the changes in the lives of black women and their families in late seventeenth- and early eighteenth-century colonial society as slavery became institutionalized. I focus on the central role women played in the creation of creole slave communities in the South. The chapter also looks at women's work and at their marriage and childbirth patterns in both Northern colonies and Southern ones, and discusses women's active role in slave resistance and revolt.

In Chapter 6, "The Rise of Gentility: Class and Regional Differences in the Eighteenth Century," my focus returns to white society and moves into the eighteenth century. Here I focus upon the increasing significance of social class in shaping women's lives throughout the colonies and on the growing distinctions in behavior and assumptions of femininity among the merchant, shipping, professional, and planter families that constituted the provincial elite.

Chapter 7, " 'Beat of Drum and Ringing of Bell': Women in the American Revolution," narrates the critical roles women played in the decade of protest that preceded the Revolution and the multiple ways in which their activism was channeled during the war. As this chapter shows, women demonstrated independent political commitment as boycott organizers, propagandists, fundraisers, and as protestors before independence; during the war they ran family farms and businesses, served as nurses and cooks in the army camps, saw battle both as soldiers and as surrogates for wounded husbands, and crossed enemy lines as spies, saboteurs, and couriers. I look at the experiences of loyalists and African Americans as well as patriot white women.

In the epilogue I analyze the ideological impact of revolution and independence in the lives of the women of the new nation.

I also analyze the debates over the definition of citizenship for white women and trace the sources, both theoretical and material, for the controversial gender ideal, "republican womanhood."

This book owes any of its wisdom to the many talented scholars who have researched and recovered for us the diverse and complex experiences of colonial women. Appropriately, therefore, the final section is a Bibliographical Essay that acknowledges their scholarship.

First Generations approaches the subject of colonial women and their experiences from a feminist perspective. Feminism, of course, admits to multiple meanings. But in all its forms it nurtures a sensitivity to the social construction of gender and compels us to acknowledge the historical dimensions of what each of us may feel is natural and eternal in women. I have tried consistently to bring this sensitivity to bear on the subjects of this book. I do not believe that this approach contradicts one of the fundamental points of departure for this study: no colonial woman I encountered was ever simply a woman. It was her multiple and sometimes conflicting identities that gave her life dimension and complexity.

A long list of debts trails behind a project that has taken as long as this one. First and foremost, my thanks to Arthur Wang and Eric Foner; their patience made Job look like an amateur. They never refused to assist me with intelligent and constructive criticism, and they never failed to lace their letters reminding me of missed deadlines with wit and humor. My thanks to them also for providing me with the best of editors, Tamara Straus, who helped make murky sentences clear and rambling ones concise—much to the benefit of the reader. I have also had the assistance of several young scholars in gathering, analyzing, and organizing the scholarship upon which the book is based. Their critiques of these resources and of my own work have always been thoughtful. And their willingness to play basketball in the foyer with my son while I searched for some citation was truly remarkable. They will be fine historians, regardless of their mediocre jump shots. To these students and former students—Penny Von Eschen, Kerry Candaele, Leslie Horowitz, Dewar MacLeod, Simon Middleton, Miriamne DeMarrais, Ariel Rosenblum, and Cindy Lobel—my thanks. My thanks also, this time as so many other times, to Mary Beth Norton, Barbara Winslow, and Philip Greven, colleagues who agreed to read the drafts of chapters that I thrust into their hands in college hallways, that I mailed to them in recycled manila envelopes, that I slipped into their briefcases as we ordered in restaurants, and that I forced on them in elevators at professional meetings. I would be much amiss if I did not also thank the former Dean of Liberal Arts and Sciences at Baruch College, Norman Fainstein, and the members of his Research and Travel Committee, who repeatedly and with steadfast confidence in me granted reductions in my teaching schedule so that I could complete this project.

Lastly, as every scholar can testify, research and writing are often painfully solitary activities. It is good to know, therefore, that there are friends "out there," beyond the study's four walls, whom we can call upon again and again. Thanks to Veronica Greenwald, who helped me learn to move from solitude to the chaos of everyday life a bit more smoothly. Also, to Andrea Balis, who swapped tales of victory and defeat in the archives with me as we drove to Jersey to grocery-shop. And to my best chum, Sally Motyka, who never failed to cheer me up with a riotous card or letter, mementos that will remain forever Scotch-taped to the refrigerator door. My friends and colleagues' suggestions greatly improved this book; my failure to heed their warnings surely accounts for many of its flaws.

Finally, I want to commend my two children, Hannah and Matthew, for their willingness to live most of their lives eating at a dining-room table covered with Xeroxes, notecards, and books, falling asleep to the irritating sound of clicking computer keys and muffled curses, participating in frantic searches for lost pages and misplaced eyeglasses, accepting abbreviated bedtime stories, forgiving missed soccer games, and surviving the occasional mood of gloom and doom in their home as their mother worked on "that book." That book is finally finished and it is dedicated to them —they have certainly earned it.

Carol Berkin
New York City, 1996

CONTENTS

FIRST GENERATIONS

WOMEN
IN
COLONIAL
AMERICA

1

IMMIGRANTS TO PARADISE:
WHITE WOMEN IN THE
SEVENTEENTH-CENTURY CHESAPEAKE

MARY COLE, the daughter of Robert and Rebecca Cole, was born in Maryland in January 1653. Her parents had come to the colony in 1652, probably from Middlesex, England, bringing with them Rebecca's two children from her first marriage and two servants as well. Rebecca may have been pregnant during the long ocean voyage, for Robert Cole, Jr., was born in Maryland before the end of the year. Thus, Mary was part of a large household, and one that would continue to grow. Within the next seven years, William, Edward, and Mary's baby sister, Elizabeth, were born at Cole's Farm.

Mary's father must have come from a prosperous family, for he was able to rent a 300-acre tobacco farm on St. Clements Bay, agreeably located near the Potomac River. His business accounts show that he was a prudent man and managed his plantation well. While Mary was still quite young, more servants and new acreage were added to the Cole family holdings, and the young Mary could take pride that her father was addressed as "Sir."

Like many of his neighbors, Robert Cole was concerned that his children learn to read the Bible. Each one received instruction at home, and Mary's brothers had a tutor who visited the farm.

The youngest child, Elizabeth, may even have attended a Jesuit school in nearby Newtown. Mary's father took care to see that his sons learned to read and also to write and do sums; for his daughter Mary it was enough that she could read and sew.

When Mary was nine years old, the Coles' comfortable and comforting family setting began to shatter. Rebecca Cole died in 1662; in the fall of 1663, Robert Cole died while visiting England. Like many Marylanders of their era, they had met their death before the age of forty. And like many Maryland children of the seventeenth century, Mary Cole was an orphan before her eleventh birthday.

Mary Cole was luckier than most orphans. Her father, always a careful man, had set his affairs in the strictest order before departing for England. He had inventoried his possessions, made out his will, and named two of his Maryland neighbors to serve as guardians of his motherless brood. Not content to see these guardians protect the children's material interest and see to their physical well-being, Robert Cole also charged them to provide spiritual training in the event of his death. If they failed, he warned both men, God would punish them on Judgment Day. Mary would know other orphans, neighbors and perhaps friends, who unlike herself suffered neglect or abuse at the hands of strangers or thoughtless acquaintances.

When they reached their majority, the Cole children would share many acres of tobacco land, four servants, and personal property assessed at over £200. But Mary and her brothers would not divide these assets equally. Like most of the men of the region, Robert Cole reserved his land for his sons; to his daughters, he gave movable property. At eighteen, Mary Cole received her legacy of eleven cattle, a bed, and kitchenware—all items that could be carried into a new household when she married.

Mary Cole did soon marry. Before she was twenty she had chosen a husband from the colonies' many eligible planters. Ignatius Warren was a native Marylander who owned property across St. Clements Bay in Newtown Hundred. Warren's family history was more typical of the region than Mary's, for his father, like many Chesapeake colonists, had come to the region as an indentured servant. John Warren had contracted to work for another man for several years in exchange for passage to America or the promise of land when his contract expired. At the end of his term, Warren had indeed become a property owner, and even a county justice of the peace. Thus, Ignatius and Mary Cole Warren began life with the complementary assets most Chesapeake newlyweds desired: Ignatius brought land, which secured an income, and Mary brought cattle and domestic supplies, which helped establish a household.

Whether the Warrens had a satisfying marriage or a troubled one we do not know. But their marriage was unusual among Chesapeake colonists in one respect: it was the only one Mary Cole or Ignatius Warren ever had. Unlike her brothers Edward and Robert, who were twice married, Mary Cole never found herself at the center of the complex family of stepparents and half brothers and sisters typical of the Chesapeake. Actually, we have no record that Mary Cole Warren had any children at all.

Ignatius Warren lived a long life for a Chesapeake native, dying at the age of fifty-eight. He earned his living planting tobacco, running an inn, and dabbling in commerce, while Mary was known simply as a planter's wife. Poor judgment or bad luck brought about Ignatius's financial ruin later in life, and although the date of Mary's death is unknown, we do know that she did not live to see her husband's downfall.

In the end, what we know about Mary Cole Warren does not make for a compelling biography. Our knowledge is largely a matter of genealogy, with Mary a modest branch on a family tree. Like most women of the early colonial Chesapeake, she speaks to us only briefly and with too distant a voice to make her story clear. The collective voice of Chesapeake women is, however, more powerful and more rich. From wills, court testimony, ship's logs, and plantation records, from baptismal certificates and tombstones, from household inventories and archaeological remains, from careful attention to community ceremonies and rituals, we can reproduce the female world in which Mary Cole Warren moved.

We can also reconstruct in some detail the larger society that the Mary Cole Warrens of the seventeenth century inhabited. We know that this early Chesapeake culture deviated from traditional English norms and also that, by English standards, many of the region's critical social institutions were unstable. As a result, women like Mary Cole Warren often found gender roles more ambiguous and fluid than women in other colonial regions did. Whether this proved to be an advantage or a burden for the women of Maryland and Virginia, historians have not yet been able to agree. But understanding these variations in women's work roles, family roles, and in their relationship to property and wealth is yet another way to bring Mary Cole Warren and her Chesapeake sisters to life.

Few seventeenth-century English immigrants failed to be shocked by the alien nature of the Chesapeake. With its intricate mazes of waterways, its vast, unbroken forest, its hot, humid summers, it bore no resemblance to the tilled fields and tamed woodlands of England. There were no towns and no manufacturing centers. The native population was at best exotic and at worst dangerous, and the variety of dialects and accents among the colonists themselves was disquieting to men and women used to the comforting sameness of parish or village life.

Society itself seemed out of joint. Whole tiers of the English social structure were missing. Immigrants accustomed to locating themselves within an old, established hierarchy could not fail to note the absence of gentry and aristocracy as well as artisans of most trades. But what surely must have struck any Englishwoman orienting herself to this strange Chesapeake society was the simple fact that it was a male world. Men outnumbered women by six to one in the earliest decades and three to one as late as the 1680s.

The explanation for this skewed sex ratio lay in the region's obsession with tobacco. Although many free immigrants were young married couples, Chesapeake planters recruited thousands of workers to plant and harvest their tobacco crops. For these planters the ideal farm laborer was young—and male. Thus, between 1630 and 1680, one-half, perhaps three-quarters, of the 75,000 indentured servants transported to the region fit this description.

The consequences of such a sex ratio were as dramatic as the imbalance itself. Chesapeake men found themselves locked into more than a competition over land, tobacco, and prosperity; they struggled to wed as well. The situation prompted one Maryland planter to remark that his colony was a "paradise for women." But was it? Indeed, unmarried women were certain to find husbands, although marriage often was delayed by the terms of indenture. A planter eager to set up his household might buy his bride-to-be's contract, but most immigrant women were not legally free to become wives until their mid- or late twenties. From that point on, their lives were consumed by childbirth and field and household labor, and certainly followed by an early death.

The short and often brutish life these immigrant women faced was not a uniquely female experience. For men as much as women a life of difficult fieldwork complicated by local diseases such as malaria produced a near-century of demographic disaster. Perhaps a quarter of all indentured servants died before their terms of labor came to an end. Male survivors could expect to live only until their mid-forties; women until about thirty-nine. These few years of difference in life expectancy—small to the demographer but significant to the colonist—were related to childbearing. Women's fecundity and mortality were ironically linked, for women's resistance to viral disease was dangerously weakened during pregnancy. Age was more critical than sex, however, since infants and small children were most vulnerable to infectious diseases. Perhaps one-quarter of all children who survived birth died in their first year. Forty to fifty-five percent of all white children born in the Chesapeake died before their twentieth birthday. Taken together, late marriage, early adult death, and high infant mortality meant that this Anglo-Chesapeake population could not even reproduce itself through the 1690s. Only the steady flow of new immigrants each season ensured that the tobacco colonies would continue to grow.

In such a death-driven society, familiar institutions took on new forms. Marriage remained the setting for the creation of a family, yet marriages were truncated and families complex. A Chesapeake couple, wedded blissfully or despairingly, could expect that death would end their union within nine to twelve years. A new marriage soon followed, and frequently a third, resulting in a crazy quilt of family relationships, with children from different marriages living under one roof. A widow brought to her second husband the heirs of her first; if he was a widower, he, too, brought sons and daughters to the home. Together, they produced offspring, and on the death of one partner, the survivor's next marriage added new children. With resiliency and flexibility, at least in their language, Chesapeake colonists spoke of their fathers' "now-wives," and mothers and fathers distinguished children in their care but not of their own blood as "sons- or daughters-in-law."

Mortality fractured every family relationship. Husbands and wives were separated abruptly, and the survivor had to be prepared to form new commitments and intimacies. Parents found themselves caring for the living as they mourned for the dead, and burying sons and daughters in their young adulthood. Few children grew to maturity under the eyes of both father and mother; those who were not orphaned were counted among the fortunate. Throughout most of the seventeenth century, there were not enough uncles, aunts, or older siblings to provide a sufficient safety net—economic or emotional—for orphaned boys and girls. The problem was so widespread that no one felt immune. Colonists in both Maryland and Virginia supported the creation of orphans' courts to oversee the care, placement, and training of parentless minors, and to guard their material inheritances.

How would men and women born in England view the seventeenth-century Chesapeake family? Had they been familiar with the vocabulary of twentieth-century sociologists, they might have remarked on the instability or deviance of family relations in the tobacco colonies. In England, a patriarchal, nuclear family had generally replaced an older, more open family based on broad and powerful kin relationships. In this newer nuclear family, the power and influence once diffused among lineal and collateral family members had become concentrated in the father's hands. The position of women diminished accordingly. In the patriarchal family, a wife was expected to defer to her husband, and a husband was expected to direct the lives of wife and children alike.

The Chesapeake family conformed neither to the older kinship model nor to the newer patriarchal one. In Maryland and Virginia communities, there were not enough kinship networks to make the older family configuration viable. Yet the newer patriarchal family could not take root in a setting where marriages were short and serial, and a man's authority as father and husband was too temporary. Chesapeake fathers simply did not live long enough to control the crucial decisions in the lives of their sons and daughters. Some historians argue that women, as mothers, held a privileged place in these households of "now-wives and sons-in-law," for they were often the single consistent thread in the complicated domestic weaving of stepparents and children. If nothing else, we have glimpses of the daily life of Chesapeake wives that suggest that submissive behavior was not the norm. Such was the case for Clove Mace, whose wife "threw [him] out of his own house in the course of a heated domestic argument."

Perhaps the constant element was the birth cycle itself. Immigrant women could expect to be pregnant every two years until they died or until menopause stopped the process. Among the creole, or native-born generations, the age of marriage and motherhood shifted dramatically, although sex ratio and mortality rates continued to shape women's life cycle. The creole* daughters of former servants, like the daughters of immigrant landholders, were born free. They could marry as soon as custom and physical maturation permitted. And marry they did—at sixteen and seventeen,

* Colonial historians use "creole" to indicate colonists born in the Chesapeake settlements, rather than immigrants to the region.

and often enough at fifteen or fourteen for the rituals of puberty and matrimony to converge. Like their mothers, these creole girls married men considerably older than themselves and like their mothers, they became mothers almost as soon as they became wives. Many were on their way to parenthood even before they were married, just as their mothers had been. Pre-bridal pregnancy ran as high as 20 percent among immigrant and creole women, for the absence of parental supervision left them with only their own judgment and their own desire to guide them in sexual relations. Marrying earlier, creole women gave birth more often, producing nine to eleven children rather then their mother's average of six.

The complex families of the seventeenth-century Chesapeake often lived in material conditions that would have shocked the poorest members of English society. On Maryland's lower western shore, it was common for parents, children, and servants to live together in two-, or at best three-, room houses. Even the most prosperous of these colonial planters built cramped six-room homes. Within these small, flimsily built, and sparsely furnished homes, families cooked, ate, made love, slept, sewed, read, played, and engaged in household manufacturing. Many colonists lay down at night on beds without bedsteads, bereft of linens, and without a chest in which to store their day's clothing.

Sparse material resources were matched by sparse human resources. As late as 1688, Virginia society could be described without exaggeration as "thinly inhabited; the Living solitary and unsociable." Indeed, the entire population of St. Marys County, Maryland, in 1675 was no more than 2,000 souls. Yet Chesapeake men and women created what community they could. Settlers on the lower western shore of Maryland, for example, clustered in neighborhoods near creeks and streams. Ties and connections were formed, cemented by mutual assistance, whether grudgingly or graciously given. In the absence of strong or adequately responsive social institutions—government, church, or courts—colonists sustained one another. Men witnessed each other's wills, appraised their neighbors' estates, raised barns, shared tools and supplies, and protected families from Indian attack. Women linked their daily lives by visiting, attending at childbirth, nursing the sick, and exchanging household products. Lacking extended kinship networks, men and women unconnected by blood served as surrogates to family in their observation and celebration of the rituals of life—christenings, weddings, and burials.

On court days or Sunday afternoons, Chesapeake residents came together to socialize. Women as well as men smoked, drank, and played cards and games of dice. When a wedding or funeral gave these colonists an excuse to interrupt the monotony of toil, they threw themselves into celebration, feasting, dancing, and drinking cider, beer, and punch until the morning hours.

Neighborliness had its price, however. Gossip exposed any misbehavior or deviance from community norms, and cooperation and assistance shaded easily into meddling, interference, and intervention in household affairs. Every woman felt her neighbors' critical eye judging her treatment of servants, her domestic skills, her marital relations, and her sexual fidelity.

Reputation counted for much in this society. The "small politics of everyone's everyday life," carried on largely through gossip, shaped the networks of trust and respect within Chesapeake communities. The reputations of the two sexes were made in different spheres and hinged on very different behaviors. For men, a reputation of reliability and honesty was critical, for they conducted much of their business by oral agreement. It was better, as Maryland planter Joseph Wickes well understood, to be known as a "whoremaster" than as a thief. For women, the litmus test of character was sexual behavior. It was primarily in the control and expression of her physical desires that a woman was assumed to be responsible for herself.

Gossip was an important weapon for both men and women in the building and destruction of reputations. However, because women were locked out of the "large politics" of government, gossip was their most essential tool in establishing their social position and regulating the behavior of others. The records from slander and defamation cases in the Maryland courts between 1654 and 1671 reflect the community's concern with men's reputation in the marketplace and women's in bed. It is in the charges and countercharges, fervent defenses and heated attacks, that we hear the voices of the men and women of the tobacco colonies.

If men spoke of each other as "rogues" and "knaves," women most often called each other "whores." While both men and women felt free to question a woman's marital fidelity, few women concerned themselves with a man's honesty in his business dealings. Instead, a woman protected her reputation, and impugned the honor of a male, by accusing him of improper sexual behavior.

Even in their manner of insult and gossip, men and women differed. Chesapeake men showed a marked preference for aggressive, public confrontation of their foes; women spread their damaging tales in private. Men defamed each other in general terms; women offered a wealth of specific details about the alleged transgression. Few women were simply "whores"; rather, they were guilty, as Jane Godson reported of Joan Balsey, of producing an "Eldest Son . . . not the son of Anthony Rawlins her former husband but She knew one at Maryland that was the father of him." Godson added a flourish to her account by citing her source. She knew Balsey had committed this adultery because "Thomas Ward of Kent tould her Soe."

Demography and economic dependency influenced Chesapeake women's concerns about morality. A married women had more at stake in protecting her sexual reputation than a single woman, as she was dependent on her husband for economic support. His respect—or lack of it—could translate easily into material comfort or deprivation. A single woman, even if she was accused of lying with a man "2 moonshiny nights under a walnutt tree," was likely to find a husband in a society where there were three men for every available woman. And so a woman was better off "caught . . . with her Coates up . . . and his breeches downe" before she took her marriage vows.

Woman's work, like her familial relationships, was reshaped by the circumstances of life in the tobacco colony. By the sev-

enteenth century, English custom drew a sharp distinction between women's agricultural activity and men's. Fieldwork was
considered masculine, and only in the most extreme circumstances
of poverty or crop-threatening weather was a wife or daughter
called upon to cross this gendered line. Women's domain was the
garden, the dairy, and the household, the locales of significant
economic productivity. This household production, or "housewifery," transformed raw materials into usable domestic products,
through spinning, butchering animals, food preparation and pres-
ervation, and manufacturing domestic supplies. The tools of wom-
en's trades included the spinning wheel and the churn, equipment
which was as valued as the plow or the hoe. In England's urban
centers, many women also engaged in housewifery production for
the marketplace and in sale and barter, as well as in the management of taverns, inns, and shops.

Inventories of Chesapeake households show that housewifery
was underdeveloped here. Although women did household chores
such as cooking, sewing, and tending the garden, few households
boasted spinning wheels or churns, and even rudimentary tools of
production were missing from most kitchens and hearths. Many
Chesapeake housewives must have spent more hours each week
grinding corn for family meals than in such skilled tasks as cloth
making or butter production. In the early decades of Chesapeake
settlement, most immigrant women also spent a part of their productive hours toiling beside men in the tedious care of tobacco
plants. Few bound servant women were taken from the fields to
assist in household work, and few planter wives were able to escape fieldwork altogether either. Manpower was too scarce, competition too great, and tobacco cultivation too labor-intensive for
the English division of male and female work spheres to be maintained.

Court records also show that this departure from English labor
norms was common. When the widow Mary Carleton recounted
that "what was produced out of ye ground" was the result of "ye
hard labor of her the said Mary," her testimony was distinguished
by her anger at her husband's apparent idleness, not by her lot

tending crops. Colonial legislation corroborates this break with tradition, for a distinct category for taxable labor included women servants engaged in fieldwork.

The tasks of childbearing and household and fieldwork were the primary physical and economic constraints in the life of a white Chesapeake woman. But there were other constraints as well. Laws regulated her action and limited her identity in society. This was true for Englishmen, too, of course, but it was peculiar to Englishwomen that the rites of passage to adulthood diminished rather than increased their legal rights. For under English common law, women were legal persons only if they reached their majority and did not marry. As *feme sole*, or woman alone, a free English-woman could sue and be sued, make contracts, earn and pay wages, own and sell property in her lifetime, and will it to her chosen heirs upon her death. Marriage—which was the primary ritual of adulthood for a woman—converted her to *feme covert*, or woman covered, enforcing the exchange of her legal persona for the protection and support of her husband. In its most pristine and extreme interpretation, the law denied married women the right to make judgments regarding their own economic circumstances. It muted their voice in the courts, restricted their accumulation and dispersement of material wealth, and made them less than responsible for their misdeeds or achievements in the public sphere. A woman was a legal incompetent, as children, idiots, and criminals were under English law. As *feme covert* she was stripped of all property; once married, the clothes on her back, her personal possessions—whether valuable, mutable, or merely sentimental—and even her body became her husband's, to direct, to manage, and to use. Once a child was born to the couple, her land, too, came under his control.

The body of law that established a husband's control over his wife's resources reflected and sustained an ideology of women's subordination to men within a marital and family system. That system was hierarchical, but it was not autocratic. Marriage was webbed by obligations and duties owed by both husband and wife. Husbands were enjoined by law and precept to protect and provide for wives; wives were required to submit to male authority and to assist their husbands by productive labor and frugality. The ideal of a unity of person, of husband and wife as one *in him*, influenced behavior—defining the choices men and women made, and setting the boundaries of what each considered acceptable action. Yet daily life rarely sustained the ideal, and the law was made malleable by a thousand informal adjustments every day as women argued with their husbands, criticized their judgments, redefined standards of household maintenance, and indulged in frivolous expenditures or, conversely, as men ignored their wives' material needs or quibbled over what was necessary. In this way, the obligations men and women owed each other became subject to daily negotiation.

That a married woman lacked a legal identity did not mean, of course, that she lacked all legal rights. The most significant of her rights pertained to property and wealth, and thus to inheritance. Although the state curtailed her rights in marriage, it became her advocate in widowhood. The state or community wished to keep the burden of a woman's support private, and thus expected a husband to extend his sustaining hand even after death. If the state could not ensure a husband's character or his marital affection, it could defend its own interests by mandating that a portion of the estate go to the wife regardless of the husband's wishes. A widow's share in that estate reinforced gender ideology by offering a woman acknowledgment of her contribution to the material well-being of the family.

The widow's inheritance share, or *dower right*, was thus well established in England by the seventeenth century, although its provisions varied from county to county and over the decades. The standard dower settlement gave a widow a life interest in one-third of her husband's real property; that is, she was entitled to the profits from the land but could not sell it or select its ultimate owner. On her death, the property passed into the hands of her husband's designated heirs. Dower was honored, in some form, in every English community and in each colony. The absence of a will signified a husband's tacit acquiescence to his widow's "thirds." Testators who designated less than those "thirds" usually had their wishes thwarted—and their wills contested. Englishwomen proved aggressive in protecting and demanding their due, and English judges proved sympathetic to their demands.

Of course, if a husband could not disinherit his wife at death, he might mismanage or squander the property she brought to the marriage while he lived. Although there were laws to prevent reckless, foolish, or irresponsible husbands from alienating property without a wife's consent, their effectiveness is questionable. In many English colonies a judge was required to interrogate a woman privately to determine if she freely consented to a proposed sale of her property. Yet as authorities frequently discovered when settling a man's estate, husbands neglected to tell their wives of impending sales. Confronted later with a *fait accompli*, she could do little but add an amen to his actions until she was widowed. And as judges and legislators evaluating private interrogation procedures often conceded, a husband could cajole or coerce his wife into a dower release that left him free to dispose of her property as he saw fit, thus subverting dower protection.

Counterstrategies to protect dower soon evolved. Concerned fathers in both the mother country and the colonies could insist upon prenuptial contracts that placed their daughters' inheritance in the care of third-party trustees; widows, wiser from sad experience, could insist upon similar prenuptial contracts with their prospective husbands. Not surprisingly, the rich were more inclined to such defensive maneuvers than ordinary folk. In the colonies, few seventeenth-century women knew of, or considered, this sophisticated option.

On the whole, colonists in seventeenth-century Maryland and Virginia respected the tradition of dower. Over 75 percent of the Chesapeake's free white men went to their graves without drafting a will, a tacit acceptance of a widow's dower rights. By 1670 inheritance was guided by a Statute of Distribution, which made the terms of property division relatively uniform in the Chesapeake. A widow's thirds in real property were honored, and her thirds of a husband's personal estate were also ensured. In this,

Chesapeake women fared better than their English sisters, for the right to dower in personalty was eroding in England just as it was expanding in the tobacco colonies. By the end of the century, as slaves became the most valuable personal property in any estate, a share in this labor force was also assured to white Maryland widows.

Demographic disaster influenced inheritance patterns as profoundly as they influenced other aspects of Chesapeake life. Deceased husbands left young wives and children, often with few relatives to rely on, and thus chose to entrust the management of their entire estate to their widows. Even older men found themselves with few options as they sat down to write their wills, for in certain areas of the region two-thirds to three-quarters of all men making wills died before any children had come of age. The great majority of such men, anxious about their families, entrusted the future to their widows. In St. Marys and Charles Counties, Maryland, for example, almost 75 percent of the men who wrote wills left their wives more than dower thirds, and most named their wives executors of their estate. If, as one historian astutely remarked, wills "document the transfer of authority from one individual to another," Chesapeake women of the seventeenth century were empowered in their widowhood.

Is it enough to say that, lacking other options, a man was forced to place his estate in his widow's hands? Or was there more at work here than expediency? Reading the wills left by colonial men, historians have found an urgent desire to preserve the household after the husband's death. By leaving the entire house and lands rather than a portion of them to his widow, by giving her control over the family resources during her lifetime, a man guaranteed the security of his wife, kept the household under the authority of a parent, and ensured that his home would remain the focal point in the lives of his sons and daughters.

This insistence on the family as an economic *and* emotional unit runs like a leitmotif through seventeenth-century wills. Henry Clarke of Surrey County gave his wife a life estate in property that ultimately would belong to his son, Sampson. Yet Sampson had to "keep and maintain his mother" or lose his birthright. Laurence Simpson of Westermoreland County insisted that "Sons Michael, Rupert, and Matthew are to obey their mother, follow her orders, or they ar not to get their Land." And Daniel Reagan left "to eldest son Francis, 70 acres of Land, after decease of his mother," but, Reagan carefully added, "they must agree to live together." Such concern may be read in darker ways, of course. Were families so strife-ridden, were sons so avaricious and impatient, were the ties within these complex families of "now-wives and sons-in-law" so tenuous, the sense of obligation so weak, that a man had to stipulate respect and responsibility or expect its absence?

Other questions hang in the air. Some historians have argued that a husband's reliance on his widow to manage his estate reflected his respect for and confidence in her. These scholars have also emphasized the relative power and autonomy these widows enjoyed. Others, however, have read the evidence differently, reminding us that a "life estate" ensured, after all, that a woman's power would be temporary. She was a caretaker of property rather than an owner, and lost even that role when her children came of age.

It was true that men with heirs rarely gave their widows land in fee simple, that is, provided them outright possession of real property. No matter how loving or intimate their marriage, the bond between husband and wife was not a bond of blood. There was always a likelihood that the widow would carry his legacy with her into another family by remarriage, as was common in the multiple-marriage system of the Chesapeake. Even if she did not remarry, a woman who received land outright might choose to leave it to heirs outside a husband's bloodline. This is exactly what Joyce Cripps did in 1679, when she left land given to her by her second husband to the children of her first marriage. Indeed, men concerned about such matters of blood and property were uneasy about a traditionally unrestricted life estate. As the seventeenth century progressed, more men chose to severely restrict their wife's right to property. They stipulated that, should a woman remarry, her use of the land or house was to be rescinded. Thus, a widow's empowerment lasted only as long as widowhood. Mathias Marriott of Surrey County typified this trend when he wrote: "My Wife Alice to Have and enjoy the Land I live on for her widowhood. After her death or remarriage the Land is to return to my son Wm. Marriott."

For the present, the questions of a widow's familial authority and economic power remain moot. As daughters, however, Chesapeake women could look forward to a share of their father's material wealth that was perhaps unusual among the seventeenth-century English colonies. In the 1670s, in York, St. Marys, and Somerset Counties, Maryland, 40 percent of the daughters whose fathers left wills received both land and slaves. In a society where land was still plentiful, and relatives to care for a man's daughters were scarce, many fathers broke traditional patterns and endowed children of both sexes with the resources necessary to survive.

By placing Mary Cole Warren in this world of Chesapeake women, we can better imagine, though we cannot document, her life. We can picture her growing up in a world where native-born women married young, where families were rent by sudden death and reconstituted by speedy remarriage, and where the domain of women's work overlapped with men's out of necessity rather than preference. We can assume that her sense of loss at the death of her parents was modified by an understanding that such losses were commonplace. We also can assume she was relieved that her judicious father had left her both a dowry and decent guardians to protect her until she reached adulthood. We can chart her daily activities, placing her, like neighboring women, by her husband's side in the fields, pounding corn, weeding the garden, and cooking her husband's meals each day. We believe she expected to give birth to several children, although we do not know what children, if any, she bore. She was, we can be sure, surrounded by women for whom frequent pregnancies, miscarriages, births, and infant deaths were integral to the rhythm of their lives. And we can better understand how unique her marital history was as we place her in the context of the now-wives and sons-in-law that made up her community. Finally, and ironically, we know that, by dying before Ignatius Warren, Mary Cole never took on the most complex female role in this Chesapeake society—widowhood—which empowered women, both by giving them control over wealth and property and by assigning to them responsibilities their society preferred to reserve for men.

2

GOODWIVES AND BAD:
NEW ENGLAND WOMEN IN
THE SEVENTEENTH CENTURY

HANNAH EMERSON DUSTON WAS THE OLDEST of the fifteen children born to Michael and Hannah Emerson of Haverhill, Massachusetts. Her father was a farmer and shoemaker, her mother the daughter of a baker and the stepdaughter of a miller. The Emersons, like their neighbors, were hardworking New Englanders, whose family history—despite the deaths of five of their children—seemed to confirm historians' claims that Puritan marriages were long, their family life stable, and their women fertile. In such demographic ways, the younger Hannah managed to replicate her mother's life, marrying a local farmer, and, in their twenty years together, bearing thirteen children. At first glance there was nothing remarkable about this frontier farm wife. Yet, in 1697, celebrity struck Hannah Duston.

In early March Hannah had taken to childbed and, with the help of Mary Neff, delivered a healthy infant. Only five days later, on the morning of March 15, Indians attacked Duston's village. Duston, Neff, and the baby were swept up among the captives forced to make a hundred-mile march into the wilderness.

Hannah Duston's infant died in the Indian camp. But Hannah did more than survive. With the help of Mary Neff and a young boy named Samuel Lennardson, Hannah Emerson Duston rose up and murdered her captors, children and adults alike. She paused only to take their scalps—each worth a sizable monetary reward from the Massachusetts government—and then made her way home.

News of Duston's exploits spread quickly, and for one dizzying year, she was the most famous woman in her region. New England's leading divine, Cotton Mather, preached a sermon in praise of her; New England's leading judge, Samuel Sewall, entertained her in his home. Yet Hannah Duston appeared little altered by celebrity. She returned to her village and to her life as a farmer's wife. If she saw God's hand in her salvation from her Indian captors, she did not take it as a sign of her own election into His grace. Not until June 1719, twenty-two years after her escape from captivity, did she seek and receive full membership in Haverhill's First Church. Thus, according to her Puritan faith, she secured a second and eternal salvation from the terrors and perils, not of this world, but of the next.

Decades after Hannah Duston's death, learned and talented men of New England debated the meaning of her captivity and liberation. They recast her story and reevaluated her character. If to Mather she was a heroic daughter of the Lord, comparable to the biblical Jael, to the novelist Nathaniel Hawthorne she was a "bloody, old hag" whose circumstances did not justify the murder and mutilation of her captors. The womanly courage hailed by the seventeenth-century minister had become unfeminine bloodthirstiness and simple greed in the eyes of the nineteenth-century moralist. Hannah Duston's experience has continued to be rewritten and reinterpreted to this very day.

To consider Hannah Duston's life is to move straight to the heart of seventeenth-century New England women's history. At first glance, Duston's experience as a resident of a small and close-knit farming community, a member of an extensive and multigenerational family, a partner in a long and fruitful marriage, and a worshipper in a strong and influential religious institution seems to stand in sharp contrast to the experiences of Chesapeake women such as Mary Cole. Duston's courage, and the pragmatism that led her to scalp her enemies, fits a long-standing, popular image of New Englanders—male and female—as practical, resourceful pioneers.

Were New England women different from the Mary Coles of their own century or from the nineteenth-century women Nathaniel Hawthorne believed he lived among, whom he saw as genteel, feminine, sensitive? Were circumstances in New England radically different from those that shaped the life experiences and defined the life choices of other colonial wives and mothers? Were Puritan gender ideals, and the behavior of the men and women who accepted and lived by them, distinctive in American colonial society? With equal degrees of certainty, historians have answered yes and no.

The disagreement does not arise from lack of evidence. More than any other region, New England has been hospitable to colonial scholars, leaving behind—in contrast to the Chesapeake, for instance—an embarrassment of evidence. Puritan culture was a culture of the diary, the letter, the sermon, and the pamphlet. Puritanism prompted New Englanders to an introspection that was intellectually, socially, and psychologically revealing. They have left us meticulous records, not only of inner journeys toward salvation or despair, but of public struggles between orthodoxy and religious dissent, even heresy and witchcraft. Occasionally it has seemed that these New Englanders lived with historians in mind: settling in villages so that we could observe and analyze community life; establishing long marriages and nuclear families to provide us with the connecting branches on their family trees; suing each other and putting each other on trial, so that we can measure tension and dissension; establishing institutions such as schools, colleges, town meetings, militias, courts, and churches, each complex enough to be meaningful but compact enough to make their interactions and interdependencies clear; and, should all else fail, writing histories of and commentaries on their own times to assist us in understanding them more fully.

New Englanders did not, of course, create their lives for our convenience. And no matter how rich the record they left, we sometimes have managed to misread and misinterpret it, to come to disparate and contradictory conclusions, and to wonder if we have asked the proper questions or found the proper answers. In each regard, the scholarship on New England women has enjoyed the same bounty and suffered from the same problems as the scholarship on New England men.

As any traveler knows, Virginia and Massachusetts present sharp contrasts to the senses. New England philosophers and poets have found their austere landscape inspirational, but seventeenth-century farmers were known to curse the rocky soil and long winters of their region. Except for the rich farmlands of the Connecticut River Valley, New England offered little opportunity in the seventeenth century for large-scale farming or profitable cash crop specialization. The men and women who settled in the region accepted the natural environment and its constraints. What they clearly did not accept, however, were the constraints placed on them by two human institutions: England's church and its government. Both the Pilgrims of Plymouth Plantation and the Puritans of the Massachusetts Bay Company were dissenters from the established Anglican Church, and both sought refuge and space to create their own spiritual community in the new world. They fled the economic penalties imposed on them by the government they criticized and the threat of imprisonment for their religious views, but they also fled what they judged to be an increasingly immoral society, whose values alienated and isolated them as surely as any edicts of bishop or king. Their departure from England was a rejection of their countrymen's lasciviousness, idleness, and extravagance and the corrupt public life they saw around them. If refuge from streets filled with drunks, prostitutes, and beggars motivated Chesapeake settlers as well, they did not articulate it as Puritans did; the rejection of English society's ills and corruptions were conscious and intentional in the immigrant world of Hannah Duston.

The ideological context for Duston's life thus contrasted with Cole's. But the demographic contrast between their two worlds may have been less drastic than historians once thought. Traditionally, scholars have portrayed New England immigration as a migration of nuclear families, which, combined with a low mortality rate, resulted in a balanced sex ratio, long and stable marriages, parental influence or control over marriage age and therefore over the legitimate birthrate, and a smaller gap between the ages of husband and wife than in the South.

New research has modified this demographic portrait. Families did indeed make up the greater part of the first immigrant waves to New England. Nevertheless, one-third of the passengers aboard Puritan ships were single adult males, young and without kin in the new world. Between 1621 and 1651, there were four single men for each single woman. For unmarried women of New England, as for those in the Chesapeake, this lack of balance between the sexes had measurable but often different consequences.

In New England, being a servant did not delay but seems to have sped women's and men's entrance into marriage. The average marriage age for single adult females was 23.4, but dependent females, that is servants, married soon after their twentieth birthday. The labor female servants performed in New England communities was not the profitable labor of the Chesapeake tobacco fields, and thus a woman's transition from servant to wife was less contested. Marriage age for daughters born to immigrant New England families, as for those within Chesapeake families, responded to the sex ratio imbalance. Puritan daughters were likely to be wives before they were twenty. And in the 1650s, the average marriage age dropped below seventeen, making Puritan brides no older than the creole brides of Maryland and Virginia. Women born in New England before 1650 thus married young, bore their last child at thirty-seven, and gave birth to an average of seven children. In this way their lives recapitulated the lives of the Southern white women. And like women of the

Southern colonies, New England women were no strangers to death arising from childbirth. At least 3 percent, perhaps 10 percent, of the women who became pregnant between 1630 and 1670 died following the birth of a child. The greatest danger came not after the birth of a first child but after the fourth, fifth, or sixth child was delivered.

In matters of mortality, however, appearances were deceiving. In its early decades, New England society was unusually youthful; two-thirds of the immigrants before 1650 were between the ages of ten and forty. In that same period, almost 8,000 babies were born among the settlers. With only a smattering of elderly colonists, illness and disease took its toll among infants, children, and young adults. Death seemed to come early, but, in fact, those who survived to adulthood enjoyed a lifespan longer than the survivors of the tobacco colonies. A generation of grandparents was being formed as Hannah Duston grew to womanhood, despite the many small tombstones in every New England graveyard.

The youthfulness of New England society meant that the Hannah Dustons of the era grew to womanhood surrounded by infants and children. Yet they were surrounded as well by two powerful institutions that enveloped, restricted, and sustained them: the patriarchal family and the Puritan Congregational Church. They also were surrounded by a native population that threatened their safety, and whose own survival was endangered by them. Within these concentric circles of instability and stability, of disorder and order, New England women shaped their lives. A closer look at the family, the church, and race relations reveals the differences in experience between women like Hannah Duston and Mary Cole.

Seventeenth-century New England society carefully replicated the patriarchal family structure of old England. Braced by religious precepts and enforced by law, the family dominated by the father and composed of a man and his immediate dependents was the primary institution in a female's life. As she moved from daughter to bride to wife and to mother, a woman negotiated various levels of dependency and authority. For the majority of her life, her place was firmly fixed beneath her husband and above her children and servants. No position she held within the family was ever characterized by autonomy.

Civil authority in the separate New England colonies—Massachusetts Bay, Plymouth Plantation, Connecticut, Rhode Island —underwrote patriarchy in the family, in principle and to varying degrees in practice. Within the Pilgrim and Puritan communities especially, the state upheld and legitimated the power of parents over children and of husbands over wives, for the family was the mainstay of social order in the American "wilderness." To transgress family rules and norms was to transgress public order. In the language of ministers and magistrates alike, the family was the "little commonwealth" on which the larger commonwealth of the state depended. The state served the patriarchal family through inheritance laws that gave preference to eldest sons over widows and through a criminal code that punished juvenile disobedience and sexual infidelity by both married men and women.

Very few white women in seventeenth-century New England placed themselves outside the limits of the patriarchal family. Within Puritan culture, as in the Chesapeake, wives were expected to perform productive and reproductive tasks. And as in the Southern colonies, New England women labored beside their husbands in the fields when they were needed. Early Salem court records document wives winnowing corn, branding steers, and tending cattle. Yet the agrarian communities and small towns of the region stressed their performance of traditional English household chores. And their Puritan culture made a more explicit connection than the Anglican Chesapeake culture did between a woman's role as "helpmeet" to her husband and her reputation within her community. In Boston, Haverhill, and New Haven, earning respect and recognition were tied to the performance of housewifely duties. The Puritan woman who executed her household duties with skill and economy won the accolade "*notable housewife.*"

In reconstructing the world of housewifery, as in so many other areas of Puritan life, the record is full although somewhat oblique. No seventeenth-century woman left diaries for us to pry into with scholarly eyes, but their sons and husbands, fathers and brothers recorded much about them in their writing. Ministers eulogized women, citing—and thus preserving for us—examples of their performance as wives, mothers, and household managers. Dutiful children recollected their mothers in moments of mundane domesticity—spinning cloth, tending the garden, sewing and mending. Artifacts of their material world—from butter churns to infant "go-carts" to linens used in childbed—make the reconstruction of women's daily life possible.

Every woman had a well-defined domain in the predominantly rural, economically interdependent society of New England. She presided over a productive universe that ran from kitchen, pantries, cellars, brewhouses, milk houses, and butteries to the garden, well, pigpen, henhouse, and orchard. Like Chesapeake housewives, each New England housewife possessed (to greater or lesser degrees, of course) a repertoire of skills for the processing of raw materials into usable goods and for the maintenance of those goods and their management. She was expected to manage resources, time, and the available labor to best advantage, balancing production against maintenance, the needs of daily consumption against long-term supply, and the particular capabilities of servants and children against their assigned chores. These duties inevitably carried a wife out into the community, for families in seventeenth-century New England lived by exchange as much as by self-sufficiency.

Although the broad outlines of the housewife role were the same for all married New England women, the details varied. Frontier households differed sharply from urban ones. A husband of middling means in a settled farming community could provide his wife with a reasonably convenient working environment: a two-story home with hall and parlor on the ground floor and two rooms above for storage of food and equipment. She would have a separate kitchen, dominated by pots, kettles, and pans, and a cool cellar for foods. Most foods she served her family were the product of housewifery, not simply in their preparation, but in their growing, raising, harvesting, slaughtering, and processing. In the course of the day, the good rural housewife not only prepared meals for immediate consumption but also replenished the supplies of the storerooms. She tended the garden and preserved its crops, raised the animals and slaughtered them, spun cloth and mended clothing. Although the New England woman exchanged some goods with neighbors, or shared work such as cloth making with friends, the rural seventeenth-century housewife and her daughters or servants ran a constant manufactory.

For women of ordinary means in New England towns, housewifery involved more marketplace exchanges and fewer productive enterprises. Trade, not home manufacture, preceded meal preparation, for these women could purchase grain or flour, even bread from a bakery and meat from a nearby slaughterhouse. Reliance on the market eliminated tasks but it did not free a woman's time: an urban housewife moved constantly through town, seeking out shops that were often widely dispersed. Knowing what merchant had received a shipment of supplies was as important as knowing who specialized in those goods. Haggling was an art form, and establishing a reputation that permitted credit-buying was an economic necessity. Spending fewer hours in household production, these women increased their concern for cleanliness and neatness. Rural women rarely washed linens or swept rooms clean, but urban households had regular schedules for what we call housekeeping. Washing, which involved boiling water, beating clothes, and hanging them in the sunlight, was followed by ironing with heavy irons that had to be filled and refilled with hot coals.

On the peripheries of the New England colonies, frontier women coped without marketplaces or adequate workspaces. A family's accumulated wealth often consisted of little more than land and livestock. A woman struggled to maintain her family in a single-story cottage, whose one room was refuge for men, women, children, and barnyard animals. In addition to cooking, milking, and baking, women on the frontier foraged for food in the forests, marshes, and streams, in order to add fruit and fish to their family's diet.

The women of New England towns, farms, and frontiers would be keenly aware of the diverse circumstances of their lives—yet they would recognize the commonalities as well. To be a "notable housewife" was to engage in a ceaseless round of sustaining and enabling activity, using whatever resources were at hand.

If these portraits of notable housewives locate women in the domestic space of home, kitchen, and surrounding garden and barnyard, that space was primary rather than exclusive. As help-meet, or companion and aide to her husband, a wife could cross from her terrain to his without staking claim to it. As his deputy, or surrogate in his absence, she exercised *ad hoc* power. The same concept of surrogacy operated in the Chesapeake, as widows managed estates for their husband's heirs. But in New England surrogacy was largely short-lived. In the Chesapeake the authority widows enjoyed might take on an independent life, but in New England the longevity of marriage and the stability of patriarchy probably operated against a woman's internalization of her deputized power.

It is important to remember how proximate and overlapping male and female spaces were in the small universe of the New England family. Men assigned daily work to servants, hired help, and did business with their peers in the parlor. Wives, daughters, even female servants were present when debts were contracted, commitments to provide goods or services made, and land sales transacted. Women thus acquired empirical knowledge of family affairs. They acquired influence as well. Salem court records show a wife not only present during her husband's negotiation on the sale of land and a house but "furthering the sale." Creditors suing their debtors called on their wives, who were "present at the bargain making," to corroborate their testimony. Women served as historians of their husbands' economic affairs, recalling under oath former ownership of property and its location as well as details of their neighbors' and kinsmen's finances. Not all New England men listened to their wives' advice—and it was always their option to heed or ignore—but in the early decades when, as one historian of court cases put it, men and women worked, socialized, and misbehaved together, it is not surprising that many did.

Personal relationships between Puritan husbands and wives have concerned historians as deeply as they concerned seventeenth-century ministers and magistrates. Puritan ideology tried to integrate seemingly contradictory commitments to hierarchy and mutuality in gender relationships much as they did in the relationships between ministers and congregations or political leaders and citizens. Men and women were exhorted to live in harmony built on love and affection. Husbands were to be obeyed, but mutual respect was the context in which their authority was to be exercised. Clearly, this affection and love had different trajectories for men and for women; men were expected to reach downward and overlook women's spiritual, physical, and social inferiority, while women were supposed to reach upward and acknowledge without resentment men's superiority and power. That some couples sought and sustained loving marriages cannot be doubted. But that others did not is equally unsurprising.

The records of marital strife reveal much about gender differences between New England husbands and wives. For example, when Daniel Ela was found beating his wife, he defended his actions to his neighbors by appealing to the fundamental power relationships of patriarchy. His wife, he argued, "was his servant and his slave." This interpretation of household hierarchy placed Ela at the margin of his community, yet his argument was not entirely beyond his neighbors' understanding. Ela's abuse of his power was extreme, but it was not alien to seventeenth-century New England culture. Likewise, when John Tillison chained his wife by the leg to a plow in order to keep her from leaving the house, or when a Maine husband kicked his wife and hit her with a club because she refused to feed his pig, they were considered to be exercising their right to discipline subordinates disrespectful of legitimate authority.

Marital violence was not limited to men, however. Court records show that women, too, were brought to trial for physical abuse of their mates. Mary Davis, who was married in the 1640s to a man far older than she, gave vent to her resentment against her husband by taking a knife to his chest and threatening to kill him, "calling him old rogue and cuckold." The latter part of the accusation was apparently true, for Mary confessed to adultery with twelve different men. Yet Mary Davis made no effort to legitimize her behavior, Puritan ideology offered her no refuge. Her contempt was naked and, in the eyes of others, illegitimate.

Historians have attempted to take the pulse of Puritan marital relations for decades, some finding the harmony ministers advocated in the daily lives of their congregants, others pointing to the resentment and discontent wives felt, which manifested itself in such symptomatic behavior as depression, adultery, and even witchcraft, or in their husband's infidelity or desertion. What is clear is this: the centrality of marriage and family to New England society, the careful and conscious elaboration of gender roles within those families, the reinforcement of gender ideals such as "helpmeet" and "notable housewife" by religious and civil authorities, and the simple reality that women had few if any acceptable alternatives to life except as wife and mother, meant that a woman's self-satisfaction and her sense of accomplishment and maturity were heavily invested in her marriage. Dissatisfaction, a sense of failure or inadequacy, resentment, frustration, and despair may well have been the risks of such a narrowly defined identity.

A New England woman did not, of course, live entirely within the confines—ideological, psychological, or experiential—of the marital household. The overlapping of male and female worlds within the family had its important parallel in the relationship of the individual and the community. New Englanders lived near each other, they depended on each other for services and skills, for protection and consolation, and the institutions they established and supported demanded not simply contact but interdependence. Community, then, was the countervailing force to family, and this had importance to women as well as men. Daniel

Ela, after all, did not enjoy the privilege of beating his wife in privacy; he defended his decision to his neighbors, but they did not feel the need to defend their intervention in his family affairs.

New England women moved freely among their neighbors' homes. They borrowed and they lent, they kept each other company while going about their chores, they assisted at the birth of one another's children, and they disciplined their neighbors' sons and daughters as if they were their own. Thus, the authority of a husband was always bounded by a broad circle of peers and dependents, and the obligations and satisfactions deriving from the role of neighbor offset to some degree the role of wife.

When fate happened upon Hannah Duston on that March morning in 1697, she was recovering from the delivery of a child. Because reproduction framed every New England woman's life, these women treated childbirth as a ritual, honored it by ceremony, and tested their faith and explored their eschatology in terms of it. Childbirth was an exclusively female social ritual. Women gathered to assist in and to bear witness to this female experience, and it was not unknown for an entire community of married women to attend a delivery. In the earliest phase of labor, the mother acted as host, serving refreshments to all who came. The humor that comes from an acceptance of the "natural" or the "inevitable," especially of a shared experience, was evident at these birthing rituals; with the pain of labor and delivery imminent, beer became "groaning beer" and cake "groaning cake."

But as the delivery grew nearer, the humor ceased and roles were reversed: the guests began to help their hostess. They used herbs gathered in the field and garden to relieve her labor pains, and they assisted the midwife in any way they could. A New England woman often gave birth sitting in another woman's lap, or supported by the steady arms of friends as she squatted on the midwife's low, open-seated stool. A friend or neighbor gave the newborn its first milk, for colonial New Englanders believed the mother was impure for several days after delivery. Rituals also shaped the child's initial experience of the world. She or he was laid on linens which had been passed down from mother to daughter, each piece embroidered, embellished, and reserved exclusively for this event. But the rituals were bawdy as often as they were sentimental. For example, a boy's umbilical cord was left long to ensure, it was said, that his penis would grow to an equally impressive length.

The arrival of an infant marked the beginning of several months' confinement for the mother. Although many New England women made journeys during pregnancy, they were housebound for the first ten months of a baby's life. A breast-fed child needed its source of milk near at hand, and colonial mothers usually found an eight- to ten-month-old baby too heavy to carry for long distances. Between the tenth and fifteenth months, however, mothers often left home for a long visit to their extended family or to friends. These trips were probably "weaning journeys," undertaken to separate mother and nursing child.

The steady cycle of pregnancy, birth, nursing, and weaning ensured that women were ever-conscious of their bodies. Colonial women of every region had to calculate their baby's protection and care into the equations of everyday life. They had to consider the impact of lifting heavy objects as they went about domestic duties; they had to calibrate how wide the circle of their movement could be, with a needy infant waiting to be fed at home; they had to adjust to the alterations in their physical appearance during each pregnancy and lactation period and the permanent changes in the shape and resiliency of their body after many births. For women who were "fruitfull vines," biology and anatomy did indeed seem to shape their destinies.

Mothering, on the other hand, did not play the central role in a colonial woman's identity that it did in the lives of nineteenth-century middle-class women. Other people held legitimate, competing interests in her children. As heirs to property, for example, children were primarily the concern of the father. To him fell the responsibility of dividing wealth and assets among sons and daughters, and in these critical matters a mother's role was at best advisory. As dependent members of the community, children were the obligation of all adults rather than the exclusive responsibility of the mother. Indeed, "mothering" was a form of expertise in discipline and instruction that, once achieved by a woman, could be employed in the interest of any child. Neighbors were entitled and expected to instruct and care for the young if the occasion arose. The community acknowledged this generalized mothering by its habit of addressing any older woman as "mother" or "gammar" (grandma). As members of the family work force, children were vocational apprentices of the parent of their own sex: fathers trained sons in agriculture or in the family trade, while mothers taught housewifery to their girls. The chains of daily command followed this gender division as the family went about its workday. Finally, as part of a numerous brood, no individual child was likely to receive the exclusive attention of a mother. Mothering was, as one historian has put it, extensive rather than intensive.

In its almost fully realized patriarchy, in the longevity of the marriage that established it, in the demographic advantages that made it multigenerational, the family of Hannah Duston's girlhood and the family of her womanhood were unlike Chesapeake families. The second, perhaps equally significant reason for her divergent experience was the strength and pervasive influence on her family by Puritanism and its Congregational Church. Puritanism was more than a theology and more than an institution; it was, as scholars have observed and documented from the seventeenth century onward, a way of life.

Not every man or woman who departed the old England for the new in the 1630s was a self-declared advocate of religious reform, but the most powerful and important of the immigrants were. The Massachusetts Bay Company had been formed by men committed to the purification of the Anglican Church and to the completion, as they interpreted it, of the Protestant Revolution in England. Their reformist impulse was not confined to liturgy or church structure, although they had strong theological and organizational agendas. Their critique extended to the moral values and behavior within Anglican society. They condemned the manners and mores of that English culture as strongly as they condemned the prayer books and bishops of its official church. They meant to create a community that fulfilled biblical guidelines and injunctions for daily life, and although they read that Bible through the prism of English social and political traditions, they read it differently from their King and his bishops.

In the model community the Puritans sought to create in America, all participants' roles were carefully defined. Yet the logic of the theology, state policy, and traditions that the immigrants carried with them produced contradictions and inconsistencies. Some were particularly important to women. For example, the extensive regulation of personal behavior, the official "prudishness" that later generations would associate as the core of "Puritanism," was confounded by a steady record of sexual and moral offenses that suggests that the bawdiness of seventeenth-century English culture had survived the transatlantic voyage intact. Traditions such as pre-bridal pregnancy and marital infidelity proceeded unabated, for, in fact, the small agrarian communities and the blending of what nineteenth-century middle-class society would call the private and the public worlds, the immediacy of sexuality and procreation in cramped spaces, gave these behaviors a logic that the Puritan code of morality could not erase.

A constellation of social problems rose from Puritan theology. The New England Puritans proclaimed the possibility of salvation equally for men and women, yet the radical implications of this theology—a critique of political and social inequality by either gender or class—were never acknowledged by Puritan religious or civic leaders. In fact, in the Puritan colonies political participation was not expanded but restricted; to the criterion of property ownership, John Winthrop's government added the requirement of full membership, rather than simple attendance, in the church. Yet women's "sainthood," as individual salvation was officially called, did not confer political rights. Second, women's participation within the church was defined ambiguously. Women were enjoined to silence during all worship services, although the same Gospel of St. Paul that justified this restriction also encouraged women to read the Bible and to teach others its word. Finally, neither the clergy nor the magistrates who regulated the life of the "city upon a hill" were able to resolve the tensions between the moral and social autonomy that sainthood encouraged and the uniformity and conformity they demanded of all colonists. Puritans did not resolve, except by fiat and force, such critical questions as how did sainthood disrupt the hierarchy of gender or of the family, or who determined the code of behavior for an individual saint. During the seventeenth century, women challenged Puritanism to clarify these issues, sometimes consciously and sometimes unintentionally, through their actions.

The most famous, or as John Winthrop would have it, the most notorious woman to challenge the authority of ministers and magistrates was Anne Hutchinson. Hutchinson's dissent followed close on the heels of another controversy, stirred by Roger Williams, who challenged the authority of Bay Colony leaders only five years after the Puritan community was settled. His three-pronged attack—challenging the legitimacy of the Bay Company's title to the land, arguing that ministerial authority was limited, and denying the right of the colony's government to compel attendance in, or obedience to, the Puritan Congregational Church—earned him exile in the dead of winter. Hutchinson's criticism of ministerial authority was similar to Williams's. And although it came from a woman and not from a minister, the threat was taken seriously. For Anne Hutchinson, like Roger Williams, had gathered strong popular support.

Anne Hutchinson was born Anne Marbury in 1591, and raised in Alford, England. Her father, a clergyman, encouraged her to read and discuss theology with him. At twenty-one, Anne Marbury married a successful Alford merchant named William Hutchinson and produced a large family of her own. Fifteen children were born to her during the course of a long and supportive marriage, and thirteen survived.

In 1634, William and Anne Hutchinson were part of the flock that followed minister John Cotton to Massachusetts Bay. She was forty-three, accustomed to a life of material and intellectual satisfaction. He was civic-minded, as befit a successful member of the gentry, and quickly entered Boston political life as a town commissioner, an inferior-court judge, deputy to the colony's legislature, and deacon in the Boston church over which Cotton now presided.

The Hutchinsons were, ostensibly, the kind of immigrants in whom the colony's leadership delighted. Yet within a year, trouble began. At first the problem centered around the pulpit of John Cotton. The Alford congregation that came to America with Cotton had their own notions of how a minister ought to be selected, and by whom. In Massachusetts, the Bay Company leadership appointed all ministers and paid them. The Hutchinsons and their friends protested that those tasks belonged exclusively to the congregation. At issue was a lay challenge to state control. When the Alford faction tried to organize a separate church but could not gain official recognition for it, they began to meet privately. The prospect of competing or alternative churches did not sit well with the authorities. Many of the dissenters resolved the matter by moving outside the Bay Colony's borders, and thus its jurisdiction. But William and Anne Hutchinson (whose father, as a clergyman, had been imprisoned twice and silenced by church courts for his attacks on incompetent ministers) chose to remain in Boston to continue the fight.

Governor John Winthrop succeeded in blocking the efforts of the Reverend John Wheelwright, the leader of the dissent and Anne Hutchinson's brother-in-law, who sought to establish an independent, lay-dominated church nine miles outside Boston. Winthrop's tactics did not appeal to one of Wheelwright's most prominent followers, Henry Vane. In May 1636, Vane opposed Winthrop and took the governorship away from him. But Vane's victory was short-lived. Winthrop and his faction rallied, discrediting Wheelwright by charging him with preaching sedition and wresting the governorship back from the young Vane. Before

1636 was over, the movement for lay control was broken and Wheelwright was banished.

The Hutchinsons had played a prominent role in Wheelwright's dissent. Their home had been used for private worship services, and Wheelwright had preached often at their farm. Anne Hutchinson's house had also become the gathering place for women's meetings at which devout Puritan women—who were denied attendance at the public lecture or weekday sermon—gathered to discuss Scripture. The women's meetings were well established before Anne Hutchinson's arrival in the colony, but Hutchinson expanded them and Winthrop and his colleagues soon saw them as a vehicle for dissident proselytizing. The magistrates wanted no such opportunities to fall into Hutchinson's hands.

What was the nature of Hutchinson's threat to Winthrop's order? Did the growing number of women, and later men, who came to hear her critique local ministers' sermons raise a challenge to established authority regardless of the content of their discussions? Or was there something specifically heretical or unorthodox in her views? Were her challenges theological or organizational? Did her criticisms address women's role in the church and women's relationship to God, or were they universal? Did her popularity reflect widespread concern over theological and institutional issues, or were social, political, and gender dissatisfactions being displaced?

On these questions, historians have long disagreed. The records of Hutchinson's many interrogations and trials come to us from Winthrop himself and are decidedly biased. Some scholars argue that Hutchinson was an antinomian, committed to the principle that no authority mediated between an individual and God, that salvation came through a direct relationship with God and that "good works" or social morality played no part in salvation. Antinomianism clearly challenged the importance and the authority of the clergy. It was a potential challenge to the regulation by any authority of a "saint's" behavior.

Winthrop's account of the Hutchinson trials suggests that he saw in Hutchinson's dissent a challenge to family order, sexual morality, and the subordination of women to men. The gathering of sixty to eighty women for discussion was, in itself, disruptive. "Though women might meet (some few together)," he wrote, "to pray and edify one another; yet such a set assembly (as was their practice at Boston) where sixty or more did meet every week, and one woman (in a prophetical way, by resolving questions of doctrine, and expanding scripture), took upon her the whole exercise was agreed to be disorderly and without rule." This practice as much as the content of Hutchinson's commentary would lead to a division between husband and wife.

If, as Winthrop insisted, Anne Hutchinson argued against the resurrection of the body, the hierarchy of sex was challenged. If believers became "demi-gods," beyond sexual distinction, and if "there is neither male nor female for you are all one in Jesus Christ," what implications did such equality have for earthly chains of command? The question was not new in Puritan thought, but the attention to it, the bald posing of it in Winthrop's Boston, was not welcome.

Finally, some historians have considered the issues raised by Hutchinson less important than the socioeconomic discontent they galvanized. They have interpreted support for Hutchinson as a veiled protest by merchants' interests against the economic and political constraints of Winthrop's government. The variety of interpretations confirms that the confrontation between Puritan authorities and Anne Hutchinson was a central event of the 1630s. It hardened the government's determination to demand conformity, not only in doctrine, but in the social arrangements between the sexes. It established the principle that religious dissent, or error, and a woman's insubordination were linked—whether the rebellion against her proper place was symptom or source did not matter. For example, in 1641 Anne Eaton, the daughter of an English bishop and the wife of the governor of the colony, was tried and excommunicated for her heretical position against infant baptism. The authorities declared that Eaton's "fall" was the result of reading and a failure to seek guidance from her husband. Sarah Keayne was found guilty in 1646 of "irregular prophesying in mixed assembly," and Joan Hogg was convicted nine years later of "disorderly singing and idleness, and for saying she [was] commanded of Christ to do so."

When the Quakers arrived in Massachusetts in the 1650s, the Puritan conviction that inappropriate feminine behavior and religious error were connected was reinforced. Quaker women enraged and shocked Puritan officials, using this Puritan conviction to dramatize their own cause. In 1662, for example, the Quaker Deborah Wilson walked naked through Salem. Her purpose, she said, was to call attention to the cruelty and immodesty of the government's practice of stripping Quaker women to the waist to whip them in public. When Quaker Lydia Wardell of Hampton was called to appear before the elders of the church for her religious views, she presented herself at the Sabbath lecture stark naked. She did it, she explained, to wake up church members who were "blinded with Ignorance and Persecution."

Most Puritan women, like most Puritan men, did not place themselves in critical opposition to their church. They entered the church by a separate door from men and, throughout most of the seventeenth century, until family pews became the norm, sat segregated from their husbands, fathers, and brothers. No member of their sex was a minister and none signed the church covenant that created a congregation. They had no formal voice in the selection of the minister and no voice at all during the service he conducted. Yet they could pursue, attain, and have acknowledged the presence of God's grace within them, and thus enter the privileged ranks of full membership in the church. Sainthood was one of the few public distinctions available to a woman, and as the steady rise in the number of women saints over men attests, this distinction was valued. Beginning in the eighteenth century, it was a New England–wide pattern that women became church members at an earlier age and in greater numbers than their husbands.

As women's numbers in the church grew, so did their informal influence. As a community expanded, women who lived on its periphery pressured their husbands to establish a new church. Burdened by infants and toddlers, pregnant or recovering from childbirth, they demanded a church within reasonable walking distance. Thus, although they were forbidden to sign the new church's covenant, they were instrumental in its birth.

Ministers understood well the power that women congregants had over their own careers. Gossip created reputation, and New England women often took on the role of watchdog of a clergyman's behavior both in the pulpit and in his personal life. A minister who could rally women's support for his tenure or for his side in a controversy enjoyed considerable advantage; a minister who alienated his female congregants faced formidable difficulties.

The church thus acted as both a conservative force and an expansive one in the lives of Puritan women. Although the equality of souls remained a theological principle, the power of men to mediate between Christ and women was expressed in the all-male clergy and in the silencing of women within the church—and outside its doors following Anne Hutchinson's trial and conviction for heresy. This subordination of women reinforced the right of husband and father to subsume a woman's interest. Yet salvation and church membership gave women an independent status, unbreachable by the men who dominated their secular life. The rising number of women in the church worked a subtle but significant change in the values extolled by its clergy. Increasingly, character traits associated with women were transposed as Christian traits, and worldly handicaps became spiritual strengths, for meekness and submissiveness readied the soul for grace.

Hannah Duston came late to the church, long after she married and produced her family. In this she differed from many of her female contemporaries. She differed as well, of course, in her celebrity, for Indian captivity and her daring escape set her apart from her neighbors. Yet the potential for violence generated by bitter race relations was present in the life of most New Englanders. During the first hundred years of colonization, New

England's white settlers pursued an aggressive policy of invasion, usurpation, and extermination which led to war, bloodshed, and a pervasive sense of insecurity for many. Even the Pilgrims, whose capacity for cooperation and respect for cultural diversity are captured in the Thanksgiving tableau, earned the reputation of "cutthroats" in later dealings with Indians. From the Pequot Wars of the 1630s to the wars against Metacomet or King Philip in the 1670s, Puritans waged brutal attacks in the name of God and their own privileged destinies. These struggles, largely for land, were framed within larger imperial struggles between European powers. French interests led to alignments between Indian confederacies and independent tribes with the Canadian colonial government, countered by English alliances with other Indian groups. Thus, New England women lived in a theater of local and international warfare.

The consequences of violent race relations were felt most immediately on the frontier, where each settlement designated one home its garrison in case of raid or full-scale attack. But when Massachusetts mobilized for war against the alliance of French and Indians, residents of settled communities and seaport towns were affected as well. It was captivity, however, not death in battle, that became the primary narrative of encounter with alien Indian and French Catholic cultures. Those taken captive during the raids over the end of the century and over the first decades of the next were intended for adoption into the tribe or into French Canadian society rather than death, and thus many stories survive. What is interesting is the gender differences that emerge.

Age rather than gender was the key factor in determining a captive's fate. Those over twenty were more likely to be returned than younger colonists. But men were more likely than women to escape or to die. Women were considerably more likely than men to remain with their captors, especially if they were turned over to the French in Canada. As one historian put it, men resisted; women adapted.

Why did women adapt and survive in greater numbers than their husbands, sons, or fathers? One-fifth of the women seized from their sleep or their household chores were pregnant or were carrying a nursing baby. Two lives, therefore, were at stake, and this may well have made the captive women less willing to behave rashly. But some historians feel there was much in the training and the life expectations of these seventeenth-century English-women that inclined them to manage this crisis through adaptation rather than resistance. Most girls assumed they would be uprooted when they married, leaving their family and perhaps their community to settle where a husband chose. Marrying a Frenchman, therefore, required a degree of adjustment, accommodation, and adaptability that was greater than normal but not wholly unanticipated. As wives within the new community, they were made welcome; women were accustomed to acquiring their status from their husbands, and European society was accustomed to granting it to them. Finally, women were supported in the early period of transition by a female network that was analogous to the networks of initiation and support they found at home. That Catholic nuns rather than Puritan goodwives made up that network was no small difference, but the similarities existed nonetheless. Indeed, some Puritan captives became nuns themselves.

Other historians read the adaptation of these women as acts of rebellion against their prescribed place in Puritan society. Those women who, on ransom and release from their Indian captors, pleaded to remain or stole away from the campfires of their "rescuers" to return to their Indian families and friends may support such an interpretation. Despite the Puritan's sure sense of the superiority of his culture over Indian society, some women found the gendered division of labor and of rights and duties within the Abnaki world more desirable than those of colonial Haverhill or Deerfield.

Whatever their motives, at least one-third of the women taken to New France chose to remain, and at least 40 percent converted to Catholicism and married French husbands. Yet other women resisted captivity and acculturation. They refused conversion to Catholicism, risking beatings and threats and imprisonment at the hands of their captors. Whipped, struck with rods, pinched black-and-blue, one·such captive would not even cross herself.

Hannah Duston was silent on the matter of her own experience. She let her trophies—the scalps she took—and her Puritan superiors—ministers and magistrates—speak for her. But others preferred to bear witness to their trials and their triumphs. From Mary Rowlandson, the minister's wife who took her knitting needles into captivity with her and practiced a groveling subservience along with feats of housewifery in order to survive among her Indian captors, we have a long narrative whose theme is not simply survival but selection for trial and travail by her God. Rowlandson carried the experience with her long after she was returned to her family and friends. In Rowlandson's insomnia, and in the hallucinations of another captive, Mercy Short, of "tawney" specter-devils who bit her and slashed her skin, the cost of living among enemies can be measured.

Although Puritan magistrates and ministers sought to create and sustain a stable, ordered community, circumstances subverted their aims. Dissent racked the earliest decades. And between 1665 and 1689, war with local Indians disrupted community life. Tax rates rose to finance King Philip's War, and in 1675–76 alone, the aggressive policy of the Puritan governments to seize Indian lands and eliminate Indian settlements led to a bitter warfare that left 600 colonists dead and 2,000 homeless. During these same decades, Massachusetts experienced a population explosion, its 24,000 colonists in 1665 more than doubling in number by 1690. Boston had 25 percent more people than any other English mainland colonial city by the 1690s, with over 5,000 inhabitants. The population growth wreaked havoc on the Puritan ideal of homogeneity; Huguenots, Quakers, Anglicans, and Anabaptists settled and did business in the port city of Boston, and commercial activity led to growing divisions in wealth. Rich merchants, poor dockworkers, black slaves, indigent widows, younger, propertyless sons of farmers—such diversity of rank and circumstance among Massachusetts's population generated considerable social tensions as well as new demands that political rights be wholly divorced from church affiliation. Signs that "the decadence of Old England" had crossed the Atlantic could also be found: men in fancy dress and wigs and women in low-cut gowns paraded city streets. Political crisis also made its way across the Atlantic. The English began to restructure the Northern colonies, creating, for a brief period, a Dominion of New England that swallowed up Connecticut and Massachusetts. By 1692 the charter of Massachusetts Bay Colony had been reexamined and revoked, and the laws of the colony were brought into conformity with the laws of England. By 1700 the Puritan experiment was formally dead; and historians have charted the shifts in community values and mores that mark the transition from Puritan to "Yankee" cultures.

And then, as the last decade of the seventeenth century came to a close, as the Puritan experiment unraveled, the Massachusetts Bay Colony was invaded by witches. A drama of suspicion and fear, accusation and counteraccusation, community disruption and eruption of social tensions and conflicts began to unfold, and women were the central actors. Witchcraft was not new to the people of the 1690s. As a tradition of folkways and religious unorthodoxies, it had a rich and complex history in most European societies. In New England communities, the belief that witchcraft was practiced was attested to formally, by accusations in courts of law, and informally (and often as effectively) by rumor and reputation, and a tacit conviction among the witch's neighbors of her guilt. In every decade Massachusetts courts tried the cases of men and women accused not so much of collaboration with the devil as of acts that disrupted the natural ebb and flow of agrarian life: the sudden death of livestock or children, the destruction of property, bad luck, and unexpected injury. What is striking is the prevalence of women among the accused. Before the Salem witch-hunts of 1692, 80 percent of the 114 New England colonists accused of witchcraft were women.

What, if anything, did these women share in common? They

were women with histories—formal and informal records of aggressive and assertive behavior—that marked them as deviants within their community. They were argumentative rather than neighborly, and their abrasiveness was felt by members of their own sex as often as by men. They had histories of domestic discord; estranged husbands sometimes began rumors of their wives' strangeness themselves, and even when the accusing husband was guilty of beating and abusing his wife, their unsuccessful marriage was used as evidence against the wife. So Sarah Dribble learned, when she was accused by a man known for "most inhumane beating of her so that he caused the blood to settle in several places of her body." Widows were often among the accused, probably because they lacked a husband's protection from their neighbors' anger. Anne Hibbens, whose religious dissent led to excommunication from the Boston church in the 1640s, was not tried, convicted, and executed for witchcraft until 1656, two years after her husband died. William Hibbens's prestige as a merchant and magistrate had shielded his wife for over a decade.

Women accused of witchcraft were often at the age of menopause—poised, as the Puritans understood it, between the preparatory stages of childhood and youth and the declining stage of old age. Women of this age were in their prime, at the height of their powers and responsibilities, and mistresses of households filled with children and servants. Witchcraft was an abuse of those powers, a malignant rather than a benign application of domestic and maternal roles. And because a woman in menopause was also a woman who was losing, or had lost, her reproductive or generative capacities, her malice was often directed—or so it appeared to the community—against infants and young children.

For many of the accused, the fertility so valued by the Puritan community had eluded them altogether. One-sixth of supposed witches were childless, and many had borne only one or two children. When children fell mysteriously ill, when a mother's milk ceased to flow or a healthy woman miscarried, infertile women were held suspect.

The New England witch violated the boundaries between

healing and harming. Many of the accused had shown a special aptitude for healing, using charms, incantations, and herbal potions to cure and to relieve pain. Some, like the widow Hale, took sick men and women into her home for rest and "nursing." Others, like Anna Edmunds of Lynn, had earned a reputation as a "doctor woman" before she was accused of witchcraft in 1673. Efforts to heal were more suspect if uninvited. Rachel Fuller of Hampton appeared at the bedside of a sick child, her face strangely covered with molasses, eager to attend the boy. When his mother refused her any contact with the child, Fuller performed a ritual that included spitting and tossing herbs into the hearth fire. She then declared the child would recover. When he died, Fuller was accused of witchcraft.

Women who had suffered or were in danger of suffering a decline in social status were also the targets of accusation. Most witches were among the poor and needy, but women who had fallen from the ranks of the respectable drew attention and suspicion from their neighbors. And the most likely to accuse her were those in positions of greatest vulnerability themselves—men and women whose security of place within the community was still not established: young, unmarried women; young, married men, untried in career or public life.

Until 1692, most New Englanders charged with witchcraft were never brought to trial. Authorities were reluctant to intervene in the internal conflicts of village life. Instead, communities were left to regulate and resolve such matters themselves, to shun or show approval of their members in the course of daily life. In 1692, however, certain judges and ministers of Massachusetts set aside their usual caution and appeared to encourage a hunt for witches in Salem. When several young, unmarried women and girls of Salem Village began to experience nightmares, loss of appetite, disorientation, and signs of physical suffering, their small farming community became alarmed. When the young women began to have violent fits, concern turned to fear, and the conviction spread that they were bewitched. Possession by the devil might be cured by a regimen of prayer, fasting, and repentance;

victims of bewitchment, however, could not be cured until the guilty were found—and punished or destroyed.

Under questioning, the victims named three local women who had revealed themselves in spirit form as their tormentors. Over the weeks and months, the number of accused grew. Salem's visitation by the devil was no simple case of black magic or individual malice. A conspiracy was implied, a network of women and men who challenged not simply community norms or state authority but God and the godly. The Massachusetts court arraigned all those accused, imprisoned them, and began to hear the cases at once. After some hesitation, the judges agreed to admit "special evidence"—testimony by the victims that they had seen the spirits of their tormentors and could thus identify them in their material form. By summer 1692, nineteen people had been convicted and executed, most of them women who pleaded their innocence to the end. Over one hundred more men and women were crowded into cells, awaiting trial.

Older patterns of accusation gave way under the pressures of the Salem witch-hunt. If the first of the accused fit the profile of a witch—poor, deviant in behavior or social status, involved with healing, middle-aged—the majority of the newly accused in jail did not. Many were respected members of the community, men and women whose histories showed no taint of disruptiveness, contention, or marital discord. Despite this, few colonists were willing to challenge the proceedings openly. The challenge came privately. Leading Salem merchants were skeptical not only of the trial procedures but of the existence of witchcraft itself. They were disturbed by the disruption to their trade as well. They took advantage of the political situation within the colony, appealing to the new, non-Puritan, royal governor to intervene. By October, Governor William Phips had banned any further arrests and had dismissed the court that tried the earlier cases. A new court, convened in January 1693, acquitted the remaining prisoners. The witch-hunt was over.

The Salem witch-hunt has fascinated Americans of later generations as much as it disturbed and confused those who lived through it. Many of the participants—judges who heard the cases, young women who made the accusations, and the surviving accused—painfully reviewed and evaluated their roles in the affair. But playwrights and scholars, medical experts and psychoanalysts have tried to explain them as well. Modern medicine would confirm that the victims were indeed victims, not of witchcraft, but of conversion hysteria, which transforms extreme anxiety into physical symptoms. Modern historians remind us that neither the victims' sincerity nor their suffering holds the key to the witch-hunts; the arrests, the trials, and the executions were the result of decisions and policies made by religious leaders and magistrates, not by the servant girls and the daughters of local ministers who fell to the ground in fits.

Scholars also remind us to consider the context in which the witch-hunt occurred. The trials took place during the transfer of power from a Puritan to a royal regime and as the fault lines deepened between an agrarian, religious society and the newer, commercial, and secular society of the port cities and towns. The conflict between these two cultures was evident in Salem itself. Salem Village, where the bewitched lived, was an offshoot of Salem Town, and was settled by men and women who rejected the commercial spirit of the larger community. Yet in 1692 that commercial spirit had invaded the village, creating division and dissension. That division was evident in the pattern of accusation: the accusers lived in the western part of the village, where the pious and increasingly poorer families lived; the accused lived in the eastern section, home to the richest and the most entrepreneurial. The victims' anxieties—centered on their marital prospects—were thus closely linked to the social anxieties of the decade.

Salem Village was believed to be invaded by witches five years after Hannah Duston's frontier community was raided by Indians. Duston's response—violent and seemingly merciless—was praised by Judge Samuel Sewall, who had presided over the Salem trials. The Puritan minister Cotton Mather lauded Duston's willingness to fight the enemy when the males captured with her would not.

In these men's praise perhaps a wish lingered that the Puritan community could defeat its enemies from both without and within as Duston had defeated hers. And perhaps Hannah Duston, a goodwife of New England, understood this as the true engine of their accolades. Women of a more secular eighteenth-century Massachusetts, like women of the seventeenth-century Chesapeake, probably would not.

3

THE SISTERS OF POCAHONTAS: NATIVE AMERICAN WOMEN IN THE CENTURIES OF COLONIZATION

WETAMO WAS BORN in the seventeenth century into an old New England family—her ancestors, men and women of the Wampanoag people, had roots deep in the history of the region, deep enough to make the Cabots and the Lodges, even the Winthrops and the Bradfords, look like the newcomers they indeed were to North America. Wetamo spent her childhood in the relative peace and security forged between the English colonists of Plymouth Plantation and the Wampanoag sachem, or leader, Massasoit. When she reached womanhood, she took as her husband Massasoit's oldest son, Wamsutta, who became the sachem of the main Wampanoag village, Pokanoket, on his father's death. Seen through the prism of English culture, the marriage was a joining of two aristocratic families, for Wetamo, like her new husband, came from a long lineage of leaders in both civil and military affairs.

When Massasoit died in 1662, Wetamo's husband took on the increasingly difficult task of sustaining the peace between the Europeans and the Wampanoags. Much had changed since William Bradford and Massasoit had met in 1621. The English were no longer a struggling and incompetent community of refugees.

Neighboring Massachusetts Bay Colony numbered in the thousands, and Puritan claims on the land extended as far as Maine; New Haven, Wethersfield, and other Connecticut towns were firmly entrenched and eager to expand. Wamsutta's own village of Pokanoket was now located in what the English new-comers called Rhode Island. The constant demand for land cre-ated rivalries among the New England colonies and led to warfare between settlers and local Indian populations. The massacre of the Pequot in the 1630s drove home the danger to Wamsutta and his people.

If Wamsutta and Wetamo feared the worst, they were correct. In 1664, Plymouth officials heard rumors that the Wampanoags had sold land to the white colonists of Rhode Island. It was their contention that treaties between Plymouth and the Wampanoag gave their colony exclusive rights to any land the tribe might be willing to give up. Outraged, the colony's government had Wamsutta seized and marched at gunpoint to Plymouth for in-terrogation. Whether his answers were satisfactory or not became irrelevant, for Wamsutta died mysteriously among his former allies.

In this manner, Wetamo became a widow. Soon after, she became the sachem of the Wampanoag town of Pocasset, a po-sition of authority that placed over 300 warriors under her guid-ance and thus made her a political power in her own right. During the next ten years, as Wamsutta's successor Metacomet tried to accommodate English demands, Wetamo and her soldiers carefully kept the peace. By 1675, however, both sides had armed them-selves for war. When Metacomet abandoned diplomacy for battle, Wetamo was among the first to cast her lot with him.

Few who knew Wetamo were surprised by her decision. The ties that bound the two Wampanoag leaders were many: Meta-comet was Wamsutta's younger brother and the husband of Wetamo's own sister Wootonekanuske. Friends and critics alike knew her as an implacable enemy of the English, firmly opposed to the concessions of land and independent authority already made by her people. She herself controlled lands that several colonies desired. When her second husband, Petananuet, decided to declare his loyalty to the English, Wetamo left him to join Metacomet's campaign.

The Wampanoag resistance went badly from the beginning. By the end of June 1675, Metacomet—or Philip, as the English called him—had fled to the temporary safety of Wetamo's territory. Soon, however, Wetamo and her people were also in flight, seeking refuge among the Narragansett. Wetamo's arrival played havoc with the carefully nurtured Narragansett neutrality: to deny a request for refuge violated New England Indian ethics; yet the English interpreted her protection as a hostile act. When a combined army from the English colonies invaded Narragansett territory, the matter of loyalties was settled. Wetamo once again took up arms—this time with a new husband, the Narragansett sachem, Quanopin.

Together, Quanopin and Wetamo successfully raided the town of Lancaster, Massachusetts. But few Indian victories followed. By mid-July 1676, Quanopin had been captured, court-martialed, and shot. Wetamo's sister Wootonekanuske and her nine-year-old son were taken soon after and—along with almost a thousand others from the Algonquin tribes—were sold into slavery. The Wampanoag and their allies had fled or were in captivity.

What became of Wetamo is uncertain. She and three dozen other surviving followers were ambushed as they tried to reach their home village of Pocasset. All were killed or taken except Wetamo herself, who, according to the Puritan minister Increase Mather, escaped alone. Later, however, Mather gleefully reported: "Some of Taunton finding an Indian squaw in *Metapoiset* newly dead, cut off her head and it happened to be *Weetamoo*." The colonists who stumbled upon the body may not have realized the prize they had impaled upon their pole, but Mather did not need to rely on their knowledge of Wampanoag leadership. For when the head was displayed in Taunton, "the Indians who were prisoners there, knew it presently, and made a most horrible and diabolical Lamentation, crying out that it was their Queens head."

Mather took satisfaction in Wetamo's death, for he believed

her responsible, second only to Metacomet, for the "mischief" that had been done and the blood that had been shed. And he found divine justice in the manner of her death. "Now here it is to be observed," he wrote, "that God himself by his own hand, brought this enemy to destruction. For in that place, where the last year, she furnished *Philip* with Canooes for his men, she her self could not meet with a Canoo, but venturing over the River upon a Raft, that brake under her, so that she drowned, just before the English found her." Mather ended with the prediction: "Surely *Philips* turn will be next."

So it was. Metacomet was killed before the end of the week, not by an Englishman, but by a Pocasset Wampanoag named Alderman. Philip's head, like Wetamo's, was stuck on the end of a pole, where it remained on display in Plymouth for twenty years. Metacomet's attempt to block English expansion into the Algonquin world had ended in dismal failure. His followers had killed some 600 colonists and destroyed twenty frontier towns, but perhaps 5,000 members of the Algonquin tribes had been killed or taken captive, and those not sold into slavery or captured fled westward, never to farm or hunt on tribal lands again.

If we can tell the story of Wetamo's public life, we can say little about the person that she was. What description and judgment we have come to us from her most implacable enemies rather than from family or friends. Mather's deep satisfaction at Wetamo's death—and the spontaneous mourning he reports arising from her own people—suggests how influential and effective she was as a leader in peace and war. Yet his account tells us nothing of her personal response to the destruction of the society in her safekeeping.

The most intimate account of Wetamo's character can be found in the celebrated recollections of Mary Rowlandson, a Lancaster housewife who was captured by Wetamo's army. Rowlandson gives us a portrait so negative that Wetamo resembles the fairy-tale witches and wicked stepmothers of European lore: "severe and proud," vain and domineering, a woman wholly lacking the mercy and gentleness that Mary Rowlandson believed distinguished her sex. The Wetamo of Rowlandson's imagination and perception is indeed unsympathetic. She intentionally torments her captive, canceling the effects of her husband Quanopin's kindness by her cruel threats and physical abuse. For Rowlandson, Wetamo's behavior marks her as a savage, and that savagery filled her with fear and dread. Yet Rowlandson also held her captor in contempt. For Wetamo presumed a gentility her English prisoner judged to be far beyond any Indian's birth and race. Rowlandson thus mocks a savage's pretensions in "bestowing every day in dressing herself near as much time as any of the gentry of the land."

The bias of Rowlandson's account goes deeper than personal animosity, of course. Bounded by—and, in her captivity, protected by—the standards of her own English, Christian culture, Mary Rowlandson was unlikely to appreciate the legitimate sources of Wetamo's independent authority or personal dignity. She was no more likely to understand that Wetamo's treatment of her was appropriate and carefully prescribed by Wampanoag culture. Rowlandson did not seek to understand the woman who held her hostage, and neither Rowlandson nor the colonists who thrilled to the narration of her deliverance felt the absence, as we do, of Wetamo's voice.

Had Wetamo searched for herself in the reflections offered by Mather and Rowlandson, she would face distortions much like those we have experienced standing before a carnival funhouse mirror. In this, Wetamo is no different from most Native American women—or men—of the colonial era. Catholic missionaries, Protestant ministers, European government officials, traders, farmers, soldiers, and housewives drew the portraits and wrote the histories of the Wetamos and the Metacomets—Anglicizing their names, assigning them values and the related virtues and vices of European culture, and forcing their rituals and customs into the molds of a European religious and social heritage. These ethnocentric portraits cover the East Coast Indians like a badly fitted suit, disguising the contour of the body, eliminating its natural grace and style, diminishing the wearer's dignity.

Historians have come to understand that they must handle the journals, government reports, sermons, books, and diaries written by Europeans about Native Americans cautiously, as artifacts of European adjustment to cultural diversity rather than true guides to Indian societies. Challenging the authority of these traditional sources, historians have searched for alternative ones. They have leaned heavily on the work of cultural anthropologists and ethnographers, and on the archaeological tools useful in reconstructing material culture. Yet these sources, too, give us the Indian observed rather than the Indian as she saw herself. At best, scholars so far have been able to use the newer insights and information in order to intelligently critique the older, biased records. They are able to suggest alternative interpretations not only of events but of cultural patterns such as child-rearing, the divisions of labor and power, rituals of war and peace, and the meaning to a society of such fundamental concepts as love, loyalty, and death. The best of the scholars who offer these interpretations offered them tentatively, aware that a sympathetic reading is not immune to distortions.

Wetamo's distant ancestors came to what we now call New England around 12,000 years ago. By 4,000 B.C. (as Europeans denote the passage of time), these Paleo-Indians had begun a slow transition from a hunting culture to a culture based on plant products and fish. Populations settled at advantageous locations, choosing sites good for fishing or agriculture, technology improved, and a division of labor along lines of gender, family, and age began. With this fundamental change came greater variation in the social organization of communities, and thus the societies along the Atlantic Coast became more diverse.

Just as in Europe, the influence of powerful nearby cultures worked changes within these communities. Between the eighth and fifteenth centuries, the Archaic cultures of much of eastern North America were slowly absorbed into the Mississippian culture. Only the North Atlantic coast remained outside the direct influence of this Mound Building civilization. Over time, even these communities adopted many of the agricultural techniques of the Mississippians, especially the cultivation of maize, beans, and squash. Each reworked this technology to its own advantage.

By the time of the first encounters between Europeans and Indians, distinctions among the coastal societies were as sharp and as important as similarities. There were, for example, at least four distinct language families—Algonquian, Iroquoian, Caddoan, and Siouan—and, within each, endless possibilities for variation. Four distinct dialects marked New England alone. Differing political structures and family organization could be found as well. Yet Europeans have been content to label the people of the Atlantic coastal region "Eastern Woodland Indians," sacrificing variety to comprehensiveness.

Throughout most of the region that the English colonized, agriculture was well developed, and Indian communities were organized around the sedentary needs of its farmers rather than the nomadic patterns of its hunters. By Wetamo's time, a well-developed sexual division of labor was basic to the gender identities of both men and women. A man hunted; a woman tilled the soil. Particular character traits, physical skills, attitudes, and values were connected to each of these occupations. Secondary responsibilities, honors, rituals, and taboos were attached to each as well. As a general rule, the more central hunting was to survival, the more extensive were male prerogatives; the greater the dependence upon cultivation, the greater the realms of authority and autonomy for women.

As in European society, the consequences of the sexual division of labor were many and complex. Male life was strikingly peripatetic, for the hunt and warfare, and to a lesser degree diplomacy, carried men away from the village and the town. Agriculture and child-rearing rooted women in a more sedentary life. The responsibility for maintaining group continuity often fell on women, and in many instances led to the creation of matrilineal kinship systems and matrilocal residence. Thus, children of the societies of the Middle Atlantic and Southeastern regions acquired their family connections through their mother, and marriage carried a man into his wife's family home rather than removing a wife from hers.

If the division of labor within these societies were based on sex, community bonds were determined by a powerful system of kinship. Indians of the East Coast regions identified themselves first in terms of their lineage, and their strongest loyalties remained to those they acknowledged as kin. Interkinship marriages wove together several clans, creating the villages or towns, bands or tribes that worked and lived together.

The principle of kin as the building block of society was not alien to the European colonizers. Nor, for that matter, was the notion of a sexual division of labor. What seemed profoundly wrong was the particulars of both. In Europe, kin relationships were carried through the father and households were patrilocal. Underlying much of the commentary and observation on Indian culture, therefore, was the conviction that matrilineal and matrilocal arrangements undermined marriage, inheritance, and the authority of the proper head of the household. To Europeans, Indian family patterns raised the specter of promiscuous women, freed from accountability to their fathers and husbands for the offspring they produced. Observers and commentators found ample evidence of the social and moral anarchy they predicted, noting what, by European standards, was Indian women's sexual freedom, their shocking lack of chastity and modesty, and the ease with which a wife discarded one husband and took another.

Equally incomprehensible—and thus perverse—to many Europeans were the work roles accepted by Indian men and women. In the world the English knew, farming was labor and farmers were male. Masculinity was linked, inexorably, to agriculture: femininity was defined by household production and family reproduction. That Indian men hunted was not a sufficient counterpoise, for, in the England of the seventeenth century, hunting was a sport, not an occupation. The judgment made against the Indian division of labor entered into the accounts of traders and missionaries alike. Many concluded that Indian men were effeminate, lazy; Indian women were beasts of burden, slaves to un-manly men. Dissent from this judgment came largely from observers of Northern tribes, who still relied heavily on hunting for survival and who were therefore patrilineal and patrilocal.

The Europeans' cultural provincialism was often reinforced by the circumstances in which they encountered Indian gender roles. For example, European traders rarely visited a Southeastern village except in the summer months, since the Indian men they hoped to do business with were absent in the fall and winter hunting seasons. During these warmer months, women's labor was con-stant and highly visible; for this was the planting season. For men, summer was the time to make war or to protect their kin against attack by their presence in the village. To keep in condition for both fighting and hunting, Indian men engaged in a steady round of sports activities, especially ball games. Although they did chores related to their work—crafting bows, arrows, canoes, or fishing nets—they were most often found playing games, gossiping, and smoking, killing time until their turn to work came around in the fall. Thus the alien tableau was interpreted by its European ob-servers: women were engaged in masculine labor; men idled the day away like fops and dandies.

Such a construction of Indian reality produced many contra-dictions and confusions for European colonists. Seventeenth-century English settlers, for example, had few doubts as to the virility of the Indian as warrior, although this did not jibe with the summertime image of his sloth and effeminacy. Nor could Puritan ministers or laymen explain why Christian women, cap-tured by Indians and adopted into a tribe, often preferred to re-main within a culture that degraded women with male tasks. These anomalies, however, did not shake the firm conviction that the Indian culture they encountered was profoundly wrong in both its gender structure and its values.

We have no evidence that Wetamo read or concerned herself with the judgments of her European enemies. Nor can we assume that her cultural bias was any less rigid. Had she written of Mary

Rowlandson, the lens of Wampanoag culture might have produced a portrait of Puritan New England life unrecognizable to her famous captive. Had she written of her own world, however, her story would have been cradled within the context of kinship, an economy based on subsistence agriculture, a ritual-bound sexuality, and a complex division of power and influence between men and women.

The degree to which agriculture sustained Native American life on the East Coast varied. In the northernmost regions of what is today Canada, hunting remained central to the Indians' survival. In southern New England, where women continued the earlier hunting culture's traditions of setting up and breaking camp and taking home the game killed by males, their planting, harvesting, and foraging actually provided 90 percent of the calories consumed in their villages. In the Middle Atlantic areas, Algonquins of the Iroquois tribes combined farming, fishing, hunting, and gathering in a life geared to the seasons and in settlement patterns geared to the waterways of their region. In the Southeast, as in the middle region, agriculture was the central economic activity, dominated by women, but not without cooperative activity by men and women. Here men helped clear land and plant corn—just as, in the English settlements of the Chesapeake, women joined male family members in the field at planting and harvest time—although women weeded, tended the gardens, gathered the firewood and wild foods, and prepared the meals.

Another captive, Mary Jemison, left a vivid account of women's labor among the Seneca, the tribe who adopted her and whose life she embraced. Work, she wrote, was not severe, nor were a woman's chores any more repetitious than the chores that filled a colonial housewife's days. Household duties were simple and Seneca women, unlike English wives and daughters, were not slaves to the spinning wheel or the needle. In summer, the women went out each morning to the fields, accompanied by their children, to work cooperatively and in the company of friends and relatives, planting and tending the corn, beans, and squash at a pace geared to their individual rhythms and skills rather than to the demands of an overseer. They moved from field to field, completing the same tasks in each before returning to the first.

Women were not simply the agricultural labor force within Indian societies. They controlled the tools of production and, in most cases, the land as well, and they determined the distribution of the food they harvested. Because extra foodstuffs often constituted the only surplus wealth of their societies, women's control over the underground silos in which crops were stored brought them clear social and political power. For example, men of the Iroquois could not undertake war if Iroquois women refused to unlock the treasury of cornmeal needed to sustain their raiding parties or armies.

Particularly among the Iroquois, woman's primacy in agriculture appeared to some observers a sign of her primacy in political and social spheres as well. Both contemporaries and historians of this powerful and influential confederation of Indians have gone so far as to call its culture matriarchal. One eighteenth-century French commentator effectively argued the existence of an Iroquois matriarchy. "Nothing," he wrote, "is more real than this superiority of the women. It is of them that the nation really consists; and it is through them that the nobility of the blood, the genealogical tree and the families are perpetuated, all real authority is vested in them. The land, the fields and their harvest all belong to them . . . they have charge of the public treasury . . . the children are their domain."

Much of what European observers wrote would ring true to Iroquois women and men. Where they might demur would be in the universality of women's power and the degree to which it was directly wielded. Not all Iroquois women enjoyed the power to distribute public resources. This fell only to matrons or elderly heads of households. Formal and institutionalized political power belonged to these clan matrons as well.

It is the evidence of women's formal political power, even by a small elite, that was most striking to Europeans. Iroquois matrons nominated the male candidates for chief, and they could initiate a chief's removal if he did not meet their standards of performance. Thus, Iroquois women served as watchdogs over the behavior of male leaders, much as the Puritan women of New England monitored the righteousness of their ministers. Although no woman could sit in the highest governing body of the Iroquois Confederacy, the Council of Elders, women could address that body through a male speaker designated as their voice in its deliberations.

Women's political power was thus well established, but its character was more reactive than active on the tribal and confederacy level. Women policed behavioral boundaries, they were a legitimating authority and an interest group to be heeded; but men acted directly on diplomatic and military issues and engaged in the give-and-take of debate, discussion, and the arrival at consensus.

Such distinctions between women's and men's political role were honored within all the Algonquin societies, but there were exceptions. Women could, and did, make claim to direct political authority based on a variety of circumstances thought to be more compelling than gender distinctions. Elizabeth I of England no less than Wetamo could make such a case for their leadership. Thus "sunksquaws," or female political and military leaders, do appear in the historical record. Wetamo is one, and she is joined—at the least—by John Smith's "Queene of Appamatuck," mentioned in his first report from Virginia, and by seventeenth-century New England's Qualapan and Awashonks.

The entire question of women's relative political power may be misguided. For Europeans, politics and the system of laws governing inheritance and private ownership of land and resources were formal spheres weighted with importance. Centralized states, nationalism and mercantilism, and territorial expansionism enlarged the arena of politics and raised the stakes involved in having access to and wielding political power. Among most of the Algonquin societies, however, such circumstances did not apply. The eighteenth-century Iroquois Confederacy and Powhatan's seventeenth-century empire-building were exceptions to a rule of limited central authority and limited, sporadic warfare. Raids to avenge the loss of clan members were more common than inter-tribal war, and these did not demand full-scale mobilization of men or resources. Territorial rights were recognized and pro-tected, but the primary concern of Indian communities was the replication and maintenance of the community rather than growth or acquisition of wealth. Without the engines of private property, a profit-oriented ethos, or expansionism, Indian societies were well served by a politics of daily life. Thus, although political organization within the Middle Atlantic societies extended through five levels—from clan to village to district to tribe to confederacy—the most active and vital area was clan manage-ment—and this was a female sphere. Ironically, this local political arena went largely unnoticed by Europeans, who sought their own recognizable counterparts in government and military lead-ership within the Indian societies. And, as a result, Europeans consistently overestimated the power of chiefs, who governed by consensus rather than by power.

It is clear that women and men shared authority in many of the Algonquin societies. Women's economic power and their in-stitutionalized role as community leaders and family heads stand in stark contrast to the temporary, informal, and often limited authority of their colonial English counterparts. As New England Puritanism eliminated any possibility of women clerics and si-lenced female theologians, Iroquois communities continued to in-clude women among their "keepers of the faith" and to celebrate women's activities and their role as food providers and childbear-ers in religious ceremonies and rites. Such a comparison across cultures tells us much, but neither this nor the calibrations of women's authority relative to men's within Algonquin society provides a complete picture of Native American women's ex-perience in the seventeenth and eighteenth centuries. For this, a closer look at their activities within the community is ne-cessary.

The life of every Indian woman was marked by rituals and ceremonies, many of which focused her attention and the attention
of her community upon her biological functions. These rituals
both honored and guarded against the powers that women were
assumed to have because of their sex. In the cycle of sexual maturation, fertility, menopause, and death, ritual taught women the
significance of the intersection between the biological and the
social realms. Young Native American girls, like the daughters of
the white settlers, spent much of their time in the company of
other females. In this setting, a young girl received her vocational
training, acquired the skills of cultivation, and learned what activities were appropriate to her sex. Thus, Iroquois girls worked
beside their mothers, learning to plant corn and to pound it into
meal in a stamping trough or mortar, how to cook, bake bread,
and make tumplines and bags. The daughters of colonial New
England settlers would recognize the pattern of their own lives in
this apprenticeship.

Among all the East Coast societies, the arrival of puberty was
marked by ritual for girls as well as for boys. In most communities,
girls were isolated during their first menstrual period, but the conditions of this isolation varied. An eighteenth-century observer
recorded that a Munsee girl was expected to retire to a hut, where
she sat with a "blanket over her head. She is given little to eat,
but regularly does with emetics . . . usually . . . twelve days . . .
At the end of the time, they bring her back into her home, looking black, grimy and disheveled, because she has been lying
around in dust and ashes." On her return, the young woman was
washed, dressed in new clothing, and allowed to reenter her
home. For two months she wore a cap that blocked her vision
and hid much of her face; at the end of this period, she was
declared eligible for marriage.

In many tribes, girls and women were expected to isolate
themselves during each monthly menstruation, but again, the degree of isolation varied. Both the patriarchal hunting tribes such
as the Ottawa and the agricultural society of the Chickasaw set
apart "moon houses" to which menstruating women retreated.

The Shawnee and the Mingo allowed women to remain in their houses and prepare food, but did not allow them to eat that food. Despite these differences, it remains clear that Indian cultures believed menstruation signaled a moment of heightened power in women. For some, like the Micmac, that moment was considered dangerous, the blood itself was a "source of pollution," and even one glance from a menstruating woman could bring illness or bad luck. For all, the power of menstruation deserved attention and cautious ritual control.

Marriage was the most significant rite of passage for most Indian women. It was publicly recognized as a transition, a movement between families and households, from youth to adulthood. As shocked European commentators noted, however, marriage was not expected to be an introduction to sexual intercourse for wife or husband. Premarital sex was permitted in almost all Indian societies, sometimes even before the partners reached puberty. What was not socially acceptable was any public display of emotional attachment, and kissing was unknown until Europeans introduced the practice to the New World. Young couples experimented with sex, but they met at night for that experiment. In daylight hours, neither their expressions nor their actions revealed who their lovers might be.

Courtship, which was a male prerogative or obligation, followed local traditions. In most cases, if a young man wanted to marry he sent intermediaries—a brother, uncle, or parent, depending on his tribe—to ask permission from the parents of his bride-to-be. Occasionally the ritual was more complex. Among the Huron of Ontario, for example, the prospective husband not only asked the parents' permission, he engaged in an intense final courtship of his lover, improving his appearance by painting his face and showering her with jewelry.

The decision to permit or forbid a marriage was never entirely the right of either the parents or the couple, for marriage joined two clans, not simply two individuals. Important clan members had to be consulted, and sometimes the advice of shamans or religious leaders was sought. No matter how acceptable the clan and its advisors found the suitor to be, women were rarely forced into an undesired marriage.

Like many European couples, Indian couples celebrated their union publicly, with a feast for family, neighbors, and friends. In some patrilineal tribes, no women attended these feasts except the mothers of the couple. In others, the entire community was invited. Before the celebration, it was the custom in many tribes for the couple and their families to exchange gifts, an exchange that symbolized the reciprocal nature of the marriage. In this reciprocity, Indian custom and English diverged. Where one party did pay for the privilege of marriage, among the Tuscarora and Catawba of the Southeast, for example, it was the groom who offered a "bride price" to the family of his new wife.

On the whole, Indian couples came to a marriage through choice and in some measure of equality. And on the whole, they could leave it in the same fashion. Divorce was often simple in its execution, for no complex laws of inheritance or dower encumbered it, no institutional religious sanctions opposed it, women's dependency did not deter it, nor did the community condemn it. As Father Chrestien Le Clercq observed in his reports on the Micmac: "As they are all equally poor and rich, self-interest never determines their marriages. Also there is never a question of dowry, of property, of inheritance, of a contract, or of a notary who arranges the property of the two parties in case of divorce."

That divorce was an option did not mean that Indian communities made no effort to ensure a couple's initial compatibility. The Huron man who courted with necklaces and bracelets and the young woman who accepted his gifts spent several nights together before the marriage ceremony. The purpose was to test whether the suitor's "kindness is not maintained." In other communities, such as the Micmac's, young couples were asked to abstain from sexual relations for the first year of their marriage, so that they could grow fond of each other as "brother and sister," the closest of relationships within their society. The concern underlying these tests of compatibility was this: if a marriage was best dissolved, it should happen before children were born.

European observers appeared more curious about issues of infidelity and its punishment than divorce itself. Among the Ottawa,
a man could renounce his wife and take a new one if he could
prove her infidelity. The Illinois permitted a husband to kill an
unfaithful wife, but disfigurement was the preferred punishment.
Roger Williams argued that among the Narragansett the opposite
tactic was taken: the wife's lover, not the wife, was punished for
her adultery.

Emotional responses to marital problems varied. "Love charms,"
or *besons*, were used to hold the affections of a wife or husband
in some communities. Most European observers knew of at least
one story of suicide by a despairing husband or wife. "Many a
one takes her unfaithfulness so to heart," one commentator noted,
"that in the height of his despair he swallows a poisonous root,
which generally causes death in two hours, unless an antidote be
administered in good time." On the whole, infidelity was less
troubling if the expectation for a lifetime marriage was low. Iroquois and Huron parted easily by mutual consent, and as one
Miami husband told a distressed missionary: "My wife and I cannot live in peace together; my neighbour is exactly in the same
situation, we have agreed to exchange wives and are all four per-
fectly well satisfied: now what can be more reasonable."

The mutuality and reciprocity that informed most Indian attitudes toward marriage were based on the distribution of privileges and rights within the marital household. Women in most
patrilineal and matrilineal communities exercised complete control
over their households. A wife distributed the fish and game her
husband brought home as well as the products of the fields she
worked with other women. Her priorities and her discretion often
appear absolute. As one European observed: "If his wife longs for
meat, and gives him a hint of it, the husband goes out early in
the morning without victuals and seldom returns without some
game, should he even be obliged to stay out till late in the evening
. . . She may then do what she pleases with it. He says nothing,
if she even gives the greatest part of it to her friends, which is a
very common custom."

While issues of property and inheritance formed the core of English marital law and influenced even the most intimate aspects of marital life, these issues appear to have been absent or muted within Indian societies. Among the Delaware, or so one observer recorded, the personal possessions of a husband or wife did not remain within the family upon their death. Instead, friends came, divided the belongings, and quickly distributed them among their own friends. Nothing was kept by this inner circle, no matter what its worth, for the Delaware preferred to forget rather than retain mementos of the dead. Anything the husband had given his wife during his lifetime, however, remained hers. In order to ensure that property was not redistributed to others, therefore, husbands and wives tended to pool their wealth during the marriage.

The rules regarding custody of children, like those regarding property, rarely required elaborate manipulation or modification. Since, in most Algonquin communities, children were members of the mother's clan, they remained with her if the marriage dissolved. Because there are so few cases in which the Indian speaks for herself, we cannot know the emotional meaning of marriage to her or to her husband. We do know that marriage did not provide a woman with a second, essential dependency relationship, as she moved from the care of her father to the keeping of her husband. It was not the exclusive setting in which she could raise her children or give them legitimacy. It did not mark her introduction to sexual relationships nor was it the only public ritual that marked recognition of adulthood. Marriages appeared, on the whole, to be a means of establishing a sustaining companionship—material and emotional—between two adults, sometimes on a temporary basis, sometimes for a lifetime. Companionship and economic cooperation seemed to be the *raison d'être* of the short-term marriages that lasted only as long as a hunting expedition. Companionship also seemed to guide the custom of sexual abstinence in the first year of marriage, as a woman and man developed ties suited to siblings before they continued the more difficult relationship of lovers. Perhaps an interpretation that stresses companionship and mutuality helps us understand

Wetamo's marital pattern, as she joined with and parted from men whose perspective on politics and war meshed with and then diverged from her own. That there were other critical factors is undeniable but less easily deduced.

Pregnancy and childbirth, like menstruation, were female experiences believed to heighten spiritual power. Algonquins honored this massing of power and treated it with caution. Taboos were established to protect the unborn child and to protect the community, especially its male members. Among the Huron, for example, a pregnant woman who broke the protective circle of taboo by looking at an animal being hunted could cause her husband to fall at its capture; if she ate with others, they might fall sick; if she entered the cabin of an ailing person, the illness grew worse. Pregnant women, aware of their more intimate connection with the forces of nature, were taught to constrain their powers for the sake of their families and communities.

Childbirth itself took place outside the boundaries of the community. A woman in labor withdrew to a special hut in the woods, where she delivered her baby, sometimes entirely alone, sometimes with the help of relatives, shamans, or midwives. European observers seemed to have been both puzzled and fascinated by the fact that the mother rarely cried out in pain during the delivery. Many concluded that Indian physiology differed from European, but some looked to Indian cultural attitudes for an explanation. In this, they were correct.

Most Indian societies expected stoicism from a woman in labor. Some, like the Micmac, whom Chrestien Le Clercq studied, took steps to help a woman ensure her silence by stifling her cries. A Micmac mother in pain could ask to have her mouth stopped up, or if the pain persisted, she could call on shamans to assist her with medicine. Most Indian women suppressed their desire to cry out, seeing childbirth as a test of their courage in the face of adversity, much as men saw warfare and the hunt.

A newborn was frequently given a drink of animal oil, intended to flush the infant's digestive system, and perhaps to feed its "guardian spirit." The baby was then dipped in cold water and returned to its mother's breast. Indian children were weaned much later than the sons and daughters of the English colonists, sometimes not until their fifth or sixth year. Breast-feeding was probably used as a birth-control method, as it was among the European settlers, and in some tribes a complete abstinence from sex for up to three years after the child's birth was practiced to control family size. If a woman became pregnant during her nursing years, drug-induced abortion was an acceptable means of spacing children within a family.

Indian infants spent much of their first year of life swaddled upon a cradleboard. During the day, the mother carried the child on this wooden board, strapped close to her breasts or on her back, with the child facing forward, its head above its mother's shoulders. At night the child was taken out of its swaddling and either put to rest naked between the mother and father or laid in its own bed of soft skins or leaves. Northern tribes favored a night cradle or hammock made of a skin tied by its four corners to the wooden support and poles of the lodge in which the baby could be rocked to sleep.

The cradleboards were utilitarian, for they served the needs of women who worked in the fields. But they were objects of beauty and symbols of affection as well—carved and painted, adorned with beadwork, and often decorated with porcupine quills or feathers. Hopes and expectations for the child were expressed along traditional gender lines, with a tiny bow attached to a son's cradleboard and a female ornament to a daughter's. The skins used to make the child's clothing and blankets were also painted and decorated. Children themselves were beautified according to the aesthetics of the community. For some, this meant pierced ears, from which porcupine quills, feathers, or wampum were hung; for others, it meant the curving of the feet, done by positioning on the cradleboard so that the toes turned in; for others, especially among the Choctaw and Catawba, it meant a reshaping of the head by two masses of clay applied to the forehead and back of the head, which pressed and flattened it into a pleasing form.

Although practices and customs differed, a general pattern

emerges from the accounts of their birth and child-rearing practices. Pregnancy was seen as a natural process that imbued a
woman with great power, and childbirth was a testing of her capacity to bear pain bravely. Each child was entitled to its mother's
exclusive attention during its infancy and early years, an entitlement assured by the mother's sexual abstinence. The cradleboard
allowed the mother and child to remain together, even when she
returned to her agricultural work, and this link between mother
and child, socially supported, was physiologically reinforced by the
practice of breast-feeding for three to six years.

Child-rearing practices reflected the desire to reproduce community values: the ideal character, male or female, combined individual independence and autonomy with a highly developed
sense of obligation to the group. Interestingly, late-eighteenth-
century leaders of the newly independent United States would
urge that the same values be instilled in the children of their
new nation, insisting that the republic would not survive unless its
citizens were independent but civic-minded, autonomous but
patriotic.

To the colonial English, however—many of whom advocated
breaking a child's will in the earliest years, and most of whom
condoned spanking, whipping, and other forms of corporal
punishment—Indian parents seemed overly permissive and in-
dulgent. Neither fathers nor mothers struck their children, and
few threats were ever heard. Instead, children's characters were
molded by frequent praise or positive reinforcement, and by
shaming and ridiculing for unacceptable behavior. Even mothers
who "dry scratched" a misbehaving child with fish teeth meant
to embarrass him or her publicly with the visible marks on the
arm or shoulder rather than to inflict pain. Guilt was also effectively used, as it was in Quaker households in Pennsylvania.
Mothers put the burden of their own reputation on their children,
arguing that a bad child advertised a failed parent to the entire
community. This emphasis on personal dignity and public honor
produced a problematic sensitivity among many children, who

were known to threaten suicide if a parent's reprimand humiliated them too deeply.

Independence and self-reliance were sometimes inculcated through an emphasis on physical resiliency. Mohawk Indians left young children naked in cold weather so that their bodies would adapt to discomfort. Some societies identified and then carefully trained potential leaders by deprivation and challenge. In southeastern New England, these selected children endured both physical and mental tests, ending with a ritual involving hallucinogens and physical abuse. In the Southeast, girls as well as boys endured a testing ritual called *Huskanaw*, a ceremony of discipline to identify future leaders. Young boys and girls were sent to a House of Correction, where they were given intoxicants and deprived of food and light for five to six weeks in order to drive out childhood memories and weaknesses. Such tests of endurance and drug-stimulated rituals of visions sometimes became part of the celebration of puberty.

The character of Indian women and men was, like the character of the English of both sexes, shaped by their treatment as children, at the hands of those they loved, respected, or feared. Indian women like Wetamo learned to value independence of action and judgment, stoic acceptance of adversity, or at least public acceptance of it, and to desire the approval of their community through service and loyalty. Adult life produced no disjuncture with these values for women, for in marriage they were not called upon to renounce autonomy or self-reliance nor were they excused from civic obligations.

To see and understand themselves clearly, Native American women looked to the traditional images of their gender in work, family relationships, and religious cosmology. In the accounts of the creation of the earth and its inhabitants, in the defining and the honoring of the sacred and the spiritual, and in the parts women played in the enactment of ritual and ceremony, they found much of their identity. The degree to which women were central rather than marginal both to their people's religious vision and to the conduct of their rituals was roughly correlated to the kinship and household structure of the tribe.

In the matrilineal Iroquois society, women enjoyed both respect and formal authority. The Iroquois creation story hinges upon the actions of a woman who falls from the Sky World and creates the earth. On this earth she gives birth to a daughter, who in turn bears twins embodying good and evil, and from whose breasts spring the "three sisters" who sustain life—corn, beans, and squash. The inclusion of women's daily life within the sacred circle can be seen clearly in Seneca rituals that stressed life-sustaining natural forces. The Women's Dance, for example, centered on the cycle of corn; women danced while men chanted about the planting, growing, harvesting, and use of corn in the Iroquois diet. In winter, Seneca held the Thanks-to-the-Maple ceremony, officiated at by women whose role it was to tap the trees and process the syrup for consumption. At this ceremony, the Chanters of the Dead, a priestly body led by a woman, sang songs that belonged exclusively to that group. The Chanters of the Dead played a central role throughout the year, helping women or men who were troubled by dreams of relatives or friends who had died. In a culture that paid close attention to the unconscious as it was manifested in dreams, the Chanters were important religious figures.

Among Wetamo's people, women were more peripheral to religious vision and less likely to hold formal religious authority. The shamans of the Wampanoag were male, as were the shamans of the Canadian tribes. Yet, in witchcraft, when spiritual energies were wielded as curse rather than celebration, women were equally as powerful as men. Huron sorcerers, both those who bewitched and those who lifted the curse, were of either sex; soothsayers who foresaw the future through rituals of pyromancy and hydromancy could be women as well. Catholic priests, attempting to convert the Indians of Canada—but often frustrated by the Native American's capacity to incorporate Christian symbolism, biblical figures, and Christian theology into their own religious context rather than renounce their "heathenism"—were especially annoyed when women laid claim to positions of religious authority. "It is a surprising fact," wrote one missionary, "that this ambition to act the patriarch does not only prevail among the men, but even the women meddle therewith." The ready acceptance of these women as religious leaders among the Micmac, for example, was based on a long tradition acknowledging women's spiritual powers. "They look upon these women as extraordinary persons," the priest conceded, "whom they believe to hold converse, to speak familiarly, and to hold communication with the sun, which they have all adored as their divinity."

English colonization cast a long shadow over Wetamo's personal history. During her lifetime, the pace of change set by these newcomers was both swift and deadly: the Wampanoag saw their claim to the land eroded, their independence of action denied, and their culture bent to the demands first of military preparedness and then devastating war. In the end, the shadow covered Wampanoag society completely, leaving only a few survivors, who ended their lives as slaves in the West Indies or refugees among other tribes. Change, gradual or dramatic, adaptive or destructive, was part of the equation in the lives of all Algonquin women during the seventeenth and eighteenth centuries. No portrait, no matter how rich in detail or how illuminating, is accurate if it leaves the impression of stasis rather than flux.

Historians have documented the most dramatic changes wrought by the European invasion of America, especially the decimation of the Indian population by disease and later by warfare. Other forces operated more slowly to transform Indian cultures, redefine work and gender roles, reshape family, and reinterpret the relationship of the natural and the supernatural. Contact between Europeans and Native Americans, for example, often produced demographic changes that resulted from intimacy rather than mortality or combat.

In Canada, French fur traders and farmers created families with Algonquin women; in the Carolinas and Georgia, Englishmen did the same. The "She-Bed-Fellows" of these English traders played more than sexual and domestic roles; they were liaisons in the local community. The result of this arrangement was the creation of a wholly new, specialized role for some Indian women. As "Trading Girls," women were expected to satisfy English traders and earn money "by their Natural Parts." The designation of a small group of women as trading girls helped preserve the racial integrity of the Native American communities, for no other women were made available to the traders but these. Few other English colonies developed a significant mixed population. In some the Indians were under no compunction or necessity to enter relationships with white men. In others warfare effectively diminished the availability of Indian women, and in others Englishwomen were plentiful.

Englishwomen entered Indian communities, too, primarily as captives who, like Mary Jemison, chose to remain and create families among their adoptive people. The impact of these women was muted, for assimilation was unambiguously welcomed and encouraged. Jemison's membership in the Seneca required no adjustment of racial attitudes or examination of community identity, for the process of adoption was well established by the time the English arrived in America.

Ironically, the Indians' encounter with English culture often intensified and distorted existing social patterns rather than introduced novel ones. For example, the fur trade between Indians and the English left work and gender roles undisturbed at first. Men hunted and trapped, as they had always done. Women led more sedentary lives, which included the preparation of the skins or meat. But England's demand for furs was insatiable and the appeal of European products soon led to a dependency on these manufactured goods that transformed many tribal cultures. Thus the expanding fur trade forced a redistribution of resources and energies and altered gender relationships and family structures. Indian men spent more time away from the village in pursuit of beaver, marten, or fox, and determined the location and permanence of a village, and the pursuit of good trapping ground pushed entire communities into the nomadic life once restricted to adult males.

These changes disrupted traditional gender arrangements: the stable village life that women directed was more difficult to sustain, and the logic of matrilineal and matrifocal family organization was weakened as whole communities dispersed or became peripatetic. Women's work activities were redefined and given new priorities. The scraping, dressing, trimming, and sewing of skins into salable goods took precedence over agricultural tasks, sometimes leading the tribe to abandon self-sufficiency and rely on other tribes for its food supply.

By the eighteenth century, Anglo-American culture had enveloped Algonquin culture, pressing new norms and values upon the women and men of the remaining East Coast tribes. Native Americans faced the options of adaptation, resistance, or marginalization, each with its costs and its advantages. What Anglo-American culture never held out to them was the promise of full acceptance, which Indian societies had always proffered to those who entered their world.

If the Indians' choices were limited, their responses were nevertheless various. Among the Seneca, whose strategies for survival have been traced by scholars, traditional life retained its vitality until the English colonists won their political independence. The Iroquois Confederation had cast its lot with the British, and American victory meant the loss of political and military independence for the Seneca, Cayuga, Onondaga, Oneida, Tuscarora, and Mohawk tribes. Iroquois men, whose gender identity was closely tied to the tasks of war, trade, diplomacy, and politics, faced a difficult adjustment. Many Seneca withdrew deeper into their own subculture, but reformers like Handsome Lake pressed for adaptation to Anglo-American ways. Handsome Lake's followers were urged to redesign their family to meet Anglo-American standards and ideals, including patriarchal nuclear families, the buttressing of the father-son relationship, and the quest for domestic tranquillity. The weakening of kinship ties and the sanctification of the husband-wife relationship, reinforced by Handsome Lake's injunction against divorce and the use of abortifacients, required that women cede autonomy and accept dependency. The Seneca who became Handsome Lake's disciples reshaped the world of the Algonquin beyond recognition.

For many Native American communities, the tug of war between traditional and dominant patterns of behavior and beliefs became a way of life in itself. To the Indian women of the late eighteenth century, Wetamo's unambiguous perception of English culture as invasive and entirely alien must have seemed simpler than this now familiar but still dangerous colonial society.

4

IN A "BABEL OF CONFUSION"
WOMEN IN THE MIDDLE COLONIES

MARGARET HARDENBROECK WAS BORN into a
Dutch trading family in the early seventeenth century. Her
parents, Maritje Caterberg and Adolph Hardenbroeck, were based
in Evervelt, Netherlands, but their lives were tied to the new
colonies of North America and the Caribbean and to the prosperity these places promised. Their immediate family was small;
they had only two sons, Abel and Johannes, and, of course, Margaret. The three children were schooled in writing, reading, and
arithmetic, and Margaret, no less than her brothers, learned to
apply these skills to the entrepreneurial world her parents inhabited.

Margaret appears to have been the most adventurous of the
Hardenbroecks, for she was the first member of the family to leave
home and settle in the Dutch outpost of New Amsterdam. She
arrived in 1659 and presented herself to the authorities as the agent
of a cousin who was an Amsterdam trader. She quickly established
herself as a presence in the colonial port, appearing in court to
collect her cousin's debts and establishing a brisk and varied trade
in pins, cooking oil, and vinegar, all exchanged for the colony's
most marketable resource, furs.

Soon after she arrived, Margaret met and married Pieter Rudolphus DeVries, a fellow merchant. Her new husband was no struggling settler; his success and status in the trading community was established by his ability to pay fifty guilders to the city for the privilege of joining the ranks of its Great Burghers. Neither her marriage nor later her motherhood interrupted Margaret's mercantile activities, however. While Pieter plied lumber, paper, bricks, tobacco, sugar, wine, and prunes, his wife continued to build her connections within the fur trade. When Pieter died in 1661, Margaret and her infant daughter, Maria, inherited his property and his business.

Twenty months after the death of her first husband, Margaret Hardenbroeck married Frederick Philipsen. Philipsen was a carpenter by training but, like many countrymen and women of Margaret's circle, a trader by choice. By the terms of the traditional Dutch *usus* marriage contract, Margaret preserved both her legal identity and her financial prerogatives, an arrangement as routine under Dutch law as it was unusual to seventeenth-century English marriage codes.

There are no clues as to the emotional quality of Margaret's second marriage, but there is much evidence of its continuing success as an economic partnership. Frederick and Margaret became partners in the acquisition of property and in diversifying and expanding the inventories of their trade. Together they built a transatlantic packet line, including in this fleet two ships that carried their own Christian names.

The conquest of the colony by the English in 1664 did little to disrupt the thriving Philipsen–Hardenbroeck business. Indeed, Frederick was sanguine about the altered political fortunes of his colony—as well he might be, for his own career flourished under the new regime. He willingly swore allegiance to the King of England in 1664 and again in 1674, and showed his openness to acculturation by Anglicizing his name. When the governor of New York, Edmund Andros, appointed him to the colonial council in 1674, he entered the political records as Frederick Philipse.

Margaret Hardenbroeck's experience was less satisfactory. She remained the aggressive, parsimonious businesswoman she had always been, yet she felt the constraints of English domination. The autonomy of a married woman in matters of trade and profit, common enough to escape comment in Dutch society, was an anomaly within English culture. The limitations forced on her under a system of law which did not recognize the custom of *usus* marriage and defined her instead as *feme covert* were disturbing to her. Although she could continue to act as legal agent for her husband, Margaret Hardenbroeck could no longer transfer power of attorney to him. Under English law, she had no such power to delegate. Nor could she continue to purchase or hold real property in her own name. To add to her properties in New Jersey, Margaret had to have her husband buy and claim title to the land. The transformation of New Netherlands into New York did nothing to deter this Dutch couple's accumulation of wealth and prestige. Yet from the English conquest until her death in 1691, Margaret Hardenbroeck found herself steadily relegated to her husband's mate rather than his partner, forced to rely on him as an intermediary in matters she had proved herself more than competent to manage directly.

Margaret Hardenbroeck's story might be used to illustrate the cultural diversity of the middle colonies. Here, in what became Pennsylvania, New York, New Jersey, and Delaware, Swedish and Dutch settlements preceded the English, and the Society of Friends, or Quakers, a marginal religious sect within English society, became a dominant force in the formation of this Middle Atlantic region. The middle colonies' seaports had, from the beginning, the cosmopolitan air associated with transatlantic trade and commerce: Jews and French Huguenots found homes in New York City, and German immigrants were accepted in Philadelphia without restriction. Thus, distinctive patterns of worship, family organization, and formal and informal legal and value systems of various ethnic and religious groups met in the middle colonies on a competitive, though never entirely equal, ground. The history of their intersections has been well told and carefully traced by colonial scholars. The historians have documented the process by which the Swedish settlers of Delaware or the early Irish Quakers of Pennsylvania became part of the dominant English culture through intermarriage. They have charted the slow, unevenly paced acculturation of the Dutch in New York after the conquest of New Netherlands in 1664. And they have distinguished the legacies of the Pennsylvania Quakers, who dominated the political and economic landscape for a significant period and sustained their power to define themselves even when their hegemony was lost.

The lives of women within these Middle Atlantic colonies were accordingly diverse. As Margaret Hardenbroeck could surely testify, the boundaries of a woman's life were culturally constructed, and their perimeters were made clearer in the contrast and clash of the legal and ideological assumptions and expectations of immigrants from different European traditions. For Hardenbroeck, the transition from Dutch to English norms was restrictive. For the historian of the period, it is opportune: it allows us to add counterpoint to point and variations to theme in composing women's experience.

In 1581 the states of Holland abandoned their allegiance to the King of Spain and began a forty-year struggle for independence. Their political rebellion was no more spectacular than their economic revolution: even before independence, the Dutch had wrought a remarkable transformation of their economy, based on commercial expansion. By the end of the sixteenth century, Amsterdam—with its wealthy entrepreneurs and its skilled artisans—was the center of an aggressive global trading network, its merchant class seeking new markets and new products in Africa, Asia, and the Americas. The Dutch republic into which Margaret Hardenbroeck was born, with its decentralized political structure and its powerful commercial oligarchies, was the greatest trading nation in the world.

The Dutch empire in North America was, however, modest. Henry Hudson's voyage in the *Half Moon* in 1609 established the Dutch claim to the Hudson River Valley area. The Dutch East

India Company (which had sponsored Hudson's exploration) was too busy with other enterprises to pursue the matter further. When, a dozen years later, the newly chartered Dutch West India Company acquired the rights to exploit the North American regions, its directors were more interested in the profits to be made from their monopoly in the West African trade.

Thus, the colony of New Netherlands grew fitfully. A post at Fort Orange (Albany) and another on Manhattan Island were established. But at the end of the 1620s, there were only 270 white settlers, almost all company employees. A new charter in 1629 granted land to voluntary colonists and bonuses to those who sponsored others. But with little unemployment in Holland, and little religious persecution there either, the impetus to relocate in America was not strong. The Dutch reached out to less satisfied neighbors, inviting English, Norwegian, and German settlers to their colony. From the beginning, therefore, New Netherlands was the most heterogeneous of all the North American colonies, producing what one critic called a "Babel of Confusion."

In 1664, when the English ships aimed their guns at startled New Amsterdam residents, there were 9,000 colonists in New Netherlands. Margaret Hardenbroeck was a prosperous entrepreneur, wife, and mother when Peter Stuyvesant surrendered the colony to Richard Nicolls. She represented, even if she did not typify, the possibilities for Dutch women given the economic and cultural contours of their society. She was the product of an entrepreneurial ethos that did not distinguish too rigidly between male and female capacities for economic activity. Her education had prepared her, just as it had prepared her brothers, for a role in trade and commerce. And, most important, the Dutch legal system did not force Margaret to choose between marriage and the marketplace; it allowed her to pursue success in both.

In part, Margaret Hardenbroeck could claim a civil identity after marriage because Dutch law, unlike English law, was based on the Corpus Juris Civilis, or the Justinian Code of the sixth century. But Dutch women also retained their civil identity because marriage was interpreted as a partnership of equals. English marital laws confirmed women as dependents upon their husbands, placing their material well-being and their property into their husbands' hands and making their husbands responsible for their maintenance even in widowhood. Dutch law, however, carried the logic of marriage as a "community of goods" and considered marriage partners equally responsible caretakers and developers of family wealth.

Thus, in Dutch marriages, partners had equal claim to their original combined wealth and to any wealth later acquired, claims made good by the custom of writing joint or mutual wills. On the death of husband or wife, the widowed partner was entitled to half of the entire estate and had the right to administer the remaining half for the heirs. Dutch widows were not mere custodians of their deceased husband's property, nor did they continue in widowhood as in marriage to be maintained by their husband's sense of affection or obligation. No one knew this better than Margaret Hardenbroeck, who had, after all, made excellent use of her first husband's wealth when he died.

In marriage, Dutch women could continue to function as buyers and sellers of goods and property. They could contract debt and earn income. They could determine the heirs who would benefit from their industry. The chasm between *feme sole* and *feme covert*, sometimes bridged in English society but never filled, did not exist for Dutch women, who could choose a *usus* marriage that preserved intact these critical legal rights. Thus, until the English conquerors arrived—and changes in her social context were set in motion—Margaret Hardenbroeck faced neither categorical exclusion from the public sphere because of assumptions about "natural roles" for men and women nor formal exclusion because legal and familial structures demanded that women choose between marriage and economic autonomy. She viewed the conquest much as any important property holder and trader might, having as much to lose as her husband or her male peers. It was not until later that Margaret Hardenbroeck would realize she faced other risks specific to her gender.

The 1664 Articles of Capitulation signed by Nicolls and Stuyvesant were reassuring to the Dutch of New Netherlands: all inhabitants, regardless of nationality, would remain "free denizens" and enjoy claim to their lands, houses, inventories personal and commercial, and to their ships as well. They were guaranteed freedom of conscience, and their inheritance laws were to remain intact. Nevertheless, a slow but persistent process of acculturation began for the Dutch communities within this now English colony. Rural farmers and traders were perhaps less ready to Anglicize their names or their customs than Frederick Philipsen, but he was far from atypical within the prosperous merchant class of New York City. Old family names disappeared; intermarriage between Dutch and English became more common; children learned English as their first and sometimes only tongue. By 1743, Cornelius Van Horne could observe with regret that "the Dutch tongue Declines fast amongst us Especially with the Young people . . . All Affairs are transacted in English and that Language prevails Generally amongst Us."

The tempo of change varied, of course, as did the perception within Dutch and English communities of the meaning and significance of some changes. Acculturation was not always a gendered process, for there were certainly areas of adaptation that affected men and women in the same ways. Yet the question remains: why did the life of Margaret Hardenbroeck change so radically?

The Dutch were not immediately receptive to the English notions of gendered obligations and privileges. Not until the early eighteenth century did the practice of mutual wills disappear among Dutch New Yorkers. Yet the notion of a community of goods that propelled fifteen of the twenty-three New Amsterdam men who made wills with their wives before the English conquest had already weakened drastically by the 1680s. By the eighteenth century, women's role in the dispensation of property had shifted from the formal arena to the informal realm of influence and suggestion.

Wives steadily lost ground in other ways as well. Where once a couple's estate was divided into two equal parts, with one half going to the surviving spouse and the other divided equally among sons and daughters, eighteenth-century Dutch husbands and fathers began to adopt English patterns that restricted widows both in the amount they received and in their entitlement to their inheritance. Margaret Hardenbroeck did not lose any of Pieter DeVries's wealth when she remarried less than two years after his death, but a Dutch widow in New York in the 1730s was likely to encounter a will that made her forfeit all of her first husband's property should she marry again. By mid-century, even if a woman did not remarry, her widow's share had become not one-half but one-third of her husband's estate.

All women within the family, not simply wives, began to feel a disadvantage based on gender. The Dutch tradition of equal portions to sons and daughters was eroded over the last decades of the seventeenth century. Even the Dutch farmers of the Hudson Valley had abandoned the practice by 1750, choosing the now common English option of bequeathing the land to their sons and a cash settlement to their daughters.

Did specific changes in family ideology or economic strategies precede and prompt this erosion of women's power? Or did the transfer of political power to the English, despite the apparent tolerance for Dutch structures and values, make it impossible to sustain a dissenting cultural tradition? Historians are uncertain. They point to the practical effects of a change in government personnel: without officials trained in Dutch law, the drafting of mutual wills became an esoteric rather than a routine legal transaction. Thus, a loss of expertise may well have led to the abandonment of a practice. Other scholars believe they have found a shift, particularly among the Dutch urban merchant class, from a couple-centered marriage to a child-centered one. The commitment to launch children early and advantageously led men to siphon resources away from wives and widows. The English legal system conveniently gave them the mechanisms to do so. But these explanations are incomplete. Perhaps changes in the availability of land, the nature of economic enterprises, growing pressures by the English authorities to conform to their customs and codes, whether indirectly or out of convenience and efficiency, and the increasing complexity of credit and debt relationships—perhaps these variables led to the steady decline in Dutch women's status within marriage and in the range of legitimate activity outside its sphere.

One thing is clear: when Margaret Hardenbroeck died in 1691, she was a relic of an older tradition. Forty-six women traders had tested their skills in the commercial world of Albany in the decade before the English conquest. By 1700 not a single woman was identified among that city's traders. The decline in New Amsterdam was even more striking, falling from 134 to 43 between 1653 and 1774, when Frederick Philipse shed his *n* and joined the colonial council. Women disappeared from the ranks of tapsters, brewers, launderers, and bakers, as the number of female proprietors of businesses shrank from fifty in the preconquest decade in New Amsterdam to seventeen in the decade that followed. Dutch women who, like the young Margaret Hardenbroeck, had appeared in court as both plaintiff and defendant for themselves and others dwindled in number after the English flag was raised at Fort Orange and at Manhattan's Battery. In the four years from 1661 and 1664, 383 women sued or were sued in New Amsterdam courts; in 1673–74, only 50 had legal claims to press or deny. Perhaps the arrival of the English, and the growth in the colony's population that resulted, left no space for the Margaret Hardenbroecks of an earlier era.

As her community made the transition from a dominant to a marginal one within New York colony, Margaret Hardenbroeck focused her energies on sustaining a dying way of life. In neighboring New Jersey and Pennsylvania, however, Quaker women were busy helping to steer their marginal culture to a position of ascendancy.

From its earliest days, Quakerism had gone against the grain of most English Protestantism. Like the Puritans, George Fox and his Society of Friends renounced the elaborate hierarchy of the

Anglican Church and the role of the clergy as intermediaries between worshipper and God. But unlike the Puritans, the Friends did not believe that the Scriptures were the source of religious authority. The Bible was evidence of God's presence but not the essence of His Spirit. That Spirit resided in every human soul, and it made every man and woman a potential member of the "priesthood of all believers." Most seventeenth-century English Protestants rejected the radical implications of Fox's argument, for Quakerism was too much a mystical religion to fit the intellectual climate of the times.

The early Quakers earned a reputation as evangelicals, traveling across England, exhorting men and women to give up the sins and vanities of the world and listen to the voice of God within them. These injunctions to abandon the world of flesh and material comfort could be brushed aside by most who heard them. But as the fundamental tenets of Quakerism became known, their radicalism and potential for social disruption became less tolerable. Quaker insistence upon the equality of all men and women, which prompted the use of a "plain language" acknowledging no one person's social superiority, grated against the accepted social hierarchy. Quaker commitment to the "simplicity of Truth," which led them to refuse the double standard in truth-telling they saw in any judicial oath, disrupted legal and political affairs. Finally, the Quakers' belief in the principle of peace, which produced a pacifist resistance to all military service, made them unreliable citizens in the eyes of many Englishmen and -women.

Quakerism remained a marginal movement within English society, drawing most of its followers and proselytizers from among those whose poverty set them at the periphery of society. Yet the Society of Friends won the hearts and minds of a few influential and wealthy men, among them the son of Admiral Sir William Penn. In 1682 William Penn won a charter from the King of England to establish a colony in America. In Pennsylvania, the Quaker community would have its moment as a dominant culture.

Quaker culture was centered on the family as a religious institution and around the pressing obligations of parents to ensure the orthodoxy of the next generation. For women, the task of transferring "holy conversation"—which entailed quiet receptivity to God's Word—to sons and daughters was paramount in their life. This emphasis on the family within the Quaker movement was due as much to necessity as to doctrine, given the social class of most converts. In northwestern England, for example, the Quaker movement sank its deepest roots among the livestock-farming families untouched by the dramatic commercial development in the south. Because these Quakers were members of impoverished and widely dispersed agricultural communities, with few strong or influential institutions, movement leaders relied on the single vibrant institution, the family, to preserve orthodoxy and perpetuate what Quakers believed to be the "sacred life."

As they made the family central, George Fox and his inner circle also redefined it. Fox preached the need for morally self-sufficient households, established by husbands and wives who were bound by spiritual rather than carnal ties and sustained by both, for women's spiritual authority and rational capacities were declared comparable to men's. This authority and the accompanying self-discipline expected of Quaker mothers were to be mobilized toward the religious education of Quaker children. Children's capacity to find and to develop their inner light, to hear the inner voice, depended on proper upbringing. No institution existed to sustain Quakerism if the family failed in its mission. Thus, Fox's emphasis on the family as agent of and sanctuary for the faith produced a child-centered culture more intense than the mainstream culture, which emphasized the material well-being of sons and daughters. Not surprisingly, as one scholar has put it, "Quaker parenting was a frightening responsibility which required access to, yet control of, all emotions and all situations . . . and full insight." When migration allowed the Quakers to flourish and to prosper in colonies of their own, this emphasis on the family as the spiritual and social center of Quakerism was not abandoned but reinforced.

The oldest Quaker settlements in the middle colonies were

the result of migration from other colonies, rather than immigration from Europe. The first settlements sprang up in the 1660s in East Jersey, populated by New England converts seeking relief from Puritan persecution. British Quakers began to settle in West Jersey, in the 1670s and early 1780s. But when William Penn launched his "holy experiment" in Pennsylvania, Quakers from northern England and Wales immigrated to the new colony. Before the century ended, almost 200 Cheshire and Welsh families had made their way to Pennsylvania, sometimes paying for their ocean voyage with contributions from their Highland communities. Penn's offer of 5,000 acres of farmland for £100 was an abundance undreamed of and profoundly welcomed by Highlander families who had been forced in the past to apprentice younger sons and daughters to the non-Quaker world. These children, sent to learn trades in a hostile religious environment, had been either lost to the Quaker fold or fined and jailed for their persistence in Quaker belief and practice.

By the end of the 1680s, the Quaker colonists had developed a thriving grain economy. Their prosperity brought material comforts, but these were secondary to the spiritual comforts it ensured. Their goal was to amass, and thus be able to distribute, enough land among their children to hold the family together physically and spiritually. Well into the eighteenth century, Quaker patterns of land acquisition and distribution to their heirs differed noticeably from their neighbors'. And in those patterns, the strategy was clear: to prevent the need or desire of Quaker children to enter the non-Quaker world.

The difference between Quaker and non-Quaker inheritance strategies can be seen clearly in York County. Among neighboring German communities, conflicting desires to keep land holdings intact and to provide equally for all children led to two familiar compromise strategies. The first was for German fathers to exclude some children from the inheritance of real property in order to provide enough acreage for a working farm to others. The second was to sell off land in order to ensure an equal and adequate legacy for all sons and daughters. Either choice indirectly promoted the dispersal of the second generation. Within the Scot-Presbyterian community of the county, the preferred inheritance strategy encouraged second-generation mobility, both physical and social, by converting land into cash settlements for the heirs. The Quakers of York County rejected both alternatives. Like the Highlanders of the Welsh Tract or the Chester Friends, they tenaciously held on to their land, constantly adding acreage so that no son would be tempted to strike out on his own—to break free of parental power—or to fracture religious unity. When land scarcity, the disruption of war, and other factors made it impossible for Quaker families to continue to amass ample acreage, married couples chose to limit the size of their family, thus consciously ensuring the orthodoxy of the few rather than losing even a small number to the outside world.

The Quaker parents' ability to provide the material context and the spiritual guidance to ensure the commitment of the second generation remained the central goal of the Quaker community for years to come. Yet a second institution soon developed to help sustain them: the monthly meeting. Quaker leadership envisioned the meeting as complementary to the family. Yet because it represented the collective interests of the community, its power and influence proved greater than that of an individual couple. As Quaker husbands and wives discovered, the meeting set the standards by which the family would be judged.

Within the meeting as within the family, women played active and independent roles. Quaker women and men organized themselves separately, each holding a monthly meeting that ran from a few hours to a full day. These monthly meetings were charged with basic oversight of the local community. Quarterly meetings brought together representatives from local monthly organizations, and they, in turn, sent representatives to the yearly meeting held in Philadelphia.

Through the men's meeting, Quakers negotiated their place within the larger English and colonial society. The men had the exclusive right to make policy on broad, and pressing, economic, political, or legal issues, such as slavery, taxes raised for military expeditions, the purchase of land from the Indians, and imperial trade regulations. In addition, they attended to internal matters, such as regulating the conduct of the male members of their community and attending to the needs of the poor.

The women's meetings had no authority to debate the larger, public issues, but they were far from ceremonial or social auxiliaries. Quaker founders had intended the women's meeting to serve as a training ground for Quaker wives and mothers. Here, older women would instruct—and if necessary, discipline—younger ones. Within the meeting, emulation would be encouraged and dedication rewarded with status and respect.

As George Fox had hoped and envisioned, respected matrons of the community did lead the colonial Quaker women's meetings. Chester County's Martha Thomas was perhaps typical of this "female spiritual aristocracy," in her energetic and self-confident use of her considerable authority. For thirty-three years she could be seen riding sidesaddle on the best of the county's horses, traveling the Pennsylvania countryside to investigate, expose, condemn, and punish "carnal talk" among female Friends. Most of Thomas's peers within the meetings shared her social profile if not her energy. They were married to Friends of good standing, usually officers in the men's meeting, and they began their active role within the women's meetings in their thirties, after proving themselves successful mothers and household supervisors. And once they achieved leadership within the meetings, most remained in positions of authority for twenty years or more.

That Martha Thomas rode the countryside on the finest horse in the county offers a clue to the leadership's wealth as well as to their devotion. Within the Philadelphia meeting, the tendency for wealth and leadership to go hand in hand was more pronounced than in the countryside, yet everywhere, wealth provided a woman with the time to visit sinners or interview brides-to-be. Sixty percent of the leadership of the colonial Philadelphia women's meeting had slaves, and over 50 percent of the Chester County leaders had servants or slaves for household duties.

The women's meeting concerned itself exclusively with intra-community affairs, but in handling such matters, they were an autonomous and self-governing body. They policed their own sex with regard to dress, deportment, and speech, exhorting the young to "labour to keep out of pryd and superfluities." Dangerous behavior for Quaker women included parting their hair, pinching their caps too tightly around their faces, wearing elaborate clothing, or making suggestive gestures. At the meetings, Quaker women also focused on care of the poor of both sexes and demonstrated particular concern for widows and daughters from needy families.

The power of the women's meeting could be gauged by its authority in two critical areas. First, the meeting controlled the preparation of certificates for women planning to move or transfer to another monthly meeting. The right to judge and evaluate was explicit in the granting or denial of this religious passport. Second, women regulated the reproduction of the community itself by investigating those who wished to marry and determining if the couple conformed to Quaker standards of matrimony. The importance of this activity can be measured, in part, by the amount of time allotted to it. The Chester County monthly meeting devoted 54 percent of its business time to marriage; only 19 percent was devoted to charity.

Quaker couples acknowledged the authority of the women's meeting to determine their fate in both serious and humorous ways. In the Welsh tract, young women announcing their intentions to marry lobbied for approval by filling the meetinghouse with supportive peers. This "love politicking" confirmed Quaker women's control over the formation of new households.

Although "love politicking" was sometimes helpful, the Quaker standards that women upheld allowed for little compromise and little argument. Sometimes the records show us acts of resistance against the intrusiveness of the meetings' authority. In 1691 Susanna Robinson, a Chesterfield widow, announced her desire to marry again. The request was not greeted warmly, for the women's meeting had received reports that the widow Robinson had a tendency toward "disorderly cariages." Robinson did not meekly accept the judgment of her spiritual superiors. Instead, she dismissed the reports as lies and declared that "she was dame enough to goe and doe whether and what she pleased." She even threatened to appear at the next monthly meeting and challenge its members directly.

More disturbing and more damaging challenges came from younger Quakers who chose to marry outside the faith. Despite the material incentives offered to children to remain close to home, despite the exhortations and urgings of loving but perhaps overly admonishing mothers, many Quakers of the second and third generation did marry outside the fold. When the outmarrying reached crisis proportions in the 1740s and 1750s, Quakers responded with severity, choosing to preserve their ideals rather than accommodate their children. Between 1750 and 1790, Pennsylvania's Quaker community disowned almost 50 percent of the rising generation for marrying "irregularly."

For women whose life choices were in harmony with Quaker prescriptives, the opportunity for leadership and public recognition far exceeded those in the non-Quaker world. Opportunities did not lie in the economic sphere, however, for unlike the Dutch of New York, the Quakers were inclined to insulate women from economic authority. Quaker women rarely handled or managed the money their products brought to the family, even though colonial Pennsylvania had an extensive trade in home manufactures. As widows, Quaker women were also less likely to enjoy the authority that Dutch or other English Protestant women could expect. Male co-executors restricted Quaker widows' actions, and husbands relied on male overseers and trustees to guide their widow's administration of the estate. A widow's guardianship of her own minor children was also closely monitored. She was expected to submit a complete account, with vouchers, for every shilling spent on basic necessities as well as education. Unlike Dutch widows of the seventeenth century, who had great latitude in managing their children's legacies, Chester County Quaker women could not sell any land unless they persuaded a court that all other existing resources—their husband's personal estate or the rent earned on lands—were inadequate to pay debts or maintain the family.

How do we explain the constraints placed on Quaker wives and mothers in a culture that acknowledged women's rationality as equal to men's? The answer probably lies with two overriding concerns of Quakerism: that parents, particularly mothers, devote their lives to the spiritual education of their children and that sufficient material wealth, especially in the form of land, be amassed and distributed to retain those children within the circle of the faith. The logic of the former discouraged women's involvement in economic affairs; the logic of the latter produced an anxious and protective attitude toward inheritance and its management among those responsible for economic affairs.

No such constraints operated within the religious sphere, however. Women became elders within the Quaker meeting and ministers as well. In such roles, they were celebrated by women and admired by men. Indeed, female spiritual leadership was often a path to social mobility, for a woman's poverty was no deterrent to an elite marriage if she was a "talented vessel of truth." The wealthiest of Quaker men were known to seek out these women to be the mother of their children.

Susanna Hudson was such a woman. She was born into poverty in northern Ireland in 1728 and spent most of her youth as a domestic servant. At the age of twenty-one she married a poor linen weaver named Joseph Hatton. When her husband's shop went bankrupt, friends found the growing Hatton family a farm to lease. Here, in the Irish countryside, her husband kept two looms going while Susanna milked the cows and nursed her own children. Over the years the couple managed to save some money, which they planned to use for their passage to Pennsylvania. But the Quaker community they lived in did not want to lose Susanna Hudson Hatton, for she was no ordinary farmer's wife but a Quaker minister who had been called to give testimony at the age of seventeen. Over the years her reputation had grown, so to keep Susanna in Ireland, friends subsidized the Hattons, paying apprenticeship fees for all their sons.

In 1759 Joseph Hatton died. Susanna took a small inheritance, left to her in appreciation for her ministry by another Irish Quaker, and visited William Penn's "holy experiment." There, she met Thomas Lightfoot, the second-wealthiest farmer in Chester County. Lightfoot was so impressed by this Irish widow's testimony that he followed her to Ireland, courted, and eventually married her.

Susanna Hudson Lightfoot lived the rest of her life in comfort. Did material ease soften her commitment to simplicity and truth or diminish her capacity to listen to and give testimony to the Inner Voice? She denied such change in herself. Before her death, she wrote to old Irish friends, intent upon assuring them that she had remained true to her calling.

> I would have my Friends to know in the land of my nativity, as some there (though very few) said I should grow proud, if ever I grew rich; therefore, I would have them to know (not for my sake but for the precious testimony's sake) that the southern breezes have not yet soothed so as to make me forget myself; it is true, this has been a pleasant spot to live in, with an agreeable companion, and I believe it was nothing short of the good hand which so provided for me, but my heart has not been in it.

Whether Susannah Hudson Lightfoot spoke with conviction or in uneasy defense we cannot know. But her life confirms the respect Quakers of both sexes willingly accorded women who were exemplars of the faith.

Born to poverty or comfort, religiously prominent women were depicted as satisfied individuals. They were energetic, happy, and faithful women who integrated their spiritual and material lives, reading the Bible in the course of their daily chores. When a moment of respite came, one matron was remembered as retreating to her room "with a Bible or some religious book; where a portion of her time was spent lone; from which retirement she often returned with evident tokens that her eyes had been bathed in tears." On their deathbed, many pious Quaker women enacted a final lesson in life for friends and family; with husband, children, and friends gathered around their bedside, they gave their last testimony on the peace that came from a Quaker life. "I can freely give up husband and children and all this world," Eleanor Smith said on her deathbed, "to be with the Lord, whose presence I feel flowing as a river into my soul."

What comes across to us from these reminiscences may not be the message that these Quaker matrons intended. The historian cannot fail to notice the independent space these women were able to create for themselves; the time for reflection and thoughtfulness they had; and the calm with which they accepted and integrated authority and respect into their character and daily life. Even if, by the mid-eighteenth century, the "holy experiment" had unraveled and Quaker hegemony in Pennsylvania politics had been broken, women such as Susanna Hudson, Eleanor Smith, and Martha Thomas had been significant figures in the creation and shaping of their religious culture.

Religion or ethnicity defined the context of many middle-colony women's lives. Yet social class was no less important in determining their circumstances. In the commercial, urban centers of Philadelphia and New York and in the Pennsylvania agricultural economy which some historians laud as the "best poor man's country," a woman's position within the social hierarchy delimited her choices and her opportunities and established the possible within her own history.

The fertile valleys and rich farmland of Pennsylvania quickly yielded a grain economy. Quakers and non-Quakers alike participated in a commercial agriculture that made the middle colonies the breadbasket of the British Empire during the eighteenth century. This grain economy required an expanded labor force, not only in the production of wheat and rye, but also in the performance of other farm chores and household activities. Home manufacture was an increasingly important part of this commercial agricultural economy. And by the 1760s, for example, counties like Chester were shipping butter to colonial cities and to the West Indies. In the cities, flour milling and textile manufacture expanded urban employment. New York and Philadelphia were becoming major colonial ports, generating growth in intracity commerce and trade between the rural and urban areas of each colony. These cities were magnets for the poor as well as the rich, and those who made their fortunes here exploited the labor of those who did not. Each of these broad economic developments would have consequences for women's productive activities.

Women of the "best poor man's country," even mistresses of the household, worked in the field in the course of their daily lives. Like the seventeenth-century Chesapeake women who labored beside their husbands and fathers, Pennsylvania farm women took part in the harvesting of the crop, wielding the sickle alongside the men. Women pulled flax as well; indeed, this plant was harvested exclusively by females.

Working with and under these Pennsylvania farm wives were a variety of free and bound female laborers. The wives and daughters of tenant farmers, more numerous than historians once realized, were hired for both harvesting and household chores. "Inmate" women—whose husbands had contracted their family labor in exchange for a place to stay on a landholder's farm—were obligated by the terms of the contract to help with harvesting, dairying, and the care of domestic animals. On the wealthiest farms, slave women were also part of the work force that the household mistresses commanded. Between 1729 and 1758, there were 104 slaves in Chester County alone, and most of them were owned by Quakers. Even after the Revolution, when the Quaker emancipation policy created a small community of free rural blacks, young black girls continued to work as indentured servants in Quaker farmhouses. And although indenture and slavery were on the decline in many counties by the mid-eighteenth century, a steadily growing and cheap supply of female labor remained to be drawn from the tenant, inmate, and landless families of the colony.

The carefully kept records of commercially minded Pennsylvania farmers give us our best glimpse of these rural working women's lives. Benjamin Hawley of the Brandywine Valley, a wealthy eighteenth-century farmer, kept records of both the wages paid and the tasks assigned to his many female employees. "Rachel Seal came here paid her ⅔ a Quire of paper is for making 3 caps & 2 hoods & 6d for Bleeding Betsy make total in Cash 3s." In the same year Hawley paid Mary Mullen to wash and Mary Lion to bake and wash. Other farmers hired local women to spin, reap, sow, pull flax, and gather apples, to wash, make shirts, and turn hay. And women often earned money from the sale of their products, marketing butter, cheese, eggs, candies, stocking yarn, and even featherbeds.

There were many women, however, who were unable to sustain themselves through their labor or a skill. The ranks of the poor grew throughout the countryside in the eighteenth century, and relief policies were often as humiliating as they were charitable. Anyone receiving relief in the Brandywine Valley region was required to wear a red or blue badge marked with a *P* on the upper right sleeve, along with the first letter of the county or city providing the relief. The penalty for failure to wear this badge was the loss of assistance, imprisonment, whipping, or hard labor. Women seeking public charity could be forced to work, and poor children of either sex could be bound out to an employer at any age.

Poor women of the cities fared no better than these women of the countryside. More often than not, those who began in need ended in desperation: women servants in eighteenth-century Philadelphia were more likely to follow a downward path to the poorhouse or a city hovel than enjoy even modest comfort or prosperity. And because Philadelphia lacked industry well into the nineteenth century, there was no factory alternative to domestic or menial jobs for women.

Throughout most of the colonial period female servants were less desirable than male ones. While men could be employed in construction, at the docks, and in crafts, the demand for white female servants rose only as the city's elite expanded and slavery became unfashionable in the wealthy Quaker households. In 1745 less than one-fifth of the city's servants were women; by the end of the century, they were 40 percent of that work force. Scarce or numerous, these women struggled on the margins of society.

Domestic servants were peripatetic, moving from job to job as work became available or leaving a household because of abuse or conflict. Many jobs were understood to be temporary. Poor women were hired for a day or a week for spring cleaning, kitchen work, or when guests in a household strained the resources of the permanent staff. Others offered—or demanded—steady employment; for the indentured servant, this often meant being on call twenty-four hours a day, six days a week.

The discipline or punishment a woman servant might face depended on the terms of employment. A hired servant could be lectured, complained to—or fired. Bound laborers could be physically disciplined. Whippings were common occurrences within Quaker as well as non-Quaker households. The laws regulating indentured servitude, however, showed some sensitivity to both the employer and the servant. Servants were forbidden anything that interfered with their work obligations, including sexual activity, drinking, or marriage. Masters, on the other hand, were denied the right to harm a servant's future life by selling her out of the colony without her consent or failing to pay her freedom dues at the end of the indenture.

Resistance also depended on the servant's status. Free, hired labor simply quit, but bound servants ran away. Masters and mistresses most often blamed a servant's flight on pregnancy and the weak and sinful character this reflected, but pregnant runaways were often seeking to rejoin their husbands. Other servants fled because of abuse or insult. Whatever the motive, the price for failure was high: here, as in most colonies, the courts extended the term of service if a runaway was captured.

In the struggle for control over a servant's personal life, the servant was frequently outmatched by her employer. So Sally Brant learned in the years she spent in the wealthy Quaker household of Henry and Elizabeth Drinker. Elizabeth Drinker was no stranger to the role of mistress, for fifty different women worked for her family over forty years. Only eight remained for more than a year. One of these was Sally Brant. When Sally Brant became pregnant, Drinker was visibly upset. She was particularly disturbed by Brant's apparent lack of remorse; as Drinker noted in her diary, the young servant "appears to be full of Glee as if nothing ailed her." Drinker felt embarrassment enough for two, and when the household moved to their country home for the summer, Drinker forced Sally to remain in that rural retreat until her delivery. The experience of motherhood was slowly taken away from Sally Brant. The Drinkers insisted on naming the baby Catherine and refused to even consider the mother's request that the little girl bear her father's surname. Instead, the Quaker couple chose Clearfield, the name of their country house. When Joe, the baby's father, tried to visit Sally Brant or see his daughter, Henry Drinker prevented it. Joe never saw Catherine, nor did Sally Brant ever see her child again. The baby was left at Clearfield with a wet nurse, and there she died.

Sally Brant paid dearly for her brief experience of motherhood. She was required to pay, in the form of added service, for the expenses of her pregnancy, the time lost while she recovered from the birth, and for the wet nurse's salary. The emotional cost is not known, for she kept no diary, as her mistress did. Elizabeth Drinker's feelings were preserved, however; she was, she recorded, "sad" about the death of the infant, yet it is her offended propriety that dominates her diary account.

Sally Brant left the Drinkers a year later. What became of her we do not know. But we do know that many of Elizabeth Drinker's other ex-servants returned to her home over the years, coming to her door as beggars rather than employees. Their stories were similar. Married to other former servants, many of them had sunk into the deep poverty known to widows with children. The records of the Guardians of the Poor confirm Drinker's personal knowledge that women were a disproportionate number of the desperately poor. Two-thirds of the residents of the almshouse were female; some resided there temporarily in order to give birth; others, homeless or ill, stayed longer. Many would have understood the hopelessness of Mary Johnson, whom the constable brought to the poorhouse just as she was about to "Drown her Child on Sunday."

Perhaps in no region of colonial America did race, religion, ethnicity, and social class crisscross with gender in more striking patterns than in the middle colonies. Surrounded by so many different expressions of women's proper work roles, family and community roles, and legal rights and restraints, few communities in this region were able to deny that alternative notions of womanhood existed. Some, like the Quakers, tried to isolate themselves from the competing values around them; others, like the Dutch, willingly or hesitantly abandoned traditions and ideas which defined women within their culture. The price of self-assertion was high for servants and slaves. We know from Elizabeth Drinker's own diary that her servant lost all control over her marital and maternal life when her actions offended her mistress. We do not know how African-American women negotiated gender in the rural world of Pennsylvania that kept them isolated, limited their access to motherhood, and assigned them work roles without any reference to their own cultural divisions of labor. It is not so much that this competition to define womanhood was unique to the middle colonies; it is the number of competing models—the "Babel of Confusion"—that is striking.

5

THE RHYTHMS OF LABOR: AFRICAN-AMERICAN WOMEN IN COLONIAL SOCIETY

MARY CAME TO VIRGINIA aboard the *Margrett and John* in the spring of 1622, soon after the Powhatan Indians launched an attack on the English tidewater settlers. She entered a community still reeling from the violent death of 350 colonists killed in a single morning. That the slaughter took place on Good Friday added to the horror these colonial survivors felt, but the day carried no special meaning for Mary. She was, after all, neither English nor Christian. She was one of a handful of Africans brought against her will to this struggling Chesapeake colony.

We can say very little about Mary; her age when she arrived in Virginia, her physical appearance, her temperament, her abilities are all unknown. Yet her experiences before arriving in Virginia could not have differed greatly from those of other Africans wrenched from their homeland and carried to America. The accounts we have of the brutality of the slave traders, from both black and white witnesses, of the painful forced march to the Atlantic coast of Africa in which women and men were chained together, of the humiliation of branding, and of the horrors of the "middle passage" allow us to envision her distress even if we lack her personal testimony on such matters. The knowledge we have of her adjustment to America—mastering a foreign tongue, adapting to a new climate, to strange clothing and food, a new physical environment, and a culture whose customs and values were alien—make the loneliness and isolation of her situation certain even if it is undocumented. Her circumstances, then, are more vivid than her personality.

Mary was taken to Richard Bennett's large tobacco plantation on the south side of the James River. Here she witnessed the full consequences of hostile relations between the English and the Indians, for only five of the fifty-seven servants who worked Bennett's Warresquioake plantation had survived the Good Friday assault. Although her English master needed every able-bodied worker he could muster, Bennett may not have set Mary to work in the tobacco fields. His culture identified agriculture with masculinity, and in these earliest decades of Chesapeake society, some masters may have been unwilling to overturn the gendered division of labor they held to be natural. Mary surely demurred from such notions, for in most West African societies women dominated agriculture. These very different traditions produced a surprising harmony in the matter of slave importation. Faced with demands for captives, African villages preferred to surrender up their males and protect their female agriculturists; faced with a need for fieldworkers, Europeans preferred to purchase men.

What we do know of Mary's life in the colonies is that she had good fortune. Despite the scarcity of Africans of either sex in the Chesapeake, one of Warresquioake's five lucky survivors of the Good Friday attack was a black man named Antonio. Mary took him as her husband, in fact if not in English law. In a society where early deaths routinely interrupted marriages, Mary and Antonio enjoyed a forty-year relationship. Together they made the transition from bound service to freedom, although how and when is unclear, and together they raised four children, whom they baptized in the Christian faith.

Like most freed servants, Mary and her husband—known in their freedom as Mary and Anthony Johnson—migrated from Bennett's plantation, seeking arable land of their own. The John-

sons settled on the Pungoteague River, in a small farming community that included black and white families. By mid-century,
they had accumulated an estate of over 250 acres on which they
raised cattle and pigs. In 1653, their good luck was threatened by
a fire which ravaged their plantation and brought the Johnson
family close to ruin. Mary's neighbors responded with sympathy,
and local authorities helped by granting the Johnsons' petition that
Mary and her two daughters be exempt from local taxes for their
lifetimes.

This considerate act by the courts is the first concrete evidence
that race set Mary and her family apart from their English neighbors. In seventeenth-century Virginia, taxes were assessed on people rather than on possessions, and Virginia's taxable citizens were
those "that worke in the grounde." Such a definition was intended to exempt the wives and daughters of Virginia planters,
whose proper occupation was domestic. By the time of the Johnsons' devastating fire, however, the earlier unity of gender had
been severed by race and "Negro women" were denied this exemption. And yet the racial distinction was not so rigid, the practice was not so uniform that Mary's neighbors could not embrace
her as a proper woman if they chose.

Whatever else race meant to Mary or her neighbors, it was
not yet the basis, or the product, of a broad official policy of
exclusion and hierarchy. Africans were clearly a minority, for no
more than 300 black Virginians lived among the 15,000 white
ones in the year the court granted the Johnsons' appeal. The identity created by members of that minority could still draw on experiences shared by the English majority. Black men like Anthony
Johnson made their appearances in court just as white ones did;
white and black intermarried, and bound servants of both races
found their way to freedom as Mary and Anthony had done.
White masters left property to black servants, black masters hired
white laborers, and black planters participated in the scramble for
labor by purchasing the labor of newly imported Africans "for
life."

In the 1660s, the Johnsons, like other eastern shore colonists, pulled up stakes and moved to Maryland in search of fresh land. The Johnsons may have arranged to have someone else finance their move, for they were claimed as the headrights of two wealthy planters. They were not, however, claimed as servants. Instead, Anthony was a tenant, leasing a 300-acre farm in Somerset County, Maryland, which he named Tonies Vineyard. Anthony and Mary's now grown sons and daughters soon joined them in Maryland, establishing farms nearby. Thus when Anthony died shortly after the move, Mary Johnson was surrounded by her family.

In 1672, when Mary sat down to write her will, a new generation of Johnsons was making its mark in this farming community. But a new generation of English colonists was making their task harder. Bad signs were everywhere: in a new colonial policy that forbade free blacks to employ white indentured servants, and in the Virginia and Maryland laws that lengthened terms for servants without indenture, a category to which almost every new African immigrant belonged. Mary's grandchildren, to whom she lovingly willed her cows and their calves, would grow to adulthood in a strikingly biracial society, for the number of African immigrants was rapidly growing. But few of these Africans would enter the world of free men and women as Mary and Anthony had done. The society that had once found room for "Mary a Negro," to become the matriarch of a comfortable family, could spare no such space for Mary's descendants. If it was accidental, it is apt that when Mary's grandson John died in 1706, the Johnson family disappeared from the historical record.

Court and legal records allow us to piece together the general circumstances and some of the critical events in the lives of Mary Johnson and her family. Such records also survive for other seventeenth- and eighteenth-century African Americans, and to them historians have added other sources both written and material, formal and informal, and they have employed the methods and insights of such related disciplines as anthropology and linguistics in analyzing them. Much of our knowledge carries the bias of the sources from which it is drawn: slave masters and mistresses and the legal and political institutions of their dominant white culture. It is not only a bias of judgment but of affective content; we know more about the feelings of masters than slaves, more about the meaning of slavery to those who instituted it than to those who lived under it. Our scholarly interpretations of these sources carry bias as well, formed from our own assumptions about normative behavior, our adherence to particular political or social values, and from the culture-bound vocabulary within which we think and write.

If we can rarely recapture the motivations or feelings of African-American women like Mary Johnson, we can at least delineate the conditions under which they made their life choices. A seventeenth-century English writer once declared that a woman—by nature, divine intention, and the rules of human society—must bend to her husband's needs and wishes. She must look upon this circumstance as "Conjurers upon the Circle, beyond which there is nothing but Death and Hell." Such were the direct and immediate constraints encircling any colonial woman by virtue of her gender. Yet there were other circles—especially social class—that held women captive. Mary Johnson made her choices in life within both these conjured circles of gender and class, and occasionally she found herself entrapped by yet another: race. This circle of race was both tighter and more constricting for the generations of colonial African-American women who came after her. Most of these women lived their lives in a bondage based on race, and the choices they made as they created families, established intimate relationships, defined and abided by community norms and values, practiced religion, engaged in work, and altered or adjusted to their material circumstances had to be made within these three powerful, overlapping, concentric circles.

In 1623 Mary Johnson was one of only twenty-three Africans in Virginia. By 1650, she was one of perhaps three hundred. Together, free blacks like the Johnson family and servants "for life" like their fieldworker John Casor made up only 3 percent of the colony's growing population. Most had made the transatlantic voyage from Africa to the West Indies and only later arrived on the North American mainland. In the decade of Mary Johnson's death, the African population in the Chesapeake began to rise sharply, reaching 3,000 in Virginia by 1680 and continuing to grow until, by 1700, the colony had almost 6,000 black settlers. African population growth in Maryland was no less dramatic: in 1658 there were only 100 blacks in four Maryland counties, but by 1710 the number had risen to over 3,500, or almost one-quarter of the local population. Nearly 8,000 of Maryland's 43,000 colonists that year were black. Yet the mass involuntary migration of Africans had only begun. Between 1700 and 1740, 54,000 blacks reached the Chesapeake, the overwhelming majority imported directly to these colonies from Biafra and Angola rather than coming by way of the West Indies. Immigrants from the west, or "windward," coast of Africa poured into South Carolina as well. By the time of the American Revolution, over 100,000 Africans had been brought to the mainland colonies. For the overwhelming majority, their destination was the plantation fields of the upper and lower South.

The relentless demand for cheap agricultural labor spurred this great forced migration. As the English economy improved in the 1680s and 1690s, the steady supply of desperate young men and women willing to enter indentured servitude in the colonies dwindled. The advantage of African servants over these English workers was already evident, for by this time, white servants had effectively exerted their "customary right" as English citizens to control working conditions. Planters were forced to abide by customs that prevented labor after sunset, alloted five hours' rest in the heat of the day during the summer months, and forbade work on Saturday, Sunday, and many religious holidays. On the other hand, local courts would not acknowledge or uphold any claims to such "customary rights" by African servants. And as life expectancy increased for black as well as for white colonists of the Chesapeake, the initially larger investment in an African laborer began to make good economic sense. Yet the supply of "black gold"—as Chesapeake planters called these slaves—was limited until the monopoly of England's Royal African Trading Society was broken by slaving entrepreneurs. By the turn of the century, the English African slave trade offered a steady, seemingly endless supply of reasonably priced, highly exploitable labor—and mainland colonists leaped to take advantage of it.

Slavery—as a permanent and inheritable condition—developed unevenly across the colonies and within individual colonies. In the Chesapeake, the laws that sharply distinguished black bound labor from white were accompanied by laws that limited the economic and social opportunity of free blacks. Together, these laws established race as a primary social boundary. The process began before the greatest influx of Africans to the region. The 1672 law forbidding free black planters to purchase the labor of white servants squeezed those planters out of the competitive tobacco market. This disarming of African Americans in the economic sphere was echoed in Chesapeake laws that forbade blacks to carry or possess firearms or other weapons. In 1691, Chesapeake colonial assemblies passed a series of laws regulating basic social interaction and preventing the transition from servitude, or slavery, to freedom. Marriage between a white woman and a free black man was declared a criminal offense, and the illegitimate offspring of interracial unions were forced into bound service until they were thirty years old. A master could still choose to manumit a slave, but after 1691 he was required to bear the cost of removing the freed woman or man from the colony. Such laws discouraged intimacy across racial lines and etched into social consciousness the notion that African origins were synonymous with the enslaved condition. By 1705, political and legal discrimination further degraded African immigrants and their descendants, excluding them from officeholding, making it a criminal offense to strike a white colonist under any circumstances, and denying them the right to testify in courts of law. While Mary Johnson had never enjoyed the rights of citizenship available to her husband, Anthony, eighteenth-century African-American men of the Chesapeake lost their legal and political identity as well. Thus, the history of most

African Americans in the Chesapeake region, as in the lower South, is the history of women and men defined by slavery, even in their freedom.

Much of a newly arrived slave woman's energy was devoted to learning the language of her masters, acquiring the skills of an agriculture foreign to her, and adjusting to the climate and environment of the Chesapeake. Weakened by the transatlantic voyage, often sick, disoriented, and coping with the impact of capture and enslavement to an alien culture, many women as well as men died before they could adjust to America. Until well into the eighteenth century, a woman who survived this adjustment faced the possibility of a lifetime as the solitary African on a farm, or as the solitary woman among the planter's African slaves. Even when there were other Africans on the plantation, the sense of isolation might persist, for "saltwater," or newly arrived, slaves had no common language, nor did they share the same religious practices, the same kinship systems and cultural traditions. Creole, or native-born slaves, were no less strange to a "saltwater" survivor.

Under such circumstances, African women found it difficult to re-create the family and kinship relations that played as central a part in African identity as they did in Native American identity. In fact, the skewed sex ratio—roughly two to one into the early eighteenth century—and the wide scattering of the slave population, as much as the heterogeneity of African cultures and languages, often prevented any satisfactory form of stable family. Until the 1740s, those women and men who did become parents rarely belonged to the same master and could not rear their children together. The burden of these problems led many African-born women to delay childbearing until several years after their arrival in America. Most bore only three children, and of these, only two were likely to survive. With twice as many male slaves as female, delayed childbearing, and high mortality among both adults and infants, there was no natural increase among the Chesapeake slaves in the late seventeenth or early eighteenth century.

There was little any Chesapeake slave woman could do to rectify the circumstances of her personal life. While women of any race or class in colonial society lacked broad control over their person or their actions, the restraints of slavery were especially powerful. A woman deprived of physical mobility and unable to allocate the use of her time could take few effective steps to establish her own social world.

Although Mary Johnson may never have worked the fields at Warresquioake plantation, the slave women who came to the Chesapeake after 1650 were regularly assigned to field labor. Organized into mixed-sex work gangs of anywhere from two to a rare dozen laborers, slave women and men worked six days a week and often into the night. Daylight work included planting, tending, and harvesting tobacco and corn by hand, without the use of draft animals. In the evening, male and female slaves stripped the harvested tobacco leaves from stems or shucked and shelled corn. The crops were foreign to most African-born slave women, but the collective organization of workers was not. Indeed, slaves resisted any effort to deny them this familiar, cooperative form of labor.

By the middle of the eighteenth century, slave women on the largest Chesapeake plantations would wake to a day of labor that segregated them from men. As the great planters shifted from cultivation by the hoe to the plow, and as they branched out into wheat and rye production, lumbering, milling, and fishing, they reinstituted a gendered division of labor. Male slaves were assigned to the new skilled and semi-skilled tasks. While men plowed and mastered crafts, women remained in the fields, left to hoe by hand what the plows could not reach, to weed and worm the tobacco, and to carry the harvested grain to the barns on their heads or backs. When new tasks were added to women's work repertoire, they proved to be the least desirable: building fences, grubbing swamps in the winter, cleaning seed out of winnowed grain, breaking new ground too rough for the plow, cleaning stables, and spreading manure.

If many male slaves were drawn out of the fields and into the workshops or iron mills, few black women in their prime were assigned to domestic duty in the planter's house or taught housewifery skills. Instead, throughout the eighteenth century, young girls not yet strong enough for field labor and elderly women past their productive years in the hoeing gang were assigned to cleaning, child care, and other domestic tasks in the planter's home. Thus, much of the work done by Chesapeake slave women in 1750 differed little from the work done by slave women a half century earlier.

Slave women's work may have remained constant, but other aspects of their lives did not. By 1750, some of these women had the opportunity to create stable families and to participate in a cohesive slave community. These opportunities were linked to changes in the size of plantations and in the composition of their labor forces. Throughout the eighteenth century, great plantations developed, and the number of slaves on these plantations grew, too, ending the isolation the earliest generations had experienced. Many of these slaves were native-born rather than "saltwater," and their energies were not drained by the efforts of adjustment and acculturation. As English-speakers, they shared a common language, and in Christianity, many shared a common religion as well. Both were factors in helping creole slaves begin to create a distinctive community. The gradual equalization of the sex ratio among creoles also helped, and, so did the lower mortality rate. Finally, the evolution of this slave community and slave culture in the Chesapeake was aided by a growing opportunity for slaves to live away from the intrusive eyes of their white masters. The retreat from contact was mutual: many white colonists sought relief from the alien impact of Africanisms by creating separate slave quarters. In these slave quarters blacks acquired a social as well as a physical space in which to organize everyday domestic activities, establish rituals, and develop shared values and norms. Most important, they were able to establish families through which to sustain and uphold this shared culture.

Newly arrived Africans found it difficult to participate in this developing community. On Robert Carter's plantation in 1733, for example, creole slaves lived in families of wives, husbands, and children, while saltwater slaves were housed in sex-segregated barracks. Although the plantation master established these barracks and viewed them as the most efficient way to deal with new arrivals, the isolation of African-born males was not entirely the master's decision. The truth was that few creole women were willing to establish households or families with an African male, preferring to take their husbands from among the creole population. From their point of view, the steady influx of African males may have been a disruptive force in their community. By mid-century, however, this issue was growing moot, for importation slowed dramatically and what one historian has called a "black life cycle" came to define the social world of many creole slaves.

This black life cycle did not develop evenly or uniformly across the Chesapeake, although it was evident in the pre-Revolutionary decades. And while gender ties rarely diminished racial distances, black and white women of the Chesapeake did have life-cycle experiences in common. The earliest creole generations of both races married younger and bore more children than their immigrant mothers' generation. And like white women, creole black women were frequently impelled by an imbalanced sex ratio to marry men considerably older than themselves. Black women delivered their children in the company of other women, just as English colonists continued to do throughout most of the eighteenth century, and midwives saw the mother through these births. The differences are perhaps more telling than the similarities, however. African nursing customs, retained by many slave women, produced wider intervals between children than English weaning patterns. Slave women bore an average of nine children, giving birth every twenty-seven to twenty-nine months. The power of masters to separate wives and husbands—through hiring-out practices or sales—led to wide gaps in many slave women's childbearing histories. Conception and birth cycles in King William Parish, Virginia, reveal other ways in which race interposed upon gender. Two-thirds of the black births in King William Parish occurred between February and July, while white women bore their children in the fall and early winter months. For black women, this meant that the most disabling months of pregnancy often fell in the midst of heavy spring planting chores. Perhaps this accounts for the greater risk of childbirth for slave mothers and the higher infant mortality rate among slave children.

Family organization depended on the size of the plantation. On the larger plantations, children under ten could expect to live with both their father and their mother, often in two-family slave cabins. When the parents came from different small plantations, the children lived with their mother, sometimes in cabins that housed all the slaves, whether related or not. The large plantations offered other advantages besides the opportunity for families to live as a unit. Here, mothers could rely on a growing kin network or on friends to help in the complex tasks of child-rearing. When husband and wife lived on separate plantations, the couple's main concern was maintaining contact. Where their master's regulation permitted and where there were roads linking plantations, many husbands and fathers undertook nightly and Sunday journeys to visit their families.

Thus, after 1750, a Chesapeake slave woman might be able to live out her life in the company of her family, as Mary Johnson had done. Yet she knew that powerful obstacles stood in her way. Husbands often lived on other plantations. Children between the ages of ten and fourteen, especially sons, were commonly sold. Sisters and brothers were moved to different slave quarters. And on a master's death, slaves were often dispensed along with other property to his heirs. A master who might never separate a family during his lifetime thought it his obligation to his survivors to divide them at his death. Hard times could prompt a master to sell a slave woman's family members in order to provide for his own. A planter's widow might keep her family intact by hiring out her slave's sons or daughters. Even the wedding celebration of a planter's daughter might mean the tragic separation of a slave woman and her own young daughter, sent to serve in the bride's new home. In the 1770s, the westward expansion of agriculture into the Piedmont and beyond led to mass dispersal of slave fam-

ilies among the new farms and plantations. Slave women, and their
men, could succeed in creating effective family structures despite
the many demands of slavery, but they could not ensure their
permanence.

Few modern scholars disagree that interplantation and intra-
plantation networks of kin grew more dense as the century passed,
or that a regional slave culture spread and was passed down to
new generations. Yet historians do disagree over the pace of community and family development, and they debate how best to
interpret the evidence available on the subject. For example, it is
true that large plantations did become part of the Chesapeake
landscape in the eighteenth century, but the smaller ones did not
vanish. In the 1790s, many planters on Maryland's western shore
still held fewer than a dozen slaves, and only one in ten held
twenty slaves. Indeed, in some communities over half the free,
white population lived in poverty and in the crowded, barren
surroundings common to tenant farm families. Throughout the
century, therefore, many Chesapeake slaves were destined to live
in their master's home, surrounded by a white majority and enveloped by English colonial culture. Even on large plantations, the
division of slaves into small groups, living and working in separate
quarters, may have made the creation of a community difficult.
And even when the slave population on a plantation was both
numerous and densely quartered, we cannot always be confident
of its composition. There may have been an equal number of
males and females, but were the majority of males youngsters of
ten to fourteen? Were many of the females elderly or still children
themselves? Nor can we always assume that the presence of adult
males, adult females, and young children was synonymous with
the presence of families. Not all planters kept meticulous records,
and the hiring out of slaves meant the creation of transitory
groups, with children from one plantation paired for a year or two
with adult women or men who were hired from other planters'
holdings. As yet, scholars do not know how slave quarters were
organized on many plantations. Nor do we know the intimate
relationships of the men, women, and children we find living on

these plantations. And we are also not certain if the solutions to the problems of divided families, such as regular Sunday visiting by fathers and other family members, were widespread. In its own way, our uncertainty mirrors the uncertainty that was a central fact of slave life.

Perhaps it is most useful to say that while legal codes created a uniform definition of enslavement in the Chesapeake, there was no uniform set of conditions under which slaves lived. Nor could there be as long as uniform living conditions for their masters and mistresses failed to exist. The circumstances and the choices made by great planters and struggling ones, by tobacco growers and wheat farmers, by residents of the Piedmont and those of the tidewater, by cruel men and kind ones set the parameters of life for the enslaved. However, if the black life cycle and the slave culture that emerged on larger plantations do not account for all eighteenth-century slave women and men, or even for the majority, they are still significant. Their reconstruction reveals basic social choices that slaves made when conditions permitted. The culture that emerged shaped the expectations and channeled the energies of slaves throughout the Chesapeake.

The slave quarters were the heart of the slave community, the houses and the yards surrounding them were the focal points of daily life. Inside each cabin were straw beds, seats made of barrels, pots, pans, and a grindstone for beating corn into meal. The older women looked after the children, the men hunted to provide extra food, and the women defined themselves, in part, by taking up domestic chores and housewifery. The culture that developed within these communities suggests a flexible adaptation of both African and European customs and beliefs. In this Chesapeake slave community dominated by creoles, African traditions were more muted than they would be in the Lower South. But on Virginia and Maryland plantations, slaves preserved African folk traditions of magic and magic charms, much, of course, as English colonists preserved their own magic traditions. In music and the instruments used to make it, and in the rhythms and patterns of dance, the slave community drew distinct lines that separated them from the dominant white culture and linked them to their African roots. Christianity, however, became the primary religion within the quarter, and sometimes this produced tensions between African values and European ones. In the Piedmont, in particular, where many slaves embraced the teachings of the Baptists, evangelical codes of morality condemning adultery and fornication conflicted with an African-based tolerance for premarital intercourse and older sexual mores arising from traditions such as polygyny.

Many slave quarters were bordered by plots of corn and tobacco and by gardens, all cultivated in the residents' limited free time. Using Sundays and the rare holidays they were granted (including, after 1776, Independence Day), Chesapeake slaves made this small-scale agriculture an integral part of community life. In the Piedmont area, historians have traced the rise of an internal economy, built upon the raising and trading of surplus food and livestock from the quarters, upon hunting and foraging, and upon materials stolen, or liberated, from the master's stock of supplies. Slaves on a plantation traded with each other, but they also traded with peddlers traveling through the Chesapeake region, with neighboring plantation workers, and with white masters or mistresses who found it easier to purchase pies or chickens from their slaves than to compete with them in these areas. Slave women played active parts in expanding and sustaining this internal economy, raising and selling poultry and eggs, baked goods, garden products, and handmade baskets. Thus, although few slave women in the pre-Revolutionary Chesapeake were employed in housewifery by their mistresses, they developed a repertoire of household production skills within their own community economy. The records of one general store in Orange County, Virginia, show that by the 1780s, slave women were able to purchase kerchiefs and scarves, calico cloth, ribbons, thread, and even tableware with money made from production and trade.

Whatever initial reaction Piedmont masters may have had to

the rise of this internal economy, they soon realized its benefits. The crops produced in the quarter allowed a master to reduce rations for his labor force, and in many cases the yield from slave gardens and fields helped reduce the pilferage of storerooms and the theft of livestock. Masters could demand that older slaves, no longer valuable in the fields, provide for themselves by gardening, farming, or keeping chickens. These masters saw the internal economy as a means to shift the burden of subsistence onto the slaves. For slave women and men, however, it was a means to carve out more autonomous space in their constricted world. This secondary, or internal, economy, in which women played active roles, had the potential to strengthen the slave community, as much because slaves established its protocols and regulated its operation as because of the material benefits it provided. Working collectively and cooperatively, slaves were able to carve out other autonomous realms. Slave midwives and slave doctors shaped the medical care of the quarter, and slave communities established their own burial societies and burial rituals. Slave women and their husbands also took the initiative in naming their children, using naming patterns to reinforce the kinship structures their community had developed. Mothers named their sons and daughters for their own brothers and sisters and for their husband's siblings. By naming sons for their fathers, slave mothers attempted to reinforce the most often violated and thus most fragile link in the slave family chain: the paternal line.

Physical and psychological distance from the master and from his white culture surely aided the development of a slave culture. Indeed, historians have found that urban slaves and household slaves who lacked this cultural space were more acculturated than the slaves of the quarters. Yet if proximity to slave masters had its costs, distance could exact a price of its own. In the Piedmont, for example, absentee owners often relied on overseers who proved to be both crueler and more intrusive into the personal lives of the slaves than masters. These overseers allowed the men and women of the quarters fewer opportunities to develop distinctive communal patterns in leisure time, in sexual practices, or in family organization. When Piedmont slaves murdered a white man, their most common victim was not a master but an overseer.

When and where it was well established, the slave community influenced the decisions of the more powerful white community around it. For example, in 1793 a Petersburg, Virginia, slave sentenced to die for robbery won support from white residents of the town. These colonists opposed the slave's execution on practical rather than moral grounds: his death would have too unsettling an effect on his large family and thus too unsettling an effect on their lives as well. And in 1774 the master of a twenty-five-year-old mulatto woman named Sall took into account the reality of a dense social network based on kinship when he tried to track her down. She came, he noted in his newspaper advertisement for her return, "of a numerous Family of Mulattoes, formerly belonging to a Gentleman of the Name of Howard in York County . . . and where probably she may attempt to go again, or perhaps into Cumberland, or Amelia, where . . . many of her kindred live."

The planters of the Lower South also relied on an African slave-labor force. Indeed, the slave-based agriculture of this region developed with remarkable speed in the early eighteenth century. In 1708 there were only 4,000 slaves in South Carolina, many of them brought to the colony from the West Indies when their masters migrated to the mainland. Yet by 1720 the number of slaves had tripled, and by 1740 the colony had a black majority of over 40,000 women and men, most of whom worked in the rice paddies that produced one of the American colonies' most valuable crops. The growth of slavery in Georgia was even more spectacular. Despite clear laws against slaveholding, the Georgia settlers were, as one observer put it, "stark Mad after Negroes." Illegal sale of slaves took place right under the nose of colonial authorities, eventually forcing the ban to be lifted. Between 1751 and 1770, the slave population of Georgia rose from 349 to 16,000; these slaves were imported directly from Africa or purchased from traders in South Carolina.

In the region's showplace city, Charleston, a largely creole population of African Americans swelled to over half the population, filling positions as house servants, boatmen, dockworkers, and artisans of all kinds. The highly acculturated Charleston slave women shared little in common with their rural sisters, for the slaves who worked the large rice plantations had almost no contact with white society. The plantation slave society that developed was the product of an isolation more pronounced than in the Chesapeake. And because of the steady importation of Africans throughout the eighteenth century, this community differed significantly from the creole-dominated world of the Chesapeake slaves. West African traditions shaped the rice and indigo culture in fundamental ways. Plantation slaves spoke Gullah, a language which combined English and several West African dialects, and they preserved the African custom of naming children for the day of the week on which they were born. Chesapeake girls and boys came to recognize themselves in the diminutives of English names—Lizzie, Betty, or Billy, but among slave children in the Lower South names like Quaco, Juba, and Cuba linked them to their African past.

Like Chesapeake slave women, Lower South women worked the fields. But as rice growers, the women of Carolina and Georgia labored under a task system rather than in gangs. This system assigned specific tasks to each slave but did not regulate the time in which it was to be completed. Thus, slaves on the rice plantations controlled the pace of their workday. The task system did provide a measure of autonomy, but no slave who worked the rice plantations would call their occupation an enviable one. "The labor required for the cultivation [of rice] is fit only for slaves," wrote one frank observer, "and I think the hardest work I have seen them engaged in." The most grueling of all the tasks was the pounding of grain with mortar and pestle—and this was a woman's job. It was also the deadliest; mortality rates were higher in the Lower South than in the Chesapeake, and the women who beat the rice were more likely to die than the men who spent hours stooping in the stagnant rice-paddy waters.

By the middle of the eighteenth century, each slave was responsible for a quarter of an acre. Other activities on the plantation—pounding the rice, making fences, and later, in tidal rice cultivation, digging critical irrigation systems—were tasked as well. The task system was not designed to accommodate the women and men who worked in the rice fields or paddies, of course. Its logic lay in the fact that effective rice cultivation did not require the constant supervision of workers. Yet the task system allowed slaves to develop a lively domestic or internal economy. South Carolina and Georgia slaves were given land on which to grow a variety of crops, including corn, potatoes, tobacco, peanuts, melons, and pumpkins, all of which they marketed. This agriculture within an agriculture quickly became entrenched, despite efforts by lawmakers to curtail it. By 1751 Lower South authorities were fighting a staying action, insisting that slaves could sell their rice, corn, or garden crops only to their own masters. These restrictions were ignored. Slave women and men continued to sell everything from corn to catfish, baskets, canoes, and poultry products. But here, unlike in the Piedmont, slave agriculture reflected the community's active African tradition, for Low Country slaves grew tania, bene, peppers, and other African crops. When local slave crops reached Charleston, slave women took charge of their marketing. These female traders were known for their shrewdness in bargaining with customers of both races, to whom they hawked poultry, eggs, and fruit at sometimes shocking prices. Slave women willingly paid their masters a fee for the privilege of selling the pies, cakes, handicrafts, or dry goods they made or brokered, for any profits after the fee was met belonged to them. These women drew on a West African tradition of female traders not unlike the female market-town traders of England.

The task system provided the women and men of the Lower South a measure of autonomy. But here, as in the Chesapeake, the opportunity to create a family and protect its integrity was subject to the slave owner's circumstances and choices. The difficulties were greatest in the newer settlements of Georgia. Well into the post-Revolutionary decades, importation, not natural increase, accounted for the rising slave population there, and that population was overwhelmingly male and young. The demand made by Georgia rice planters for "prime" workers translated into a demand for slaves under the age of twenty-five. Only 4 percent of the almost 2,500 adult slaves listed in Georgia's pre–Revolutionary War inventories were "old." The distribution of these young saltwater slaves accounted for some of the difficulty they faced in creating family or community. Into the second decade of the nineteenth century, only 6 percent of Georgia's planters owned fifty or more slaves, while 13 percent owned only one. Yet by the time of the Revolution, perhaps three-quarters of the slaves lived on plantations with populations of more than twenty. The real problem was not the concentration of the slave population but its composition, for not only did men outnumber women but the larger the slaveholding, the greater the sexual imbalance. Some plantations were virtually single-sexed, and only about 17 percent of those we have records for could claim a balance of the sexes.

Slave masters showed little interest in creating circumstances favorable to natural increase as long as new slaves could be imported. The African women who found themselves in Georgia were treated as workers not potential mothers, and they were put to work in the rice and indigo fields during childbearing years. Despite these obstacles, slave women and men who worked in proximity did form sexual relationships and bonds of affection, and families followed. Generally, Georgia planters allowed slaves the right to choose their own partners, and they made few efforts to disrupt a monogamous relationship. They did place restrictions upon those choices, however, for most of these planters refused to allow interplantation visiting. Thus, couples had to be formed from within the slave community of an individual plantation. Only a little over a quarter of the slave women whose lives can be traced through inventories in the pre-Revolutionary era were married and lived with their husbands. Over half these couples had one child living with them. The rest, however, had none, possibly because the children had been separated from them.

Conditions in Georgia were extreme, but slave women in the Carolinas also found it difficult to establish the relationships they desired or to create the family circumstances they thought best. What these women did want is evident, in part, from the choices they made whenever choices were possible. Historians have long argued about when slave women became sexually active and whether they delayed childbearing until marriage, but the most detailed study of South Carolina slave women suggests that in the twenty-five years before the Revolution, they bore their first children between the ages of sixteen and twenty-three. The median age was nineteen, well after a typical Carolina slave woman reached puberty. This deferral of motherhood suggests that slave women sought a stable relationship before creating their family. It also suggests that the slave community endorsed restraints on a woman's sexual behavior. Thus, black and white women shared the close identification of morality with sexual behavior.

In South Carolina, the master's power to disperse its members was the greatest danger to a woman's family. Here, as in Virginia, Georgia, and Maryland, male sons were at greatest risk. Indeed, 60 percent of men between twenty and twenty-nine were separated from their mothers. Sixty percent of a slave woman's daughters, on the other hand, were likely to remain with her. Almost all children under five were also allowed to stay with their mother. The result of these dispersal patterns was that three generations of women were likely to live together, from infant daughter to young mother to the elderly matron of the family. Strain and rivalry were as likely to result as harmony in this multigenerational female world, but this was a connection few men could expect with their father or their brothers.

Although South Carolina's demand for slave labor produced a black majority, only 17 percent of the mainland colonial slaves worked the fields of the Lower South at mid-century. Sixty-one percent lived, as Mary Johnson had a century before, in the Chesapeake. In 1750 61 percent of all enslaved women and men were residents of Virginia or Maryland. Together, these Southern regions were the magnet that drew slave ships to America's North Atlantic coast, and within them, distinctive slave cultures developed. But slavery was not simply a Southern institution; the remaining black population could be found in the cities and the farmlands of the Northern colonies.

Slavery in the North was an accepted tradition but not a widespread habit. The Dutch had employed slave labor extensively when New York was New Netherlands, using African labor to compensate for the scarcity of colonists from Holland. The small farmers of New England, on the other hand, had little practical use for slave labor, and where slaves were employed it was often because of their master's close tie to the transatlantic slave trade. For example, the merchant-landowners of Rhode Island who made their riches in trade liked to flaunt their prosperity by retaining anywhere from five to forty slaves. One merchant magnate boasted a holding of 238 slaves. But the majority of New England slaves, like the slaves of the middle colonies, were found in the cities, where shortages of white labor in artisan shops, on the docks, and in household or personal service were a periodic problem. The greatest influx of African slaves to Pennsylvania, for example, came during the Seven Years War, when the flow of English and other European servants was seriously disrupted. By mid-century, roughly 10 percent of the population of Boston, Philadelphia, and New York was black, although only one out of every five families owned a slave.

A slave woman in these Northern cities spent her days engaged in housework—cooking, cleaning, washing and ironing, tending the fires and the gardens, and looking after her master's children. She passed her nights sleeping in the garret or the kitchen. She might be hired out to nurse the sick, to put in a neighbor's garden, to preserve food or wait on tables for a special occasion, but few

urban slave women were ever hired out to learn a craft. Colonial
artisans considered their shops a male domain. Ironically, the
"black mammy" so often associated with plantation life was not
an authentic figure of the colonial South, but she could be found
in the fashionable homes of Philadelphia and New York. Slaves
in the countryside also did housework, but more of their time
was spent tending larger gardens, raising poultry, milking cows,
and spinning cloth than in cooking, cleaning, or serving as personal maids to farm family members. At harvest time, these
women were assigned to fieldwork.

As they worked in the wheat fields of southern Pennsylvania
or in the kitchens of Boston, Northern slave women experienced
constant, intimate contact with white society. Whether their owners were kind or callous, their values and customs were ever present, and a solitary black servant, working, eating, sleeping in a
crowded Pennsylvania farmhouse, or in the close quarters of a
merchant's home, lacked the steady reinforcement of her African
heritage. Not surprisingly, Northern slave women were more
likely to acculturate than their sisters in the plantation South.

Urban slave women had little hope of creating a family that
could remain intact. Slaveholdings were too small for a woman
to choose a husband from the household, and few urban colonists
were willing to shoulder the costs of raising a slave child in their
midst. Rural slaveholders could set a slave's child to work in the
garden or field, but in the cities youngsters were simply a drain
on resources and living space. At least one master preferred to sell
his pregnant slave rather than suffer having her child underfoot.
Other masters solved the problem of an extra mouth to feed by
selling infants—or, in one case, giving his slave's baby away. Slave
women who dared to start or add to their families were sometimes
separated from the men who fathered their children. In Boston,
a pregnant woman and her husband chose to commit suicide
rather than endure the dissolution of their family. Urban slave
women who were allowed to keep their children often lost them
quickly. Communicable diseases and cramped quarters combined
in deadly fashion in every household in eighteenth-century co-

lonial cities, but black infant mortality rates were two to three times higher than white.

A slave woman's life—like a slave man's—could be enriched by a family, an independent culture and community, and the autonomous spaces created by the task system or wrested from the gang-labor system of the Chesapeake. In a sense, these were all forms of resistance to enslavement. But there were other forms of resistance as well—rebellion, suicide, murder, escape, self-mutilation, disobedience, the destruction of tools and equipment, arson, theft of supplies, feigned illness, feigned pregnancy, and feigned ignorance or stupidity. Colonial English society rarely assumed that slaves were docile or content, and slaveholders preferred to rely on repressive laws, a show of force, and harsh reprisals rather than a belief in the passivity or contentedness of their slaves.

In many Southern colonies, women received the same punishment as men if they resisted their enslavement. Georgia's list of capital crimes, which included insurrection, murder, assault, and the destruction of property carried a death penalty of hanging or burning without regard to the criminal's sex. In 1774, when eleven "new negroes," recently imported from Africa, joined with one creole slave in the murder of four white colonists, the Georgia authorities meted out the same punishment to the two women participants that they did to the men. When, in 1754, two female slaves set fire to their master's buildings in Charleston, South Carolina, he did not hesitate to have them burned alive. And when Nat Turner led the rebellion that chilled the hearts of slaveholders everywhere, a slave woman named Lucy took and held a woman hostage until Turner's rebels made plans to execute her. Lucy was hanged as a Turner conspirator just as the male rebels were, but she remained defiant, riding to her execution on top of her own coffin.

Women poisoned mistresses and burned homes just as men did, but they were less likely to attempt to run away. There were female runaways, of course, as the 142 advertisements in the Chesapeake between 1737 and 1801 and the 61 notices of Georgia runaways between 1763 and 1776 attest, but as mothers and daughters, women proved reluctant to abandon the young and the old who were dependent on them. Even if they were willing to cut family ties and abandon family obligations, women had little chance to find employment once they fled the fields. Few whites would take an unknown black into their home as washerwoman or domestic servant, and unskilled women could not go to sea as unskilled male runaways often did. For the majority of black slave women, therefore, the bounds of family and the constraints of gender made flight less likely than endurance.

The work demanded of Northern slave women was less grueling than the work done with mortar and pestle in the Carolinas or with hoes and hands in the Chesapeake tobacco fields. Indeed, slavery in the North was generally less brutal than in the Southern colonies. Yet enslaved women in the middle colonies and New England also resisted, ran away, and rebelled. Here, too, women fled their master's home, determined to reunite with their husband or children. And here, too, women participated in the rare but violent uprisings of slaves seeking to overthrow their oppressors. When authorities moved against participants in the 1712 Slave Revolt in New York City, several women were among those arrested and convicted. And when a slave presented the first petition for freedom to the newly formed state legislature of Massachusetts in 1782, she was a woman. The woman, Belinda, pressed these Revolutionaries to make good on their state constitution's pledge to discontinue slavery, stating her case with eloquence: "I have not yet enjoyed the benefits of creation . . . I beg freedom."

Decades before the American Revolution, a small number of blacks like Mary and Anthony Johnson had known the freedom Belinda sought. Even after the shift to slave labor in the Southern colonies had institutionalized chattel slavery, communities of free blacks had survived on the margins of Chesapeake society. Tax records preserve our knowledge of them. And in every colony the most fortunate runaways managed to pass from slavery into freedom. In Pennsylvania, where Quaker conscience wrestled with the morality of slavery as early as the 1720s and 1730s, a trickle of emancipations produced a free black community in Philadelphia. Between 1748 and 1752, at least fourteen free black adults and children were baptized in the Philadelphia Anglican Church. Free black children attended the Quaker schools of the 1760s, and complaints about free black vagrants appeared in Pennsylvania newspapers. But it was the social upheaval of the American Revolution that offered slaves the most dramatic opportunity to enjoy at last the "benefits of creation."

THE RISE OF GENTILITY:
CLASS AND REGIONAL DIFFERENCES
IN THE EIGHTEENTH CENTURY

ELIZA LUCAS WAS THE DAUGHTER of a gentleman military officer, George Lucas, and his wife, Anne. By the age
of fifteen, Eliza had enjoyed a taste of life in both England and
the provinces, for her father's career took the family first to London and then to the Caribbean island of Antigua. In 1738, Eliza
arrived at her new home on Wappoo Creek, South Carolina, a
move prompted by her father's recent inheritance of three promising plantation sites in the rice colony. What we know of Eliza
in these early years suggests a bright, energetic young woman,
with little of the frivolous about her. If this is indeed an accurate
portrait, her character was well suited to the life she would lead
in Carolina. For, before her sixteenth birthday, her mother's ailing
health and her father's military commitments would leave her entirely in charge of the family plantations.

Eliza's responsibilities (and opportunities) did not arise out of
economic necessity. When Anne Lucas grew too ill to play an
active role in the domestic affairs of the family, her husband had
the resources to hire a housekeeper. Instead, he turned the management of the household over to his daughter Eliza. And when
George Lucas was called to active duty in a conflict with Spain

popularly known as the War of Jenkins's Ear, there were men available to oversee his affairs and attend to the operation of his plantations. Instead, he placed the family's fortunes in his daughter's hands. At an age when many wealthy Carolina girls were dreaming of marriage and children, Eliza Lucas was an established planter and the mistress of a complex colonial household.

George Lucas's confidence in his daughter was striking. Yet he knew her abilities and her personal character well, for he had taken an active hand in her education and training. From the start, he had encouraged her to develop into a woman of compelling intelligence rather than a woman of trivial refinements. Although he may have known little about the new, enlightened theories of nurturance or the power of emulation in shaping a child's character, proponents of these child-rearing methods would have approved of the affectionate manner in which he helped his daughter develop her sense of self. The young woman who emerged from his care had an intellectual bent, a broad education, an air of confidence, and a love of achievement that would have made her distinctive in any milieu. Yet she was not lacking in what eighteenth-century planter society considered female accomplishments. She was attentive to, and well versed in, the social skills expected of a South Carolina planter's daughter.

Eliza's new responsibilities required her to master both male and female roles within her culture. That she had her hands full there can be no doubt, but there is little evidence of the tensions such duality of roles might have produced. By her own account, she quickly established a grueling daily schedule that blended male and female spheres. She rose at 5:00 each morning, read for two hours, and then took a quick tour of the work getting under way in the plantation fields. She returned home for breakfast and then devoted two hours to the study of music or French. By midmorning she had shifted from student to instructor, giving reading lessons to her sister and two slave girls. In the afternoon she did needlework, and in the evening she wrote letters and read. From these quiet evenings alone came a familiarity with traditional works by Milton and with Samuel Richardson's controversial

Pamela. One day a week, she set aside all female duties and attended entirely to plantation business.

Under Eliza's management, the Lucas plantations prospered. From the beginning she took a bold approach, experimenting with new crops that might grow in South Carolina's climate and soil. Her father approved wholeheartedly of her unorthodox methods and assisted her in her search for potentially profitable crops. In the midst of his military duties, he found time to send her indigo seeds, from which a blue dye could be made. Later he provided her with an expert indigo maker from Montserrat. It took more than five years for Eliza Lucas to show a profit in indigo, but her perseverence paid off, and indigo became a staple crop of the colony for several years.

Eliza rarely discussed her management of the plantation with female friends. In her letters to them she usually focused on her activities as a gardener of vegetables and flowering shrubs. When she did broach the subject of her life as a planter, she spoke with confidence and authority. When, for example, Eliza described a "large plantation of Oaks" she had just created, she not only took credit for the project but also asserted her right to any profits in timber it generated. It was, she said, her business acumen that had led to the project, and she insisted that the oaks were "my own property, whether my father gives me the land or not." The men who worked for her would not have been surprised by such a claim, for they knew her entrepreneurial side well. Eliza hired and fired the overseers, who reported directly to her, and she wrote regularly to the family's agent in London on matters of property deeds, sales of land and livestock, and the purchase of goods through local Charleston merchants. In matters of business and legal affairs, as in other areas, George Lucas had laid the groundwork for his daughter's expertise. He had instructed her fully on her *feme sole* rights and encouraged her to make good use of the legal library left behind in her care. And she did just that. Many of her neighbors relied on her to make their wills or assist them in suing for their debts. Male or female, these colonists knew less about protecting their property than this teenage girl who read law books, legal treatises, and philosophers of civil society such as John Locke.

Despite his certainty and admiration of Eliza's competence, George Lucas was keenly aware that his daughter was a young, unmarried woman. To remedy this situation, he encouraged several suitors. But Eliza, always eager to satisfy her father's wishes if possible, refused to accede in the matter of matrimony. Not even "the riches of Peru and Chili," she wrote him, were enough to make any of these men her husband. She believed she was too young to marry, and she meant to remain single until she was ready to live otherwise.

In this, as in many other ways, Eliza Lucas protected her own individuality. She believed that she had a "true self," which she had to both discover and honor. When she felt uncertain or uncomfortable with her own behavior or with emotions that troubled her mind, she turned for guidance to the writings of John Locke. As she told friends, she "consult[ed] Mr. Lock over and over to see wherein personal Identity consisted and if I was the very same self." Locke confirmed her belief in rational self-scrutiny to keep her emotional balance, but it was Eliza Lucas who declared that the self she examined was unique, individual, and worthy of attention.

When Eliza Lucas did marry in May 1744, she chose a man twice her age. The recently widowed Charles Pinckney was a leading lawyer and political figure in the colony, and a friend of several years. Intelligent and erudite, he had acted as Eliza's mentor in the study in philosophy, science, and literature after her father's departure.

As Charles Pinckney's wife, Eliza turned all her energies and attention to domestic concerns, and especially to maternal ones; within five years she had given birth to four children. Of her three sons, Charles Cotesworth and Thomas survived their childhood. Eliza's second child, named George Lucas Pinckney in honor of her father, died in infancy. Her only and much loved daughter, Harriott, was born in 1747. Eliza undertook motherhood with the same energy and clarity of purpose she showed in her years as a planter and businesswoman. She resolved to be a "good Mother," by which she meant that she would "instill piety, Virtue, and true religion into them" and would "correct their Errors whatever uneasiness it may give myself." Her goal was to raise moral, honorable, and intelligent children; not surprisingly, her method was to be "Mr Lock's." She believed in Locke's theory that a child could "play himself into learning" and was confident that, through play-linked instruction, she could teach her oldest son his letters by the time he was able to speak. By contemporary standards, she could claim great success as a parent. Both sons grew up to be political leaders during the Revolutionary struggle, and both enjoyed long careers in American politics after the war. Harriott's successes were far less public and thus less well recorded, but she did replicate many of her mother's life choices. Like Eliza, Harriott was an avid reader and showed an aptitude for business matters. And like her mother, Harriott married a man significantly older than herself. She too married well, for her husband, Daniel Horry, was a wealthy South Carolina rice planter. When Horry left her a widow in 1785, Harriott took up the reins of management of her late husband's extensive estate, just as Eliza Lucas Pinckney had done in 1758 when her own husband died.

Charles Pinckney died fourteen years after his marriage to Eliza. The family had been living in England while Charles served as an agent for the Carolina colony. When he was called back to America, twelve-year-old Charles Cotesworth and seven-year-old Thomas remained behind to pursue what provincial elites considered a proper education. Although the separation from her sons was painful to Eliza, the loss of her husband soon after their return to Charleston brought her true grief. In the letters she wrote in 1758, she relived the experience of loss and spoke bluntly of her depression. Yet left to manage on her own once again, the thirty-six-year-old Eliza Lucas Pinckney revived the skills she had developed at the age of fifteen. Until her death from cancer in 1793, Eliza managed the complex business and plantation affairs that were her family legacies.

The Eliza Pinckney who emerges from letters and journals is

an accomplished, talented woman with a zest for life that is conveyed across the centuries. The fullness with which her life is documented—in her own letters and in the records of others—and the care with which it has been reconstructed—because she was matriarch of a leading political family—accounts in part for her vivid image in contrast to the sparer, or more stylized images we have been able to construct for Mary Johnson or Hannah Duston. Yet there are obvious lines connecting these seventeenth-century colonial women and this eighteenth-century planter, wife, and mother. The rhythms of Eliza Lucas Pinckney's life cycle are similar to Mary Cole's and Hannah Duston's. She was married in her early twenties to an older man. And once married, she immediately became a mother who also knew the experience of burying an infant child. Like these women, Eliza Lucas Pinckney was excluded by her sex from direct political participation and her behavior was filtered through a set of gender assumptions. Her larger world, like theirs, was bounded by its colonial relationship to the British Empire.

But there are sometimes subtle, sometimes striking differences that seem to separate Eliza Lucas Pinckney from colonial women of an earlier century. There is the matter of her erudition and her catholic taste in the ideas she sampled and mastered. She could both read and write, and she did not claim the Bible as her primary text nor did she simply recollect her daily tasks when she sat down to record her thoughts. There is her perception of herself as a competent planter and businesswoman in her own right, her unapologetic interest in politics, both local and international, her scientific experiments in agriculture, and her expertise in the law. There is a consciousness of self and a confidence in reason that seemed to serve Eliza as both guides and tools for success. Indeed, in these and other ways, she seems strikingly modern. It takes only the slightest stretch in empathy for a twentieth-century white woman scholar to feel she understands Eliza Lucas Pinckney's character, emotions, and experiences. She was, after all, a woman of intelligence and acquired learning, a woman with what today would be called a good liberal education. She had focus and drive, ambition and energy, and she took unabashed pleasure in her achievements. Even in her youth, she insisted that what she had created or produced was her own, from an oak plantation to an indigo crop. She resisted pressures to marry, chose her own mate, and, when she became a mother, consulted the experts of the day on parenting and child education. As a widow, she relied on her own skills and talents as a planter rather than depend on sons or male advisors in matters of property and trade.

There is little to suggest that Eliza Lucas Pinckney thought of herself as an anomaly in colonial South Carolina, and nothing to suggest that her friends and neighbors did either. Of course, she and her contemporaries recognized a critical, if unspoken corollary to Pinckney's image of herself: her behavior and her experiences were possible only in the context of her social class. Eliza Lucas Pinckney was, in the language of her day, a member of genteel society. If hers was an acceptable style of life, it was also an exceptional one, marked by privilege and opportunity not enjoyed by most Americans of the day. And yet there is more to understand here, for locating Pinckney within a social elite does not answer all the questions her life raises. Indeed, for historians, it threatens to cloud and confuse what we believe we know about this class-based ideal of gentility.

We have assumed that genteel women were circumscribed by and identified with the domestic sphere, that they focused their energies on such private matters as raising children, and were more invested in appropriately feminine accomplishments than publicly acknowledged achievement and activity. If the Eliza Pinckney who studied French, learned to dance, and served as amiable hostess at the dinner table of her father and her husband affirms this gentility, the Eliza Pinckney who managed plantations, hired and fired overseers, discoursed on Locke, and laid claim to the future profits from an oak plantation does not. Perhaps this is only to say that ideals and lived lives are rarely the same; perhaps it is to say that gentility, like most social ideals, was more contradictory and less rigid for those who laid claim to it than for those who try to reconstruct it as history.

It is clear that Eliza Lucas Pinckney lived within the magic circle of prestige and privilege enjoyed by her father, her husband, and later her sons. In itself, the existence of such a social hierarchy was not new. In the seventeenth century the men and women of Hannah Duston's world deferred to the ministers and magistrates who honored her after her captivity. What is new is the fact that Pinckney's social status was accompanied by a range of material comforts, luxuries, resources, and the opportunity to deploy them that went far beyond those available to most colonists. These resources separated the Lucases and the Pinckneys dramatically from other colonists, even if those of more modest means shared in the valorizing of the "genteel life." Thus, to understand Eliza Lucas Pinckney and the women of her era we must look closely at eighteenth-century society and at the distinguishing marks of its social classes. If we ask what had changed or was changing in the first half of the eighteenth century that made social space for a woman like Eliza Lucas Pinckney, we must also ask to what degree social class had become a determinate of behavior and norms, just as race, religious community, or even region had long been.

By the eighteenth century the line of settlement the English called the frontier had moved many miles west of the Atlantic coast. Changes in the physical landscape along the coast were striking. Where dense forests once stood there were now acres of cultivated farms and plantations and scores of towns and cities stretching from New England to the Carolinas. These signs of what the English would call civilization were moving steadily westward as quickly as land could be purchased or seized from Indian tribes and protection from England's European rivals could be ensured.

The sheer size of the colonial population distinguished the eighteenth century from the earlier decades of initial settlement and growth. Both natural increase and immigration in the early eighteenth century had wrought this transformation. Between 1688 and 1775, the white population of the colonies went from 225,000 to over 2.5 million. (The African-American population would reach 500,000 by the eve of the Revolution.) Every region experienced this astonishing increase in men, women, and children: New England's population rose from 170,000 in 1720 to over 570,000 in 1770; the middle colonies from 102,000 to 560,000; and the Southern colonies from over 192,000 to 700,000. Eliza Lucas came of age in the midst of a population explosion that even the economist-demographer Thomas Malthus found impressive.

Greater diversity was a striking feature of this growth. Thousands of immigrating Scots-Irish, Irish, and Germans made their way from their landing sites in Philadelphia, New York, and Charleston to the farmlands of Pennsylvania and to the Southern backcountry. Colonies such as Connecticut remained more homogeneous than New York or Pennsylvania, yet not even New England remained untouched. In addition to this increased ethnic and religious diversity, every colony was also becoming multiracial. African-American slaves were imported into the mainland colonies by the thousands each year, and although most were sold in the Southern colonies, New York City had a sizable slave population, and wealthy families in Newport, Boston, and Philadelphia purchased black men and women as household servants. Small free black communities were scattered throughout the colonies as well, and Indian communities still existed despite the decimation of the New England wars and the colonists' ever-increasing claims on Indian lands.

A diversity of population may seem an ironic characteristic for the colonies to share. Yet other forces also began to connect colonial men and women. Some were simply improvements in transportation, as the networks of busy roads that colonists traveled by horse or wagon, in carriages or on foot, helped to shrink local distances. Others arose from the complex web of intercolonial associations that included everything from shared military experience in the imperial wars to male friendships formed in college or through marriage ties. Expanding intercolonial trade, however, was probably the primary connecting link, making Rhode Island slavers and South Carolina rice planters regular business partners and establishing interdependence among the regions. Distinctive regional economies did continue, of course. Trade, lumbering, and fisheries dominated in New England, while wheat production and trade sustained the middle colonies. The South continued to build its prosperity on the production of agricultural staples such as tobacco, rice, and wheat. Perhaps even more distinctive were the regional labor systems: slavery now fueled the Southern plantation economy while in the middle colonies and New England free and tenant labor were prevalent. Nevertheless, as the eighteenth century progressed, several once significant distinctions among the regions were fading. For example, New England's "Puritan way" gave way to a "Yankee" entrepreneurship similar to the commercially minded ideology of New York or Philadelphia, and demographic changes narrowed the differences in family structure from North to South.

Colonists also shared the experience of what some historians call the eighteenth-century consumer revolution. Among the prosperous, an attention to English fashion and to genteel amenities grew, but even families of more modest means sought to purchase teapots, cutlery, and other consumer goods not considered essential for survival. While colonists still relied on European manufacturers for many of their needs and desires, there were local artisans, both slave and free, to supply some of these goods. In New York City alone, apprentices entered thirty-nine different trades between 1700 and 1730, and itinerant artisans carried craftwork to the most remote areas of every colony. The availability of consumer goods—from the mundane and necessary to the most luxurious—was greatest in urban areas. In cities like Philadelphia, Boston, and New York, streets were lined with shops offering everything from cloth to mutton chops, and hand-crafted silver to books and maps, while on the streets themselves men and women hawked fruit pies, farm eggs, and freshly churned butter.

Finally, English and European ideas, like manufactured goods, began to make their way into the eighteenth-century society of

Eliza Lucas Pinckney. Frequent transatlantic travel had become commonplace for the colonists engaged in international business and politics. The children of the rich, including Eliza Lucas Pinckney's sons, often took their schooling in England, where they became familiar with the latest fashions, both intellectual and sartorial. Private libraries grew in number in every colony. Local newspapers carried accounts of everything from English politics and European diplomacy to the use of feathers or fur in hats. If the colonies were still "the provinces," by the eighteenth century they were no longer so hopelessly provincial in attitudes and taste.

The colonial world Eliza Lucas Pinckney knew as a girl and a young wife had ceased to be a society that could be characterized by religious refugees, speculative ventures, or political experiments (although Georgia, founded as a haven for debtors in 1752 by philanthropists, briefly continued along these lines). The colonies of the eighteenth century were now viable members of the British Empire's transatlantic community. Historians speak of these decades as a time of colonial maturation, using terms that suggest transitions—"from puritan to yankee" or from a "moral economy to capitalism"—or in terms that suggest evolution—the rise of the assembly, the formation of a slave culture, the consumer revolution, or the Anglicization of colonial law. Whether these are signs of maturation or not, they provide evidence to explain the chasms between the lives of Hannah Duston and Eliza Lucas Pinckney.

How did these changes and developments affect women's lives? Such a question requires us to take a closer look at white women's experience in terms of geography, social class, and the age cycle. The starting place for this examination is not difficult to find: the household, which remained the primary setting for white women's activities in the eighteenth century.

The majority of white women in the colonies still lived in rural, agricultural settings. Although fewer worked in the fields, there were notable exceptions. In Pennsylvania, for example, the wives and daughters of landless "cottagers" and tenant farm wives could still be called on for fieldwork, including sickling wheat and rye. And on the modest plantations or backcountry farms of the South, as on the outer edges of settlement everywhere, the whole family was likely to labor in the fields at critical moments of the season. The sharp decline of white female fieldwork could be best accounted for by the shift from white indentured servants to enslaved Africans and African Americans on the larger Southern plantations, and by the tendency of farmers who prospered in every colony to exclude wives and daughters from agricultural labor.

However, white farm women were still responsible for the care of young children and the cultivation of the family garden. Like their mothers and grandmothers, these colonists were also expected to prepare and process food, sew and mend, and perform one or several—though rarely all—of the essential steps in manufacturing household necessities. The scale of these activities, of course, differed from family farm to large plantation. On Eliza Lucas Pinckney's plantation, laundry was apt to take a week rather than a day, and sewing, even of the rough and shapeless clothing provided to slaves, was a task involving more hours than even the most industrious Pennsylvania housewife could imagine. In the Northern and middle colonies, rural women continued to rely on their daughters for domestic assistance or on servants or poorer local women, hired to complete particular tasks such as laundering or dairy work. Female slaves were used as domestic servants in the prosperous farmlands of Pennsylvania, especially among Quaker families, and some Southern planters probably allowed their wives to put young or elderly female slaves to work in the kitchen, laundry, or garden and, later in the era, in the production of cloth and clothing. The number of assistants a housewife had thus depended upon her own fecundity, the availability of hired or enslaved help, her husband's prosperity, and his willingness to allocate resources to her for domestic duties.

These eighteenth-century white farm women and their assistants probably did more household manufacturing than their mothers or grandmothers. For most of the seventeenth century, colonial families lacked the resources, or the male head of household would not allocate the funds, to purchase the equipment necessary to churn butter, mold candles, make soap, or complete the cloth-making process. In Eliza Lucas's lifetime such equipment began to show up more frequently in household inventories. Not every housewife was a mistress of all trades. Nor did she need to be. Within their communities, women developed specializations and created informal networks of trade and exchange. Butter was churned by some; soap made by others; candles by still a third group of housewives. And where itinerant or locally based artisans were available, housewives often relied on their skills to provide some of the steps in the manufacture of needed goods. General stores, hubs of trade in Southern rural areas, brought English manufactured goods into homes, and household supplies also came from skilled slaves. Thus, while there were more churns and more spinning wheels and looms in the eighteenth century, this did not mean that every home boasted a full complement of the tools of "housewifery."

A rural white woman's daily life, then, was shaped by her race, her social class, and by where she was in the socially defined life cycle. Only poverty and dependence could override the social conventions and, in some colonies, the legal restrictions that kept white women out of the fields. Prosperity, on the other hand, allowed some farm wives to be household managers and directors of other women's labors. Whatever their economic circumstances, custom decreed that unmarried daughters, like servants, give assistance in a household that was ultimately not their domain. Thus, housewifery and household chores were the lot of all rural colonial white women, but not all of them were mistresses of the domestic sphere they inhabited.

When these rural women speak to us through the rare diaries or letters we have found, they seem to speak in a single dismayed voice of the repetitive tasks that constituted the "sameness" that "reigns throughout the year." They envied the variety of experience they saw in male work. Men's fieldwork was hard labor, they conceded, but the chores were seasonal, and during work breaks, husbands and sons could enjoy a change of scene, taking trips to town or going off on hunting expeditions. By contrast, women's work was constant, its cycle weekly, the days marked by a litany of chores: Monday washing, Tuesday ironing, Wednesday baking, and so on, until Monday came again. And the constant obligations of childbirth and child care kept these women bound to home. Most painful was the fact that there was little time to spare for niceties such as neatness or cleanliness, and no time at all for solitude. New England and Long Island farm wives seemed convinced that urban matrons did enjoy such niceties, imagining that all women in colonial cities and towns lived a Cinderella life of leisurely tidying up, making afternoon visits, and spending evenings reading or in quiet contemplation.

It is impossible to know if the malaise expressed in these diaries was widespread. Most of the commentaries we have were not made in diaries but in "daybooks," intended to keep track of daily chores. Perhaps complaints and comments were natural at the end of a long day, as a woman entered an accounting of tasks completed and those to be undertaken in the morning. There is usually no mention of children or of visits from relatives or friends. Thus, if these records capture genuine feelings of drudgery and boredom, they do not portray the entire range of the ordinary farm wife's experiences.

It is true, however, that urban and rural domestic routines were different. The difference arose from a city resident's more reliable and steady access to processed goods and essential household supplies. Trips to the butcher shop, the fishmonger, the greengrocer, and to merchants' establishments that sold cloth and other supplies were the common techniques of provisioning urban households in the eighteenth century—at least among those who could afford to purchase goods and services. Most townswomen continued to tend gardens and see to domestic animals, as indeed they would well into the nineteenth century, but other, tedious household chores fell to resident servants or to poorer women hired to do disagreeable tasks like washing, cleaning, and mundane rather than decorative sewing.

It was clearly not the household tasks themselves that separated seventeenth- and eighteenth-century women's experience. Yet the physical setting of many households probably would have surprised women of the earlier generations. By Eliza Lucas Pinckney's day, a consumer revolution had begun to spread throughout the colonial world, even reaching into the countryside. It was transforming the material life of the colonial family. Some scholars mark the arrival of this consumer revolution in the early decades of the eighteenth century. Others consider it a late-eighteenth- and early-nineteenth-century phenomenon. Still others view it as an ongoing social transformation, whose tempo and timing depended on the availability of goods and access to the discretionary capital that translated into purchasing power. We can assume that it, like other sea changes in society, was an uneven, erratic process, reaching some segments of the population before others. Yet a look at inventories of family possessions, or at advertisements in colonial newspapers of the arrival of imported goods, or at the architectural and related material evidence remaining from the era suggests that many free colonial contemporaries of Eliza Lucas Pinckney welcomed the opportunity to add to their worldly possessions whenever possible.

While the consumer revolution affected males and females alike, new possessions most dramatically transformed the domestic sphere and women's roles within it. Consider the changes Chesapeake scholars observe when they contrast planter homes in the seventeenth century with those of the eighteenth century. In the seventeenth century, historians have seen little to suggest that wealthy planter families lived in greater elegance than their poorer neighbors. True, a prosperous planter's family sat on chairs to eat at a table, and they lay down each night to sleep on beds raised on frames rather than cots laid upon the floor. But luxuries were rare even among the most successful; perhaps the wealthy owned some crystal, a silver plate, or hung a picture on the wall. On the whole, however, a family with greater means possessed ordinary extras such as tableware and bedsteads rather than luxuries such as clocks, curtains, or family portraits. This "rude sufficiency," as one scholar has called it, was not a temporary phase in the life of the large planter. Once the bare necessities entered the household, possessions that would have marked a higher standard of living failed to appear. What was true for the Chesapeake was true as well for rural Pennsylvania: in the seventeenth century, colonists demonstrated a homogeneity of material life that was spare by any standard.

By the eighteenth century, however, such spartan existence was no longer acceptable to many white colonists. Where once entire households ate, worked, and slept in one room, these colonists of the eighteenth century showed great interest in constructing separate rooms for separate functions. Parlors were created, and heated to invite sociality. Kitchens no longer shared space with living areas. Multiple bedchambers, encouraging privacy, replaced the collective sleeping arrangements of the earlier decades. Even in the most modest homes, communal bowls of food gave way to individual servings on individual plates. Among the wealthy, rituals of table setting included the proper placement of individual wine and beer glasses. In rich homes and modest ones, the older custom of passing a single tankard around the table was vanishing.

The consumer revolution undoubtedly affected all colonists to some degree. But perhaps its greatest impact was the increasing division between the material life of the wealthy and that of the less prosperous. The wealthy were no longer identified by their possession of sufficient ordinary goods but by their attainment of elaborate and ritualized luxury. Visitors from abroad were struck by the fact that Southern planters took pains to fill their homes with elegant furniture, china, and silver before they had even completed the construction of their house. By mid-century, couches and upholstered chairs, japanned chests and elegant mahogany tables, sideboards, buffets, screens, and clocks furnished the parlors and dining rooms, and family portraits decorated the walls.

For the women of prosperous families, a new set of burdens offset the enjoyment of this "sweeping train of luxury," since each genteel experience required considerable behind-the-scenes preparation. Walnut chests of drawers had to be dusted; cutlery had to be polished; pots, cups and saucers, jugs for cream, bowls for sugar, tongs, and teaspoons had to be washed, filled, and cleaned in order for tea to be a gracious ceremony. Where once a table could be laid with a tankard and a few earthenware bowls, now a proper meal required clean linen for the table, glasses for wine, cider, and beer, and plates and serving bowls—each sparkling and needing to be cleaned again after meals. Simple, one-course meals gave way to an elaborate procession of courses, provided from the garden, the oven, and the commissary skills of housewives as they went in search of shellfish, eggs, and poultry. This meant new domestic strategies: more planning of the garden and the orchard; more storing, pickling, and preserving of fruits and vegetables; more baking; and, especially in the cities, careful shopping and cultivation of relations with suppliers. As eating became dining, simple recipes handed down from mothers and grandmothers were no longer adequate. Cookbooks replaced custom in the kitchens of the genteel, and soup kettles, stewpots, saucepans, cake pans, and tart molds replaced the spartan kitchenware of the past. These demands on time and energy were adding to, rather than replacing, the demands of motherhood and household production. Still, such new domestic rituals had their rewards: like the young Eliza Lucas, genteel women sat down to preside over meals that had evolved into family social events rather than the hasty refuelings of the past.

The personal and social meaning of these lifestyle changes were perhaps as important as the changes themselves. The possession of individual glasses and plates could reinforce a person's new sense of individuality in other arenas. (Here, perhaps, is a clue to Eliza Lucas Pinckney's own keen sense of her self.) And, when these daily items were not shared with others, a different connection to "things" may well have emerged. At the same time, ownership of luxury goods helped signal a person's social standing to friends and particularly to strangers outside the home. An ideal of gentility, involving both a new self-image and a new encoding of social hierarchy, was being born.

But possessions alone would not mark a man or a woman as "genteel," especially since falling prices in the eighteenth century made manufactured goods more available to many colonists. Fancy clothing had to be coupled with the new manners, rituals, and social conventions that combined to express gentility. Thus, gentlemen and gentlewomen were able to recognize each other by their manners at the tea table and their civility in public places as much as by the silver buckles on their shoes and the decorative buttons on their sleeves. When Eliza Lucas left the isolation of Wappoo Creek for the intense sociality of Charleston, her evident familiarity with the rituals of tea ceremonies, formal dinners, balls, and the never-ending round of social visits marked her as a true member of South Carolina's genteel society.

A commitment to the genteel life redefined the priorities of a wealthy matron's daily work routine. Even without this new social ideal of gentility, however, the prosperity enjoyed by the urban and planter elite was likely to produce subtle but significant shifts in the education and training of their daughters. While farm daughters learned and engaged in domestic skills in order to contribute to their family's welfare, and poorer urban girls mastered specialized skills in order to bring income into the home, the daughters of the wealthy were not expected to contribute to the family economy through housewifery. Instead, their training was oriented toward the future, toward their married role as household mistresses. A very different constellation of accomplishments was added to their training, for young ladies were expected to have some familiarity with foreign languages, fancy stitching, dancing, and music. Many of these accomplishments required formal instruction, but mothers relied on exposure and experience to teach their daughters the arts of the tea table and the rules of "visiting." Farm girls, accustomed to rising with the sun and working until bedtime, would have marveled at the pace of an elite urban daughter's day. For, as one historian put it, these girls were the first American leisure class, rising late in the morning and finding time during the afternoon for socializing and reading novels. The widening differences between the experiences of daughters of the poor and the wealthy in a city such as Philadelphia can be captured vividly in their sewing tableaus: While poor girls sewed for income, alone or in the homes of employers, the daughters of the rich gathered in one another's parlors, stitching while one member of the group read aloud to her friends, turning sewing into a social event.

For eighteenth-century daughters of all social classes, marriage remained what it had been in the previous century: the female rite of passage into adulthood. While no law required that a woman marry, what colonists referred to as spinsterhood was still a decidedly undesirable condition for most girls. Daughters of prosperous Southern planters might fare well enough if land or ample support was provided for them in their spinsterhood, but the majority of unmarried adult women faced a lifetime of domestic tasks performed in someone else's home.

By mid-century, daughters of every social class seemed to enjoy the right to refuse a matrimonial candidate. The evidence we have suggests that girls did not resent but often solicited their parents' advice on the critical matter of choosing a husband. The stakes were high: from her husband a woman acquired her social standing, the quality of her material life, the position of mistress in a household, the opportunity to become a mother, and perhaps even a degree of companionship and affection. Often the criteria set by parents and daughter were different. For example, genteel girls declared that the men they sought must have high moral character, show respect for wife and family, and be dutiful sons and brothers. Frequently they spoke of romantic love as a necessity. Their mothers usually stressed mutual esteem and respect as essential requirements. For their fathers, practical matters held sway. Most parents hoped to ensure that marital candidates came from the same social class as their daughters (and, in some cases, had the same religious background and ethnicity). Like George Lucas, planter and merchant fathers found the sons and nephews of their peers more "suitable" as sons-in-law than other men. Indeed, in the Chesapeake, marriages among cousins helped sustain and strengthen the exclusive ties of a small, elite planter class. But compromise was possible. In the southern Piedmont, in frontier towns, and in areas where the demographics favored men, girls and their families seemed willing to choose grooms from lower social ranks rather than no grooms at all.

Courtship took place in different settings for members of genteel and ordinary society. For young women with Eliza Lucas's background, males and females met at dances, musical evenings, barbecues and formal dinners, and during the endless round of social visits to the homes of their peers. The majority of young men and women, however, met at events such as harvest frolics, country dances, races, or at church. In courtship, gentlemen avoided direct references to sexuality or physical attraction. They wrote and spoke instead of a romanticized affection for the woman they desired. Poorer men spoke more bluntly of the physical appeal of a woman's body. They spoke more bluntly as well about the pleasures of passion and the pains of delayed gratification. "Your coldness to me I am afrade will cause me to run Crasey," wrote one farmer to a woman who would not agree to intimacy. Another boldly asked the girl he courted to sleep with him, saying, "Let not your chiefest glory be immurd in the nice casket of a Maidenhead."

Ending a marriage, on the other hand, was far more difficult than embarking on one. Absolute divorce was rarely permitted by the courts, although legal separations, called *divorce a mensa et thoro*, were granted on grounds that varied from extreme brutality to *de facto* desertion to male impotence. Many colonial couples who wished to end a marriage settled the matter outside the law, separating by agreement rather than by decree. Most often, disgruntled parties simply deserted their mates. What defined a failed marriage depended, of course, on the expectations a man and woman carried into it. The evidence we have suggests that, for most colonists, marriage continued to be seen as an economic arrangement, a union to which men and women brought their gender-defined skills and work roles as well as their financial resources. A marriage was generally deemed successful if the partners lived up to their differing marital obligations. To be a good husband, a man was expected to provide for his wife according to his means, show her respect in public, acknowledge her and her children as his legitimate family, and cohabit with her. A good wife was expected to obey her husband's orders, manage her household efficiently and frugally, and perform her domestic and sexual duties.

There were, however, some signs that for certain eighteenth-century colonists the definition of a good marriage was changing. The new set of expectations did not appear to be centered on romantic love, however, but on companionship. Eliza Lucas Pinckney, for example, chose to marry a man who was first and foremost a friend and an intellectual companion. Over the years, her letters suggest that this companionship remained crucial to her satisfaction in marriage. The valorizing of companionship did not replace but was added to the older understanding of marriage as an economic institution, for it did not break down the gendered divisions of labor or alter the obligations and duties of wife and husband. Nor did it require the family hierarchy to be altered. Indeed, a commitment to a companionate marriage did not disturb the patriarchal privileges of the head of the household, for he continued to control the family's resources, determine where it resided, retain legal custody of the children, and enjoy the family's only legitimate voice in the political and legal spheres. A wife continued to address her husband with the respectful "my dear Mr. ———," while her husband responded using her Christian name. Finally, this tendency toward a companionate marriage did not carry an endorsement of strong emotions or spontaneous affection between wife and husband.

Companionate marriage did not become the norm in the decades that remained to America as a colonial society, probably not even among the genteel classes, where it was most likely to emerge. It remained an ill-defined ideal, its contradiction not yet resolved. What is likely, however, is that its meaning was perceived differently by husbands and wives, and its power to alter the traditional privileges and disadvantages allotted to men and women in marriage was probably contested.

No matter how a woman fared in "the important crisis upon which our fate depends," once married, she would soon embark on another critical phase of her life: motherhood. Some soon-to-be wives were already well on their way to motherhood. Prenuptial pregnancy seems to have risen steadily throughout the entire colonial period: before 1680, only 3.3 percent of all brides had children within six months of their wedding; by 1761, the number was moving toward its 1800 peak of 16.7 percent. In part, this number reflects the fact that many colonists considered sexual intercourse legitimate as soon as a couple had published their banns, or intention to be married; in part, the statistic itself cannot distinguish between a child conceived before marriage and one born prematurely after marriage. Nor can the historian discover how many women miscarried children conceived before marriage vows were exchanged. What is known for certain, however, is that most white women could expect to be pregnant twelve months after taking their vows.

Women looked forward to the delivery of this first child, and every child for that matter, with dread, fearing "that evel hour" when their baby's life and their own seemed to hang in the balance. Husbands waited anxiously outside the birthroom, where the midwife and female friends and relatives assisted their wife, aware that the events inside could lead to mourning rather than celebration. Although most women survived delivery, these fears were not irrational. Almost everyone in eighteenth-century colonial society knew of a mother who had died in childbirth.

Safe deliveries did not always guarantee a mother's health, for a host of postpartum problems were possible. And breast feeding, practiced for generations by ordinary colonial mothers and increasingly popular among the elite by mid-century, could cause additional physical problems as well. Women spoke frankly of the pain in their breasts, and concerned husbands recorded: "My wife distress'd with her Nipples." Nursing mothers watched anxiously for signs of inflammation that could turn into abscesses. Mothers sometimes relied on practices that provided temporary relief. Through "courtesy wet nursing," nursing female friends could take over the infant's feeding for a day or two if the mother was sick, in pain, or if she had to go out of town on a short trip. Not every woman, however, was willing to endure the soreness, the possibility of infection, or the restriction on her movements until weaning. In cities like Boston, wet nurses did a thriving business.

Pregnancies and infant care were not confined to an intense, limited period in a married woman's life. In fact, eighteenth-century women, like their seventeenth-century predecessors, spent most of their adult years in some phase of the birth cycle—nursing, weaning, infant care, and child-rearing. Mothers arrived at their daughter's childbed with infants of their own in their arms, and the children of a young matron played with those of her widowed mother at many a family reunion. The extent to which infant care was a constant part of daily life can be understood, for example, through the life of Massachusetts matron Hannah Parkman. Parkman provided "courtesy nursing" for her own son's daughter when her daughter-in-law fell ill.

Once again, social class played a role in determining a woman's experience of childbirth and infant care. Wealthy and even comfortably situated mothers could "lie in," or recuperate, for a month after giving birth, since servants could be called on to keep the household running. Most farm women and urban poor got up soon after their babies were born. More important, wealth allowed a woman to devote more focused and individualized attention to each child as it grew up. The hours Eliza Lucas Pinckney spent educating and inculcating her sons with what she deemed proper values and virtues were made possible by the servants, hired hands, or slaves working in her household.

The domestic servants who were the silent partners of Eliza Pinckney's gentility far outnumbered their mistresses. But women could be found as bound labor or as wage earners in other arenas as well. By the eighteenth century, the majority of these women were free rather than indentured servants, for bound white labor was declining in most colonies. In the South, for example, the number of female indentured servants had fallen steadily since 1700. In part, the problem was their availability, for as opportunities for work increased in England, migration to the American colonies diminished. Beginning in 1718, an average of only two women a year made the journey from London to the Chesapeake as bound labor, and the number did not increase until the end of the colonial period. The ratio of white servants to plantations shrank as well. In the 1690s, one in five plantation households included a white female servant, but by the middle of the eighteenth century, only one in twenty Chesapeake farms boasted such a servant. Most of these were drawn from England's convict population. As slave labor grew more common, fieldwork became an unusual task for these servants, and they were assigned instead to assist the planter's wife with domestic production. Female indentured servants had always been a small percentage of the bound laboring force in Northern cities. In Philadelphia, for instance, most indentured servants were men in the building trades. When, in the 1740s, a rise in demand for white household servants occurred, it was the result of the Quaker-dominated city's growing uneasiness with slaveholding.

It was free but poor women, therefore, who were regularly employed by their more prosperous urban or rural neighbors as domestic servants. For some of the Northern urban servants, this type of domestic employment was a transitional phase, coming in the years before marriage. For others, however, it was the mainstay of their existence, standing between them and the horrors of almshouses. In cities such as Boston, where the number of widows grew larger after each of the English imperial wars, reaching over 1,200 by 1742, the fear of abject poverty drove women not only to bind out their children to other families but also to place their daughters in domestic service. Poor women with young children at home earned what they could in these cities by providing specialized services such as wetnursing, midwifery, sewing, and millinery work to wealthier women.

In the South, a white woman might be employed as a housekeeper on a large plantation, although such positions were rare. A rural Pennsylvania woman in need of work had more opportunities, since prosperous farmers of the area hired the wives and daughters of cottagers or non-landowning men to work in local mills, in harvesting, and as temporary domestic help. When these farmers' wives acted as entrepreneurs, producing linen or dairy products for the market, they often relied on the labor of poorer, local women. The Pennsylvania farmers William Smedley and Benjamin Hawley provide glimpses of these employment patterns. Their records include payments to women for agricultural work such as reaping, sowing, pulling flax, and gathering apples, as well as domestic activities like spinning, sewing, baking, laundering, and nursing family members.

Working women could not expect to be paid well, nor could they expect wages on a par with men. In New England, the disparities were ensured by local authorities, who set the ceilings on wages for both sexes. As late as 1777, the maximum weekly wage for a New England domestic servant was the same as the maximum daily rate for male farm laborers in the summer. Female tailors could expect only 37 percent of what a male tailor earned. In the New England countryside, women's agricultural wages were desperately low between 1715 and the 1750s. Women farm laborers in Pennsylvania fared even worse. The influx of immigrants into the middle colonies at mid-century both drove down the wages for everyone and increased the available male labor

pool. Thus, Chester County, Pennsylvania, women found themselves shifted into domestic tasks such as spinning for less than
fivepence a day.

Not all women who needed to earn a living found their employment in the homes or fields of their neighbors. Some ran small
businesses of their own—dry goods or liquor shops, greengrocer-
ies, taverns, inns, or millinary establishments. Some turned to
prostitution. Others ran schools, while still others provided medical care not connected to childbirth, such as bone setting, a practice known as "doctoring." Many of these women were members
of households headed by a man of modest or dependent means,
but others came from the growing ranks of widows, unmarried
women, abandoned, deserted, or runaway wives that filled the
eighteenth-century cities and were present in the small towns,
rural counties, and parishes of every colony.

A great chasm separated an Eliza Lucas Pinckney, who lived off
the profits made on slave labor, indigo, and rice from a Rachel
Seal, who earned three shillings for making caps and hoods and
"bleeding" farmer Hawley's daughter. Yet both a plantation mistress and a woman servant were likely to be dependent on a male
for their economic status. What was true in the seventeenth century remained largely true in the colonial world of the eighteenth:
women enjoyed little unconditional control over the wealth of
their society. Daughters did receive dowries, wives support, and
widows a share of the realty and personalty in their husband's
estate. Yet the wealth that came to women was rarely theirs permanently or absolutely. A bride relinquished her dowry to her
groom, a wife turned over her earnings to her husband, and a
widow could enjoy the use of her husband's real property but
could not divert it from his heirs. Only three colonies—Pennsylvania, Maryland, and South Carolina—created the equity court
system needed to ensure that a woman could retain a separate
estate in marriage. Elsewhere, the ideal of marital unity—with its

assumption of identical interests expressed in male prerogative—
ensured white women's lifelong dependence.

Re-creating women's relationship to property and wealth is
more difficult than it may first appear. Although the fiction of
"marital unity" influenced most colonial jurists and lawmakers,
the laws drawn up by each colony were not the same. Historians
trace this lack of uniformity to a number of factors. First, colonies
settled in the early seventeenth century were guided by English
laws that had changed by the time Pennsylvania or Georgia was
established. Second, colonies often ignored changes in English law
regarding inheritance. Instead, colonial lawmakers and jurists insisted on preserving or even strengthening practices that England
had decided to abandon. Third, some colonies simply ignored
English law or custom because it did not mesh with local religious
values, with demographic circumstances, or with emerging economic patterns. For legal scholars, many of the variations that
resulted, especially between regions, make sense. But the motives
for other, equally significant legal differences are, frankly, difficult
to discern, especially when we cannot look to regional differences
or religious ones for possible motives.

The almost bewildering lack of uniformity in colonial inheritance laws is not the only roadblock to our reconstruction of the
relationship of women and property. The difference between formal legal rights and actual daily practice is equally important.
Many women did not know of the existence of advantageous
laws, and many more did not have the resources to use them.
Only the wealthiest South Carolinians or New Yorkers, for instance, created the separate estates that equity courts made possible. And, if we understand the role that property and inheritance
laws played in shaping women's lives, we cannot be certain to
understand women's attitudes toward them. An eighteenth-
century widow did not view the dispensation of her husband's
estate simply from a self-interested perspective but from her van-
tage point as mother and perhaps grandmother of her competitors
for that wealth.

For most white women, there were two critical moments of contact with inheritance law and practice: dowry and dower. Both dowry, a daughter's marriage gift, and dower, a widow's share of the marital estate, were part of the inevitable competition among family members for the resources they collectively had created. Male heads of household had to weigh the advantages of preserving the integrity of the estate against the rightful claims to it from widow and children. This dilemma was reflected in the intestacy laws developed by each colony. In New York, Maryland, Virginia, and South Carolina, primogeniture ensured that the bulk of the estate passed to the oldest son, once the widow's share had been resolved. But most colonies rejected primogeniture, substituting instead a double share of the father's real property for the oldest son. Of course, by writing a will, men in every colony could attempt their own solution to the conflict between preserving the estate intact and distributing it among their heirs. Whether a man had made a will or, like the majority of colonial fathers, died intestate, the smaller his estate, the more difficult it was to determine its ownership.

How did daughters fare when men sat down to address this problem? Most fathers with any means made dowry provisions for their daughters that were transferred before the parent's death. Thus a daughter's share of the family resources might not appear in her father's will. But whether she received her share on the occasion of her wedding, or at her father's death, alloting a daughter's inheritance was always problematic. If a daughter took land into her marriage, it generally passed into the control of her husband. As long as she remained childless, she had absolute rights to her own property and it did not become part of her husband's estate. But with the first child, her father's gift became her husband's asset; as a "tenant by curtesy"—the legal recognition that he was the guardian of their children—he acquired control over the property's use and determined who would inherit it. A bride's personalty became the property of her groom even more quickly. Faced with the possibility that "marital unity" would not be blissful, or that a husband might not always be guided by protective impulses toward his wife's welfare, wealthy fathers sometimes devised means to restrict ownership of the property they gave to their daughters. For example, a Maryland planter might not grant his daughter land in fee simple—that is, as an outright, unrestricted transfer of property—but gave it only as a life estate, naming *her* children as its ultimate owners. This ensured that a less than perfect husband could not sell the land, even if he did have the right to manage it.

Although a Chesapeake planter might view land as a risky gift to his daughters, some, especially from the wealthier classes, chose to take that risk. Between the 1730s and the 1780s, for example, more than one-fifth of all daughters of landowners in Charles County, Maryland, received use or ownership of land. In early eighteenth-century Baltimore County, two-thirds of the planters with 400 acres or more gave land to their daughters. And in Virginia, one-fifth of the testators between 1735 and 1775 provided their daughters with real property. Often, the intention was to provide security for an unmarried daughter, even if it worked to a son's disadvantage. By giving an unmarried daughter the use of property as long as she was single, a father delayed its transfer to the actual heir—her brother.

Most planter fathers shied away from transferring as much real property to daughters as they gave to sons. Instead, they provided daughters with one of the most valuable personal assets they had: slaves. Daughters of wealthy planters received more slaves than did sons in Maryland, in South Carolina, and perhaps in the other Southern colonies as well. And they received more female slaves than male. In Charles County, for example, 60 percent of the female slaves provided to children went to daughters, while 60 percent of all male slaves went to sons. The assumption was that female slaves would produce additional assets—children. To protect these gifts from abuse by irresponsible sons-in-law, fathers carefully worded the terms of their bequest: slaves went to daughters "in full and perfect property" for her use and for the use of the heirs of her body—and for "no other person."

Propertied fathers in other regions, where slaves were not as numerous and a less critical resource, had less flexibility in resolving the problems of providing for all children and protecting what they provided to their daughters. In the Northern colonies, fathers did what they could to ensure that their own death did not set in motion the dissolution of the family. Sons may have been considered the rightful heirs to property, but they were often required by their father's will to care for their mothers and their unmarried sisters until another man took up the burden of their dependency.

A daughter who remained forever single or childless might realize a measure of economic independence and autonomy from her inheritance. But most women expected to marry and to bear children. They had the satisfaction of knowing that their fathers wanted to provide for them, even if it meant the dilution of the value of the estate. But they surely understood that their parent's intention was not the same for them as for their brothers. When a colonial father wrote his will, he did not envision a permanently independent or entrepreneurial daughter; he saw instead a child who needed, and deserved, protection.

A wife was expected to relinquish all management and control over her dowry. A widow, however, could expect to take out of a marriage some portion of the wealth she had contributed to it. Eighteenth-century colonists, like seventeenth-century society, continued to protect a woman's dower rights. Dower acknowledged her economic contribution to the marriage—not simply the property she had brought into it as a bride, but also her industry and energy during her years as wife and mother. English common law established that the widow of an intestate man was entitled to the use of one-third of all land owned over the course of the marriage and, until English law changed, absolute rights to one-third of his personalty. If there were no children, the widow received half his personal estate. In either case, a widow was entitled to reclaim her own "paraphernalia."

All colonies acknowledged, and protected, dower, although they did not always calculate dower in the same fashion. The differences could be significant. For example, most colonies, when calculating a widow's dower share, included all the property a husband had owned over the lifetime of the marriage. Pennsylvania and Connecticut did not. A widow in these colonies could expect her "thirds" only in the property he held at his death. There was no agreement among the colonies on what property fell into which category. Here, too, the consequences could be serious. In Eliza Lucas Pinckney's South Carolina, and in Maryland as well, slaves were defined as personalty. Widows in these colonies thus enjoyed absolute ownership of the African-American men and women they received. This meant that Eliza Pinckney was able to will her slaves to her children or grandchildren—or to any heir she might choose, simply because her husband's home had been in Carolina. Friends in Virginia were not as lucky. There, slaves were realty and thus a widow held them only during her lifetime. Nor did the colonies always protect a woman's property rights in the same ways. Many colonies carved out the dower share before any other claims could be made on a man's estate. But neither Pennsylvania nor Connecticut was willing to exempt dower from the claims of creditors. Indeed, in Pennsylvania, a man's creditors had to be satisfied first, leaving the widow any assets that remained. Connecticut was less severe; it made creditors wait until a widow's death before collecting their due. Yet neither Pennsylvania's Quakerist tendencies toward gender equality nor Connecticut's legacy of radical Protestantism prevented these two colonies from sacrificing a widow's rights to commercial considerations.

If a man left a will that denied a widow her "thirds," most colonies allowed her to reject the legacy and sue for her rightful share. But the decision to renounce a legacy did not imply an ungenerous or an unjust husband. For the wife of a debt-ridden farmer, merchant, or planter, dower might simply be the wiser choice, since most colonies refused to protect a testator's legacy from creditors. Lawmakers may have assumed that a widow did not know the extent of her husband's debts or assets, for they gave her from six months to a year to make the decision to renounce or accept a legacy. This grace period allowed her time to discover the extent of her husband's debts. Some colonies also willingly granted extensions to newly widowed women. Such consideration was made up of equal parts kindness and practicality, for a widow deprived of her "thirds" was one more woman the community would have to support.

Dower was thus a public as well as a private concern. And most colonies took steps to protect it, even before a husband's death. Recognizing that the most significant portion of a woman's dower came from her husband's real property, the Southern colonies in particular did not allow a husband to sell any of his realty without the knowledge—and consent—of his wife. The procedures established tell us much about gender assumptions in eighteenth-century colonial America. They were based on the assumption that obedience to a husband's will was so ingrained, so pervasive, and so central to a married woman's identity that the mere presence of a husband would prevent her from expressing her true opinion or desires. Colonial courts demanded, therefore, that the wife be examined in private regarding any possible land sale.

Were the colonial courts' assumptions of women's timidity or subservience valid? We cannot say. It is difficult to picture Eliza Lucas Pinckney, who laid claim to her father's oak plantation as a teenager, meekly acceding to her husband's sale of properties. But all women were not so bold or confident. We do know that many men took their wife's compliance for granted, ignoring the private examination procedure altogether and disposing of land without her prior knowledge—and sometimes without informing her at all. We also know that few wives demanded that such sales be declared invalid. Their motives, unrecorded, remain unclear. Perhaps they were loath to publicly reprimand their spouse. Perhaps they felt it was important, or admirable, to put their faith in their husband's judgment—at any cost. Or perhaps they gave greater priority to the future prosperity of their children than to their own. To such women, profitable land sales might seem an end that justified the means.

Allowing a husband free rein to build his fortune through land investments and sales may have been one of the few positive gestures a mother could make to influence her children's future. Women owned a negligible share of the wealth in colonial society and so had little to pass on to the next generation. Like her children, a woman was a dependent, and her dependence put her in direct competition with her sons and daughters for family resources. A widowed mother—left a share of the family home, the family's land and slaves, or the profits from a family farm until her death or remarriage—was an obstacle, though perhaps a loved or honored one, to a son and his full inheritance. Wives knew this. And although they may have had limited knowledge of their husband's assets or debts, they also knew that any inheritance strategy developed by a responsible man had to balance obligations to her with obligations to his children. That some men found such choices difficult can be seen in the will left in 1757 by Virginia farmer Samuel Cobb. A man of modest means, Cobb gave his wife, Edith, all his land, not for use but in fee simple, and he gave her most of his personal property as well. He explained his decision to give Edith "extensive Power," writing: "She has been my Wife near Forty Years during which Time hath always been Kind, loving and obedient to me without affection. My children are hers I commit them to her care." Cobb understood well the choice he had made between his children and his widow. "As my circumstances are now I could not provide for both," he wrote bluntly, "and I do think it my Duty to provide for a Wife now in Decline of life who so well Deserved it from me."

Not every man of the time would make the same choice Samuel Cobb did. Over the course of the eighteenth century, colonists employed a variety of inheritance strategies. Poorer men tended to leave more to their widows. Men with small children, especially in newly settled regions, tended to do the same. Like their seventeenth-century predecessors, they relied on their widow to act as the caretaker of their estate, preserving it for their heirs. Men with adult children, on the other hand, often favored these children over their widows in their wills. In Bucks County, Pennsylvania, some men abandoned the practice of leaving the farm to their widow, giving her instead a portion of the family home and some share of the yearly farm profits. This allowed a husband to provide adequately for his wife, and a father to give his children what immediate economic assistance he could. In other areas, men took more drastic steps. In Baltimore County, Maryland, 15 percent of the men who left wills in the first quarter of the century left their widow nothing at all, dividing their estate among their sons and daughters.

Strategies were not simply a matter of what a widow or a child received but of when a son or a daughter gained control of their inheritance. Fathers could—and did—speed up the process by placing restrictions on their widow's legacy. Where once a widow's use of land extended over her lifetime, for instance, her husband now might stipulate that it cease if she remarried. For these husbands, a desire to provide more speedily for sons and daughters combined with a desire to keep their inheritance out of the hands of another man.

Wealthy men felt the strain less acutely than their poorer neighbors, of course, for they were able to provide adequately for both widow and children. Their widows did not have to sacrifice material comfort, but they may have lost economic authority. Among the elite of Baltimore County, for example, wills revealed a tendency away from the appointment of widows as sole executors of the estate. Instead, these planters assigned their grown sons the task of managing the estate, either jointly with the widow or in her place. Did this signal a lack of confidence in a wife or a gesture of concern? In a world that assumed women's dependency to be fitting, a husband's motive may have reflected not contempt but kindness. The same consideration, blended with practical considerations, may have led wealthy planters in Virginia's Piedmont counties to appoint business acquaintances or friends to manage their estate. Thus, in 1765, James Hill named fellow planter Edmund Booker of Amelia County, Virginia, as executor of his children's legacy, a vast estate of tracts of land spread over two counties. Few of his neighbors would have argued that Hill's widow was the more qualified person for the task. The simple fact that women, as mothers, were more homebound than men may have made a son, nephew, or brother seem a better executor than a wife. For reasons such as these, control of a large estate, and the fees earned by the executor, might pass from mother to child or to neighbor.

Still a considerable number of husbands, whether wealthy men or men of modest means, continued to place their family's fortune and future in the hands of their widow. The presence of adult sons, the density of kinship networks, the size and complexity of the estate were all factors that might suggest different reasons for a will maker to entrust his wife with the family fortune. Whether widows protested a loss of authority as executor, sued to gain their rightful dower share, or accepted their husband's choice of strategy also depended on factors such as their children's age, the wealth involved, and their own sense of what was just or appropriate. Scholars have found no clear pattern: in one Southern county only 20 percent of women with children demanded dower rather than the family legacy. But in other Southern counties a third to over half the widows who received less than their "thirds" fought back, demanding their due. Some wanted dower even when the legacy was greater, to compensate for restrictions in their husbands' wills relating to remarriage.

Colonial laws affecting women and property conformed to a gender ideology that assumed women's continual economic dependence upon male family members, by birth or marriage, and even after their protector's death. To a surprising degree, women's economic "rights" were a function of the cynicism lawmakers brought to bear on the notion of perfect marital unity and a husband's responsible paternalism. The legal culture of Eliza Lucas Pinckney's South Carolina, for instance, never took for granted that men would treat their wives—or their wives' property—with honor or respect. They did not believe in the efficacy of religious scruples or the internalization of gender responsibilities to prevent abuses. Instead, they acknowledged the darker possibilities. To sustain the gender structure they endorsed, lawmakers had to anticipate its worst abuses and devise corrective measures. If women had to be protected from men, society's interests had to be protected from them as well. South Carolina lawmakers and courts enforced a wide range of legal remedies: equity courts that allowed a married woman a separate estate, strict enforcement of private examinations, *feme sole* trader laws that permitted any woman to engage in self-support, and private separation agreements for couples whose marriages were no longer viable. Thus, a colony steeped in paternalism, both toward women and toward an enslaved work force, was willing to secure by law what could not be assured by individual males.

Eliza Lucas Pinckney never experienced the disappointment of failed paternalism. Both her father and her husband were mentors, advisors, and men whose affection for her remained constant. Perhaps, however, South Carolina's willingness to allow women to provide for themselves when necessary offered a positive setting for Pinckney's entrepreneurial independence. Certainly her wealth gave her access to formal education and sophisticated ideas, and the leisure to master them, which few ordinary colonial women enjoyed. But it was her social class's adoption of genteel values and mores that gave her the social and psychological vocabulary to understand her own actions and desires and convey them to others. Pinckney considered herself rational, capable of performing the complex tasks of plantation mistress and nurturing parent, and able to bring order to her life through self-discipline and self-examination. She was confident that she could control her domain and those within it, and she was successful often enough to confirm this confidence. This was not the steadfast faith in God's plan that sustained Hannah Duston; it was not the resourceful endurance of the African immigrant Mary. This was the individualist trademark of eighteenth-century gentility. In Eliza Lucas Pinckney's generation, social class shattered the unity of gender in colonial American society.

7

"BEAT OF DRUM AND RINGING OF BELL": WOMEN IN THE AMERICAN REVOLUTION

I N 1750 A PENNSYLVANIA WOMAN in her early thirties sat for her portrait. The portrait survived two transatlantic journeys and a revolution; its subject did not. If you look at the painting, however, it is hard to believe that this imperious, confident woman then known as Grace Growden was less resilient than the canvas that has preserved her image for us. The image is striking: Grace stares boldly and directly at the viewer, her head lifted high, her posture formal but relaxed, her body clearly accustomed to the weight of brocade and velvet. Her right arm crosses the front of her body, the hand resting comfortably on her lap, while her left hand is poised, shoulder high, as if caught in the familiar act of lifting a teacup to her lips. She offers a mild, polite smile, more in acknowledgment than welcome. Grace Growden's forehead is high and broad, her brows arched, her nose aquiline, her eyes sharply focused. She shows the world intelligence in lieu of beauty. The woman in this portrait knows her place in society—and expects it to be acknowledged by others.

For most of her life, others did acknowledge the social superiority of Grace Growden Galloway. It was a position based first on her father's great wealth and public service and later on her wealthy husband's reputation as a lawyer and political figure. In the decade of relative political calm before the Stamp Act crisis, she reigned as one of the preeminent social figures of the mainland colonies' major city. Such preeminence did not, of course, ensure or require personal happiness. Indeed, what we know of Grace Growden's life suggests a lonely childhood and a difficult marriage, a life dominated by powerful and egotistical men. By most accounts, her father was an overbearing man and her husband, Joseph Galloway, brilliant but unstable, temperamental, argumentative, haughty, and disturbingly suspicious of others.

It was not Joseph's possible lack of affection for his wife but his politics that finally disrupted Grace's life. Throughout his career in Pennsylvania politics, Joseph Galloway viewed the British government as an ally not an enemy. Despite the shifts in Crown policy toward the colonies in the 1760s and 1770s, he never altered his opinion. On the eve of the Revolution, he argued for compromise and patience and, in the last resort, for capitulation to British wishes.

Joseph Galloway's loyalism earned him the condemnation of his colony. His service for the British army that occupied Philadelphia in 1776 ensured him his community's enmity. Fearing for his life, Galloway fled to the safety of British-occupied New York, taking with him his daughter and only child, Elizabeth.

And Grace? Grace Growden Galloway remained behind, never to see her husband or her daughter again. Why? It was certainly not a commitment to the Revolutionary movement that held her in Philadelphia. No less than Joseph Galloway, she abhorred a revolutionary cause that endangered the two things she held dear: her family and her social position. As the wife of a now notorious traitor, she could no longer claim her place in the first tier of society. And as the wife of an officially attainted property holder, she was in danger of losing the wealth on which that place had once depended. Historians usually have assumed that Joseph, like other men of property, instructed his wife to stay behind—hoping her presence might help preserve his property from confiscation. This was a tactic of many noted, or notorious, Loyalists.

But Grace's diary suggests otherwise. It suggests a desire to pre-serve what she considered to be *her* wealth, the Growden prop-erties, which she would pass on to her daughter as a mother's material and social legacy.

Grace Galloway sought to separate her fate from her hus-band's, to demand that the punishment meted out to him for his political actions fall on him alone. With the aid of lawyers, influ-ential friends, and her own rectitude, she intended to see that the confiscating hand of revolution did not reach her daughter's leg-acy. And in the early months of her battle with authorities, she was confident that the names Growden and Galloway were shields strong enough to protect her in the face of a temporary political crisis.

They were not. Joseph Galloway's very political prominence, once a source of satisfaction, proved an insurmountable disadvan-tage. Pennsylvania rebels could not allow the wife of an officially declared traitor to win her quiet battle. Soon after Joseph de-parted, the Pennsylvania government moved to confiscate the ex-tensive holdings of the Growden–Galloway union. Estates outside Philadelphia were seized; even the city mansion in which Grace Galloway resided was threatened with confiscation. Galloway's di-ary records her vigorous, stubborn resistance, in the courts and in the very parlors of her home. In the end, she was escorted politely but firmly out the door of her Philadelphia mansion. She had little money and few possessions with her. Her dependence on the goodwill and charity of others had begun.

During the next two years, the meanness of her circumstances filled her every thought. She meticulously recorded, and stub-bornly defied, the humiliations of rented rooms and the real and imagined snubs of former friends, social equals, and eventually even her social inferiors. She watched as rebel upstarts rode by in her own confiscated carriage; she endured chilly receptions in the parlors of the elite Revolutionary families and, later, their failure to invite her at all; and she argued with lawyers and negotiated for debts from former tenants. Although she lamented to her diary that her weakness of character, her timidity and confusion, her lack of diplomacy in dealing with authorities ensured her defeat, this was far from true. It was her stubborn and intelligent resistance that prolonged these battles with the rebel government and made their simple assertion of political power so complex. There were signs that she understood this as well. For, woven into the diary, scattered among the expressions of anger, loneliness, and anxiety, were expressions of delight in a newfound independence, in a discovered capacity for autonomy.

Grace Galloway's spirit remained unbroken until she discovered that the deeds to her father's property carried only her husband's name. Marriage had made her legally invisible, just as politics had erased her social position. The woman we see in the last months of the diary bears little relationship to the woman of the 1750 portrait. She is cynical, suspicious, angry—and defeated. When she died in 1781, the war that had turned her world upside down was itself coming to an end.

Grace Galloway's experiences during the American Revolution may seem at first too extreme to be typical. Yet many colonial women would have felt a kinship with her. Like Galloway, they found that the Revolution and a protracted home-front war swept aside their ordinary life and settled expectations. Even those who did not enjoy the benefits of Galloway's social position might empathize with her intense anxiety over changes in a social order that had shaped her identity. Like Galloway, many would find themselves exercising their own judgments for the first time on legal, economic, and political matters, and testing their resources in the midst of crises, as their property was confiscated and their crops, livestock, and homes commandeered or destroyed. Some shared Grace Galloway's pleasure in this new independence and sense of competence even when their efforts ended in tragedy or personal defeat.

The impact of the Revolution on women's lives was, of course, as various as the circumstances of those lives. Social class, region, race, age, and even religion influenced what crises a woman faced and the resources she might have to resolve them. For a small number, the Revolution provided opportunities that peacetime did not, opportunities that ranged from participation in meaningful activities to the promise of freedom from slavery. Yet for most women, the war was a conflict that taxed their resiliency and endangered their husbands and their family. If few of the accounts that come down to us are as bitter and despairing as Grace Galloway's, they bear, nevertheless, the familiar grim tone of war and destruction. If we see a romance in the bravery of "Molly Pitcher" or the women who served as spies for General Washington, their actual recollections speak of a dead husband lying at their feet or of a captured friend's death on a British prison ship. Only later could these women—and their historians—try to assess what positive impact the war and independence may have had on them and on their daughters as well.

In one sense, the Revolution was a victory for women. Like many upheavals, natural or social, the Revolution generated a treasure trove of sources that have allowed historians to reconstruct women's experiences. True, eighteenth-century genteel women were likely, even under stable circumstances, to leave behind the diaries and letters that earlier generations of women could not. And it is also true that African-American and Indian women have left us less than the European women of the society. Yet as a society in crisis, Revolutionary America produced a vast and rich record, from newspaper accounts of women's prewar protests against British policy, to widow's petitions to the U.S. Congress regarding veteran's benefits, to claims filed by loyalist women for pensions from the British government, to books, speeches, sermons, and public debates over women's role in the Revolution and in the new republic. From the myriad of official and personal documents, individual lives can be captured in fine detail and women's collective experiences can be reconstructed. The narrative of white and black women's activities during the Revolutionary decades, for example, has been especially well told. Thus the texture of this chapter will appear richer than those that preceded it.

Although historians often write of the "coming of the American Revolution," no woman or man would have imagined such an event a dozen years before. Indeed, in 1763 colonists everywhere joined together to celebrate the English victory over the French in the great struggle for empire the Americans called the French and Indian War. The outpouring of patriotism—the parades, the bonfires, the toasts to the King, his country, and to the architect of English victory, William Pitt—may have been excessive but it was not unreasonable. The defeat of the French and the capture of Canada meant that for the first time in colonial memory warfare might cease to be a regular feature of the colonists' experience. New Englanders, in particular, rejoiced; generations of them had suffered the loss of sons and fathers and husbands in the hundred years of imperial struggle that preceded this victory. Few Massachusetts or Connecticut families had escaped burying a casualty of these wars, and if the devastation had been less extreme in Pennsylvania or South Carolina, here, too, lives had been lost and property destroyed in battle with European enemies and their Indian allies. Now, in the wake of England's crushing defeat of the French both in America and abroad, safety seemed assured.

Colonists in New England attributed Britain's victory to the hand of Providence, while in other regions people spoke of the bravery of their soldiers, the genius of William Pitt, and the military daring of General Wolfe. But everywhere colonists were in agreement that the obvious superiority of the British system of government and of its citizens was the deciding factor in the defeat of the enemy. Orators extolled the British constitution, with its system of balanced government and its delineation and protection of the "rights of Englishmen." That this civic satisfaction so quickly turned to protest must have seemed remarkable even to the protesters themselves.

American protest arose in response to Britain's postwar changes in colonial policy. In the wake of the war, the British government found itself burdened by staggering debts and the need to maintain an expensive military and naval presence. Efforts to raise funds, tighten control on colonial trade and production, and devise a workable governance for the new holdings in French Canada and the Ohio Valley brought colonial interests and imperial interests into immediate conflict. Over the 1760s and early 1770s, trade regulating measures such as the Sugar Act, revenue-raising efforts like the Stamp Act and the Townshend Acts, and provisions for the military including Quartering Acts in many colonies all eroded the colonists' confidence that their interests were synonymous with the interests of the mother country. A decade of escalating political protest and the failure of compromise eventually led to the independence movement and to a revolutionary war. Women played their role in every phase of this protest and the struggle for—or against—American independence.

Where and how women participated in these political struggles was determined by custom, coincidence, and necessity. In the decade before Lexington and Concord, the struggle between Crown and colonists was waged on four clearly defined battlefields. The first of these was the colonial governments themselves, through tests of will and skill between royal governors and the local interests of the assembly. Women were entirely absent from this arena, excluded as a sex by both law and custom. In the second arena—propaganda and the politicization of the citizens on the issues of British policy—women played a limited role. Writing for the public in newspapers or broadsides was a traditionally male activity, and women made few direct contributions to political strategy or discussions of tactics. Wives may have been present when political leaders gathered to draft their responses to new British legislation, but that presence was coincidental rather than intentional.

As with every social pattern, an exception can be found. Mercy Otis Warren was among the most famous and effective propagandists of the prewar period. She was also an active participant in the strategy sessions led by the cousins, John and Samuel, whom Loyalist governor Thomas Hutchinson disdainfully referred to as "that brace of Adamses." Warren had access to the inner circles of Massachusetts radical politics as the favored daughter and beloved sister of the James Otises, whose reputation as "trouble-makers" was transatlantic. Many a New England Loyalist's diary or postwar memoirs held these two gentlemen entirely responsible for the Revolution. Mercy Otis's access to radical circles was solidified when she married James Warren, for the leaders of Massachusetts's opposition forces met in Warren's home. Yet if gender determined her proximity to the sources of power, talent and intelligence determined her participation in their activities. Because she had a genius for satire, a flair for drama, and a willingness to use both, she became the opposition's most effective shaper of popular opinion save perhaps for Samuel Adams. Her plays and poems filled Massachusetts newspapers in the 1770s, and were widely reprinted elsewhere. In satires such as *The Defeat* and *The Group*, she gave her colony's growing crisis its cast of characters. The ambitious supporter of the Crown Thomas Hutchinson became Rapatio, Bashaw of Servia; General Timothy Ruggles was hounded by the sobriquet "Brigadier Hate-All"; and Crown propagandist Jonathan Sewall felt himself eternally marked as Beau Trumps. The heroes of her own cause, colonial resistance, were ennobled as Brutus or Cassius, reinforcing the theme that the opposition was acting to preserve rather than harm the British constitutional tradition.

A white woman had to step far outside her customary roles to participate in the realm of propaganda and strategy. But she had only to step into her kitchen or parlor to be in the center of the third arena of protest: economic sanctions. As early as 1765, the colonists' policy of nonimportation and consumer boycott of British-made goods became the most effective means to combat the Crown's new trade policies. This strategy reflected an awareness that the role of the colonies in Britain's mercantile economy had shifted dramatically during the eighteenth century. Where once their value to England lay in the production of raw materials, by the 1760s the colonies had grown into an important market for British manufactured goods. Shipments of everything from cloth to tea, paint, and salt, as well as reshipments of European products from British ports, were central to the economic expansion and well-being of the mother country. A blow to this commercial link was a blow certain to be felt in the halls of Parliament. As household managers and as major consumers, white women's cooperation was vital to the success of any proposed boycott.

In 1765 New York and Boston merchants organized the first of the nonimportation movements to protest Britain's first direct tax on the colonists, the Stamp Act. The idea spread rapidly. Newspaper contributors called on colonists to give up all imported luxuries and finery and to embrace austerity until Parliament repealed this first direct tax on its colonies. When the Stamp Act was, indeed, repealed, colonists laid much of the credit for this change in policy to their boycott. Not surprisingly, they turned once again to nonimportation in the wake of the Townshend Acts and the much hated Tea Act. In both instances, boycott organizers made a conscious effort to elicit the cooperation of housewives and their daughters.

The importance of women's support for these boycotts was rarely underrated, although some leaders believed it would be difficult to arouse female patriotism or stir women to act. In 1769 Christopher Gadsden spoke frankly to his colleagues in the South Carolina assembly:

> I come now to the last, and what many say and think is the greatest difficulty of all we have to encounter, that is, to persuade our wives to give us their assistance, without which 'tis impossible to succeed . . . for 'tis well known, that none in the world are better oeconomists . . . than ours. Only let their husbands point out the necessity of such conduct; convince them, that it is the only thing that can save them and their children, from distress, slavery, and disgrace; their affections will soon be awakened, and cooperate with their reason.

Gadsden's argument both complimented and insulted the women who were the indirect audience of his oratory. His assumption that women were politically ignorant and naturally indifferent to public matters ran side by side with his praise for their "notable housewifery." Such a view was common, particularly among the genteel classes. It was widely believed that women's political choices were, and ought to be, controlled by male relatives. This "natural" subordination based on gender was reinforced by a social subordination based on the absence of property. As every English child knew, a propertyless person could take no part in making political decisions.

Yet Gadsden was wrong. Before he issued his appeal, women of his own elite social class had been mulling over the political events of the era in their diaries and letters for several years. Furthermore, free colonial women expressed a clear understanding that their economic decisions—what to buy, what to declare a necessity, what to eschew—had become political decisions. This political awareness was dynamic, growing stronger and more widespread over the decade between the Stamp Act and the Declaration of Independence.

Thus, women who boycotted tea and wore dresses of homespun rather than imported cloth publicly defined these choices as political ones. When a group of Newport, Rhode Island, women substituted an herbal drink for imported tea, they declared it a matter of honor. When "upwards of 300 mistresses of Families, in which number the Ladies of highest rank and influence" signed a petition to abstain from tea drinking, they stated their motivation clearly: "to save their abused Country from ruin and Slavery," from dangers brought on by Parliament's "unconstitutional" attacks. These petitioners also knew how to give their tactic greater legitimacy. In the petition they linked their action to the actions of "the very respectable body of Merchants and other inhabitants" of Boston. And in Philadelphia, when Hanna Griffitts set the politics of tea drinking to verse, she established a direct relationship between housewives and the oppression of the British government.

> For the sake of Freedom's name
> (Since British Wisdom scorns repealing)

Come, sacrifice to Patriot fame
And give up Tea, by way of healing
This done, within ourselves retreat.
The Industrious arts of life to follow
Let proud Nabobs storm and fret
They cannot force our lips to swallow.

Even a nine-year-old like Susan Boudinot of Pennsylvania was capable of relishing a well-executed political gesture. When offered a cup of tea at the home of New Jersey's Loyalist governor, William Franklin, Susan curtsied, raised the cup to her lips, and then tossed its contents out the startled Franklin's window.

Perhaps the most widely circulated declaration of political sentiments came from Edenton, North Carolina. Here, the newspaper carried a resolution drawn up by fifty-one local women to boycott English goods. The Edenton statement was based on a sense of civic duty and responsibility. "As we cannot be indifferent on any occasion that appears to affect the peace and happiness of our country, and as it has been thought necessary for the publick good to enter into several particular resolved," wrote the Edenton women, "it is a duty we owe not only to our near and dear relations and connections, but to ourselves who are essentially interested in their welfare, to do everything as far as lies in our power to testify to our since adherence to the same." The "Edenton Resolve" prompted a broad spectrum of male response, from enthusiastic acknowledgment to satiric attack. Patriot men could hardly denounce the commitment that their own orators had urged upon the "ladies." But their Loyalist tormentors knew exactly where to aim their blows, suggesting that the colonial protest had set a sexual revolution in motion, creating aggressive women and emasculated men. Patriot ministers might continue to call on women to use their power, "to strike the Stroke, and make the Hills and Plains of America clap their hands," but American men remained ambivalent about the consequences of this political awakening. Not every man would, as the Presbyterian preacher

William Tennett III promised activist women, "rise and call you blessed."

Women's response to male criticism and male approval, but especially to male "guidance," is instructive. When male writers to the newspapers suggested that patriotic women substitute rum for tea, women fired back that they did not welcome such advice. They would replace tea as they themselves saw fit, just as they would be their own judge of what to wear in place of British finery. And although the local committee men granted an ailing Salem woman an exemption, she steadfastly refused to drink tea. Nonconsumption was, she reminded them, a matter of personal principle. Historians can find similar evidence that by the 1770s women of all ages and regions had a well-developed sense of their own political agency. Even a thirteen-year-old could speak confidently in her diary of her independent political choices. "As I am (as we say) a daughter of liberty," she wrote in the early 1770s, "I chuse to war [wear] as much of our own manufactory as pocible."

The fourth arena for protest was the streets. For many centuries the crowd had been a recognized form of political expression for those without access to formal political power in English society. In England and the colonies, protests against rising food prices, onerous taxes, and infractions of popularly held moral standards were a tradition among the poor. Not surprisingly, opposition to British policy took to the streets as well. Sometimes these mass demonstrations were organized and led by elite politicians and businessmen who saw their value as propaganda and who recognized the need to mobilize broad popular support. But the sailors, dockworkers, and servants who participated in what critics called "riots" and supporters called "demonstrations" were just as often the agents of their own political acts.

Few of these crowds were exclusively male. If women did not take an active part in acts of destruction such as the raid on Thomas Hutchinson's Cambridge home, they did not shy away from acts of physical violence. Generally, crowd actions organized by elites conformed to genteel notions of respectability and discouraged female participation. But the more spontaneous the demonstration, the more likely the participation of women. Women joined in the tarring and feathering of local merchants who continued to import British goods, and sometimes organized their own intimidation efforts against perceived enemies of either sex. In 1775, when a Massachusetts woman expressed her politics indirectly by naming her newborn son in honor of the British commander Thomas Gage, a crowd of patriot women attacked her house, fully prepared to tar and feather both mother and child.

Even when they did not participate directly, evidence of women's solidarity with the demonstrators' cause was considered critical. Women were valued as spectators or witnesses, in part because workingmen often couched their protest against British policy in terms of its devastating impact on "widows" and "fatherless" children. But the women of their class did not need to be told where their interests lay. Many felt the impact of British policy directly, especially the wives and daughters of Boston and New York dockworkers, who suffered when moonlighting British soldiers took their men's jobs away. Thus, throughout the 1760s and early 1770s, working-class women attended ritual events such as commemorations of the Stamp Act repeal, the hanging of political enemies in effigy, and funeral marches for protesters killed by British soldiers. On the evening that British tea was dumped into the murky waters of Boston Harbor in 1774, the silent witnesses lining the wharfs and docks included several women and children.

Women who supported the American protest did not hold a monopoly, of course, on activism or on an emerging political consciousness. Political involvement was evident among the wives and daughters of Crown officials and supporters who were often the earliest victims, if not the intended targets, of their neighbors' protests. Indeed, attacks on their male relatives served to sharpen the political awareness of these women and to force them to follow political developments more closely than many of their neighbors. Terrifying experience was a strong impetus to political awareness for a woman like Anne Hulton, who watched her brother, Customs Commissioner Henry Hulton, flee a jeering Boston mob. By 1774, attacks on the homes of known Crown sympathizers had become common, and while the men fled to safety, their wives often found themselves facing an angry and sometimes drunken crowd.

Women shopkeepers or merchants who supported Crown policy were directly challenged to conform with the boycott regulations or suffer the consequences. Gender was no protection for Anne and Betsy Cumming when they were accused of breaking the nonimportation agreement in 1768. When members of the local boycott committee entered her shop, Betsy defended herself firmly and directly. "I told them we have never entered into eney agreement not to import for it was verry trifling our Business," she later explained to her aunt. She reprimanded the men for trying to "inger two industrious Girls who ware Striving in an honest way to Git their Bread."

And like Grace Galloway, many Loyalist women developed a sense of the price of political commitment before their Revolutionary neighbors were forced to do so. In October 1775, a Virginia woman was called before a local Committee of Safety to answer accusations that she was engaged in Loyalist activities. When she refused to cooperate with this extra-legal Revolutionary committee, they declared her "insolent, scandalous, and indecent," judged her "an enemy of her Country," and instructed her neighbors "to break off all kinds of intercourse and connection with her." Thus, even before independence was declared, social isolation for some had begun.

As the likelihood of war grew stronger, women's activism intensified. In New England, where fighting preceded a formal declaration of war, observers on both sides remarked on women's enthusiasm for the conflict. In early September 1774, local militias were mustered in response to a false report that Boston-based British troops planned to attack neighboring Cambridge. The women, recorded one eyewitness, "surpassed the Men for Eagerness & Spirit in the Defense of Liberty by Arms." He marveled that "at every house Women and Children [were] making Cartridges, running Bullets, making Wallets, baking Biscuit, crying and bemoaning & at the same time animating their Husbands & Sons to fight for their liberties, tho not knowing whether they should ever see them again." The observer's amazement is more surprising than the behavior of these Massachusetts women. For these women knew, as did most colonial women, that the approaching war would be a home-front war. Loyalist or patriot, Indian, African, or European, American women understood that such a war allowed no civilians. Even if a family was to attempt strict neutrality, the effects of war—scarcity, inflation, danger, and dislocation—would find them.

The women of Lexington and Concord were among the first to experience the terrible realities of war. "We were roused from the benign Slumbers of the season," wrote Hannah Winthrop to Mercy Warren on April 19, 1775, "by beat of drum and ringing of Bell, with the dire alarm that a thousand of the Troups of George the third were gone forth to murder the peaceful inhabitants of the surrounding villages . . . It seemed necessary to retire to some place of safety til the calamity passed." There proved to be few places of safety. As the battle reached the outskirts of Cambridge, Winthrop saw "the glistening instruments of death, proclaiming by an incessant fire, that much blood must be shed, that many widow'd & orphan'd ones be left."

Like the "crying," "bemoaning," and "animating" women of Cambridge, colonial women of every region moved quickly to aid in the mobilization for war. Their cooperation was vital, for the newly constituted continental government had few resources and would rely heavily in the beginning on popular contributions to equip its army. Patriot women found that several areas of household production shifted easily into wartime production. Sewing circles redirected their efforts, causing fancy embroidery on fancy linen to give way to the plain stitching necessary for soldiers' shirts. As a result, continental soldiers, most of them farmers and laborers, could be seen parading in uniforms made of rich fabrics originally intended for Sunday suits or ladies' gowns. Girls and their mothers took up knitting, producing stockings and gloves for the soldiers. Acting as a sort of volunteer quartermaster corps, women of all ranks mounted drives to collect basic, essential materials, asking other housewives to contribute pewter plate, candlesticks, and ordinary window weights to be melted down for cannonballs and shot. One New England woman, eager to contribute metal for bullets, melted down not only her pewter tableware and her clockweights but all the nameplates from her family's tombstones.

As always, the most assertive efforts by women proved disconcerting to some men. While the Philadelphia physician Dr. Benjamin Rush applauded the fund-raising efforts of his wife and her genteel friends, praising them for "at last becom[ing] principals in the glorious American controversy," the newly appointed commander in chief, General George Washington, was less enthusiastic. Washington's personal vision of female patriotism belonged to those who could be passive and admiring, and who could quietly suffer through the turbulence of war. When Philadelphia's Julia Stockton Rush, Sally Bache, and Esther DeBerdt forwarded to Washington the money they had collected, he felt obligated to thank them graciously. He refused, however, to acknowledge their accompanying letter, which audaciously instructed him on the allocation of those funds.

Soon, however, the growing shortage of essential household supplies began to absorb women's energies. As Britain moved to cut off the colonies' regular channels of trade, sugar began to disappear from tables, and salt, pins, molasses, and medicine vanished. The problems were exacerbated by merchants who took advantage of the situation and began to hoard their stock, hoping to charge higher prices as the scarcity increased. Women responded angrily. In East Hartford, Connecticut, twenty women marched in "martial array & excellent order" on a shop where a store of sugar was being kept. Although the owner insisted that the sugar was being held for the American Army, the protesters were unconvinced. They "requisitioned" 218 pounds of his supply. Similar stories followed from across the regions. In 1777 a Poughkeepsie, New York, merchant was rumored to be hoarding sugar. When his wife tried to avoid a confrontation by offering to sell the cache at four dollars a pound, local women were unsatisfied. Accompanied by two continental soldiers, a crowd of twenty-two women demanded entry to the merchant's home, saying that they would have the sugar "at their own price." Armed with a hammer and scales, they proceeded to weigh the sugar they wanted and to leave behind a far smaller sum than the anxious woman had suggested. The following year, almost a hundred women assembled with a cart and marched to the warehouse of a wealthy Boston merchant suspected of hoarding coffee. When he refused to turn over the keys to his storerooms, the women seized him by the neck and tossed him into the cart. They quickly relieved him of the keys, opened the warehouse, hoisted out the coffee, loaded it into the cart, and drove off. As Abigail Adams reported, "A large concourse of Men stood amazed silent Spectators."

In the long run, attacks on shops and warehouses proved useless, for merchants' supplies rapidly dwindled. In these circumstances, women's ability to improvise proved more important than their "oeconomy." The most serious threat was the absence of a salt supply, since colonial families relied on salt to preserve meat over the winter. Experimentation proved that a lye extracted from walnut ashes could be used as a preservative, although it did little to improve the taste of the food. Other substitutes followed, including sage and herb teas and an ersatz rum made from corn syrup for local army use.

In the end, of course, it was the absence of men, not of supplies, that taxed women's resourcefulness. Some had encouraged that absence. As one Philadelphia woman proudly wrote: "I will tell you what I have done . . . My only brother I have sent to the American camp with my prayers and blessings. I hope he will not disgrace me . . . and had I twenty sons and brothers they should go." Others were filled with regret. But whether they had resisted the military service of husband or father or encouraged it, the war left women alone with the responsibilities of home, farm, or shop and family in circumstances that were daunting. Inflation quickly ate up the ordinary family's savings, and a soldier's pay, though faithfully sent home whenever it was actually received, could not support that family. By 1778 it was said that four months' pay could not purchase a single bushel of wheat. Enlisted men received letters daily, demanding or pleading for their return. In a rush of words, one such desperate wife poured out a litany of grievances: "I am without bread, and cannot get any, the Committee will not supply me, my children will starve, or if they do not, they must freeze, we have no wood, neither can we get any—*Pray Come Home.*" Faced with such realities, men often deserted, slipping out of camp as harvest time approached or disappearing at night as winter set in.

Not every husband would—or could—return home, however. Nor did every woman left to manage her husband's or father's affairs find the experience disastrous. There were, after all, profits to be made in wartime—armies to be fed and shortages of food to be overcome in the regions where fighting was concentrated. Especially in New England, where the fighting ended almost as soon as the war officially began, some women were able to turn a profit from a farm. For many more, there was satisfaction in simply preserving the family's farm or business through the long economic crisis. As one historian discovered, subtle changes in pronouns in the correspondence between wife and husband reflected larger changes in women's sense of their familial role. At first, thinking of herself as a surrogate, or deputy husband, a woman might report to her husband on the condition of "his" farm or "his" crops. As months or years passed, that same woman slipped into a discussion of "our" farm and "our" crops. Not a few of them made the transition to a sense of hard-earned ownership that the young Eliza Lucas had made, that is, to "my" farm and "my" crop.

Throughout the war, the destruction of property wrought by an army on the move amazed civilians. The usually unflappable Eliza Lucas Pinckney was shaken by the ruin she saw around her in 1780–81 in the wake of British troop movements. Suffering was universal, she wrote, "crops, stock, boats, carts, etc all gone taken or destroyed." Circumstances were the same in Georgia. "Property of every kind has been taken from its inhabitants," wrote one survivor, "their Negros, Horses, & Cattle drove and carried away." And the demand that women open their homes to the quartering of troops meant further damage. A Long Island woman recorded the daily destruction of her property by the Hessian troops she had been forced to house. The soldiers "take the fence rails to burn, so that the fields are all left open, and the cattle stray away and are often lost; burn fires all night on the ground, and to replenish them, go into the woods and cut down all the young saplings, thereby destroying the growth of ages." When the soldiers, some of them living in her kitchen, received their monthly rations of rum, "we have trying and grievous scenes to go through, fighting, brawls, drumming and fifing, and dancing the night long." Friendly armies did as much damage as the enemy, as Loyalist Elizabeth Drinker discovered when a British officer commandeered her home. He put his own horses in her stable, moved into the front parlors, took over an upstairs room and the kitchen, and gave noisy dinner parties at her expense.

The loss of property was not the only thing to be feared when an army was near. Civilians, women in particular, felt so vulnerable to physical violence and to fatal disease that sometimes the mere rumor of an approaching army was enough to produce panic. In 1776 word that the British were sailing up the Chesapeake led to frantic efforts both to flee and to defend the city of Annapolis. "What with the darkness of night, thunder, lightning, and rain," wrote one woman, added to the "cries of women and children, people hurrying their effects into the country, drums beating to arms," the arrival of ships could be no more terrible than the preparation for it.

Such fears were well grounded. Smallpox and dysentery spread through Boston during the British occupation in 1775 and moved quickly into the surrounding countryside, killing women and children as well as soldiers and militiamen. Fires during the battle for New York City in 1776 left a quarter of the civilian population homeless. Although many of these civilians were women and children, gender was not the defining factor where disease or raging fires were concerned. But being female did make women vulnerable to rape. From the large-scale rapes documented in Fairfield and New Haven, Connecticut, in July of 1779 to the individual attacks reported in New Jersey or New York, the threat of physical violence against women was a persistent fear and a historical reality. Women of all ages were victims, from the thirteen-year-old raped by six soldiers to the backcountry matrons raped by Europeans disguised as Indians.

Women who had been raped were often reluctant to report the attack. The price for public disclosure was too high. As one Princeton man conceded, "Against both Justice and Reason We Despise these Poor Innocent Sufferers . . . Many virtuous women have suffered in this Manner and kept it Secret for fear of making their lives miserable." At times the women's reluctance was based on the futility of the disclosure rather than its potential damage to their reputation. In the fall and winter of 1776, for example, officers of the British occupying forces based on Staten Island and in New Jersey did little to halt the systematic and brutal rapes of local women reported to them. Indeed, cavalry commander Lord Rawdon preferred to cast the situation in lighthearted terms. "The fair nymphs of this isle [Staten Island] are in wonderful tribulation," he wrote to his uncle. "A girl cannot step into the bushes to pluck a rose without running the most imminent risk of being ravished." The results amused him greatly, he added, for "we have the most entertaining court-martials every day."

Women's impulse to flee from the military's presence was understandable, but many commented on its futility. The lesson Margaret Livingston learned when she fled New York only to reencounter the British in Connecticut was to "never move from the place providence has placed me in come what Foe that will." A North Carolinian echoed these sentiments: "The English are certainly at Halifax but I suppose they will be every where & I will fix myself here it is as safe as anywhere else & I can be no longer tossed about." A Pennsylvania woman put it bluntly to John Adams, in terms Grace Galloway would surely understand.

"If the two opposite Armys were to come alternately ten times," Adams recalled her saying, "she would stand by her Property untill she should be kill'd. If she must be a Beggar, it should be where she was known."

The presence of the army did not, of course, strike every woman with apprehension or fear. There was a benign aspect to military occupation that was as real in the experiences of some women as rape was for others. Young women from Winchester, Virginia, to Newport, Rhode Island, to Philadelphia recorded with pleasure the presence of an occupying army whose officer corps provided dancing partners, dinner guests, and opportunities for flirtation. One young woman admitted that "she wishe[d] there was to be [more war] if it were not for the shedding of blood." The war, as she understood it, was a seasonal ebb and flow of discomfort and delight: "They had a little fighting, to be sure, in the summer, but when winter came they forgot all the calamities of war and drowned their cares in assemblies, concerts, card parties, etc."

For African-American women, the impact of military occupation was equally unpredictable. For some, the opportunity for freedom arose from the disruption of white society's daily life. But in many cases, military occupation separated black families. As white families fled an enemy, they took their slaves with them—dividing black husbands and wives, parents and children in the process. In New York City, for example, few enslaved wives and husbands shared the same master. When rebel families fled from the city and Loyalists from the surrounding countryside fled to it, many black families were thus broken apart.

Not all wartime damage was due to the demands of the military or to its thoughtless abuse. As Grace Galloway could testify, Loyalist women suffered the loss of property and the fall into poverty at the hands of former neighbors. Their houses were plundered, their shops destroyed, their families sometimes ejected naked from their homes. For these women, the enemy never broke camp and moved on.

If the Revolutionary War came to the majority of women, it

is also true that a sizable minority went to it. Well over 20,000 wives, lovers, fiancées, and prostitutes filled both the American and the British army camps throughout the war, transforming these sites into bustling towns. The motives of these "camp followers" were various: some feared starvation if they remained at home, others Indian attack; some could not bear the loneliness or anxiety of not knowing their husband's fate; and some saw profit to be made from both sex and theft. Black women, sometimes accompanied by their children, came to the British army camps in a bid for freedom from their rebel masters. British officials encouraged these desertions by Southern slaves, offering sanctuary less out of humanitarian motives than in hopes of demoralizing rebel planters and disrupting the Southern economy.

Camp followers were considered necessary evils by British commanders, who understood the value of women. Their mercenary soldiers were less likely to desert if their wives and families came to war with them. Thus, the British institutionalized camp following, especially among their German troops, and allowed female civilians rations and supplies to bring aboard their transport ships. In their ledger books, ship officers carefully recorded the women and the expenses they accrued as "baggage."

The American commanders liked camp followers no better than their enemies did, although they, too, acknowledged their usefulness. A wife in camp could promise a reliable soldier. Indeed, American commanders were not above keeping enslaved African-American women hostage in the camps to ensure that their soldier-husbands did not desert. And women in the camps could be enlisted as nurses, cooks, launderers, and food foragers —a menial labor force skilled in domestic arts and also willing to take on the unpleasant duty of stripping the enemy dead for useful items. Despite women's service to the army, supply sergeants begrudged the extra rations, skimpy though they were, that they doled out to women. Their concerns were not entirely unreasonable, of course. Supplies at winter camps such as Valley Forge were scarce and women and children were unwelcome extra mouths. In addition, army officers had to grapple with the very real problems caused by campsite prostitution: disease, theft, and black-market sales of soldiers' liquor to the Indians in exchange for supplies. The prostitutes who flocked to Washington's army in New York reached alarming proportions, and several soldiers were killed at or near their reputed meeting grounds. The colonel responsible for breaking up fights between soldiers and women called his mission "Hell's work." Frustrated by the endless trouble, he railed against the "bitchfoxy jades, jills, haggs, [and] strums" who defied his regulation.

General Washington, in particular, fumed about camp followers, regularly complaining that pregnant women, small children, chickens, dogs, and domestic paraphernalia drastically diminished his army's mobility. On occasion, his orders that women march separately from men and through a city's back streets and alleys sparked resistance. One Philadelphia observer reported that the women and children were "spirited off into the quaint, dirty little alleyways and side streets. But they hated it. The army had barely passed through the main thoroughfares before these camp followers poured after their soldiers again, their hair flying, their brows beady with the heat, their belongings slung over one shoulder, chattering and yelling in sluttish shrills as they went and spitting in the gutters."

This observer, like many commentators, saw the camp followers through a biased lens of gentility. As many soldiers were drawn from the working or impoverished ranks of society, their wives were unlikely to exhibit the social graces of the eighteenth-century lady. And the presence of prostitutes among their ranks marked the soldiers' wives as "sluttish" by association. When the wives of high-ranking officers, including General Washington's Martha, arrived to spend the winter camp months with their husbands, these ladies were treated far differently than the wives of enlisted men.

Enlisted men, on the other hand, and sometimes their immediate officers, developed an admiration for camp followers. A soldier's wife asked no special treatment—and received none. Her rations were sparer, her blanket no warmer, and she was expected to endure the misery of lice, dysentery, and long marches without complaint. When a woman proved more durable than her husband, the soldiers readily acknowledged her fortitude. A sergeant's wife won the admiration of one observer as they crossed a swamp on Benedict Arnold's harrowing march to Canada. "Now Mrs. Grier," he recalled, "had got before me. My mind was humbled, yet astonished, at the exertions of this good woman. Her clothes more than waist high, she waded before me to firm ground." Despite the lifting of her skirts, this camp follower remained "a virtuous and respectable woman" in the eyes of the soldiers she accompanied.

Many of the Mrs. Griers saw combat and did battle. As water and ammunition carriers, the wives of soldiers sometimes observed the moment of their widowhood and took up their dead or dying husband's place on the battlefield or beside the cannon. Known generically as "Molly Pitchers," because of the water they carried to cool the cannons and to quench the men's thirst, a number of these women filed for pensions from the government for their service. Among them were invalids left crippled by their war wounds. Few were compensated, although in July 1779, Congress did grant a military pension to Margaret Corbin, who had been hit by grapeshot at her husband's post, captured by the British, and left completely disabled by her injuries.

Wives like Margaret Corbin, Mrs. Grier, and Mary "Molly Pitcher" Ludwig may have participated in the Revolution out of loyalty to, or dependence on, their husbands rather than out of a political commitment to national independence. They also may have entered the military camp with loyalty to a political cause as well articulated and elaborated as their husband's. Since they have not left a record of their personal motives, we cannot be certain. Women's applications for military pensions, and the many petitions received from women by local, state, and national governments requesting compensation for requisitioned property or relief from poverty suggest that women were deeply conscious of the services given and sacrifices made to the creation of an independent nation. Whether patriotism is synonymous with political consciousness is perhaps the question. What can be said is that these women had made direct individual contributions to the public good, to the larger commonwealth rather than to the "little commonwealth" of family, and they wished their role to be acknowledged.

Some women found other ways to serve the military. A few set aside their society's gender boundaries completely, donning men's clothing—assuming a male identity—to enlist in the American Army. The most famous of these women, Deborah Sampson Gannett, saw active service as Robert Shirtliffe until she was revealed as a woman by a physician tending to her fever. Gannett slipped with similar ease back into a female role, marrying in the postwar years and bearing several children. How many other white women saw battle as men is unknown.

A significant number of white women chose to use their society's gender-based assumptions to advance the cause they supported. As spies and saboteurs, some women used their femininity as a disguise to gather intelligence and convey sensitive information. Their stories are numerous and frequently told. Some of these spies acted spontaneously, seizing the opportunity to obtain critical information about the enemy in their midst. In South Carolina, for example, a fifteen-year-old farmer's daughter named Dicey Langston outwitted the Loyalist troops who had camped beside her family's farm. As she went about her daily chores, she took careful note of the troops' number, their supplies, and even their morale. She conveyed this information to American forces in the neighboring county. It was several months before the Loyalists realized who the spy among them was. And in Philadelphia, Lydia Darragh made similar use of the enemy's shortsightedness to serve General Washington. Officers of the British occupying army paid little attention to Darragh as she served their evening meals. While they talked strategy and made plans for their spring campaign, Darragh listened and remembered. She passed along almost verbatim accounts to George Washington, smuggling messages past unsuspecting British soldiers by sewing them into the linings of her pockets.

Sometimes it was a girl's youth, sometimes a woman's old age that made her invisible to an enemy who assumed that women, being women, were passive onlookers rather than Revolutionary participants. Not infrequently, however, American forces made the same mistake. One of General Henry Clinton's most dependable spies, Ann Bates, spent three years visiting American army camps as a peddler, counting men, supplies, and artillery as she sold her wares.

Most of these women spies acted on their own initiative, unable to resist or to avoid the opportunity and what they saw as their obligation to sabotage the enemy. But there were organized spy rings as well. The most elaborate of these, the Culper Ring, was based in New York, where fighting in the first year of war was fierce and the British occupation of the area was long. The ring established itself in 1778 on the strategically located Long Island Sound, which linked Connecticut and New York. At the center of the operation was a Mrs. Anna Strong, whose property, at Strong's Neck, Long Island, lay near several inlets where supply boats from American-held Connecticut might land and remain overnight undetected. Mrs. Strong acted as a signal woman, employing the most mundane domestic chores to fulfill her assignments. When the coast was clear of British patrols, she went to her clothesline and hung her black petticoat along with an agreed-upon number of white handkerchiefs. Although the head of the ring was a man, the majority of its operatives were women, for they were better able to enter and leave occupied New York City without raising suspicion. The domestic tenor of the Culper Ring activities—its baskets of fruit and food carried to city relatives, its laundry-line messages—belied the dangers of participation. In 1779 one of the women, known to us only by her code number, 355, was captured and imprisoned on the British prison ship *Jersey*.

Like most of the prisoners of war crammed into the ship's hold, agent 355 did not survive.

In 1781, General Lord Cornwallis surrendered to General George Washington and the British abandoned their efforts to restore the rebellious colonies to the empire. Sporadic fighting continued for months, but Americans and their former rulers understood that independence had been won. If defeat was a blow to English pride and to British power at home, it was far more intimately experienced by Loyalist women and men, whether European, African-American, or Indian.

Throughout the war, much of white Loyalist women's experience was a mirror image of patriot women's experience. During the pre-Revolutionary protests, some Loyalist women had been drawn into political activism, defending their rights to sell or consume British goods as they saw fit. Some had stood beside the windows of their homes, watching patriot crowds gather, waiting to see if their houses would be destroyed, their possessions looted, their husbands and fathers harmed. When the war began, Loyalist women served as spies, saboteurs, and couriers for the British; they flocked to British army camps; and they died or were wounded during battle. Like patriot women, some made self-conscious and autonomous choices to preserve their political loyalty. Among them were the newspaper editors Margaret Draper and Anne Catherine Greene, who fully and publicly asserted their loyalism, and three New York property owners—Margaret Inglis, Susannah Robinson, and Mary Morris—who were cited in the 1779 New York Act of Attainder and who lost their entire estates as a result. Some came to Loyalism as a consequence of their familial or marital ties. Even then, a woman might feel the pull of conflicting loyalties. Esther Sewall, for example, was a daughter of the patriotic Quincy family and sister-in-law to John Hancock, but the wife of Massachusetts's leading Crown propagandist. Marital loyalty carried her into exile in 1775.

For African-American women, the choice of loyalties was based on different considerations than those of white women. In a search for their own freedom, enslaved women took advantage of any opportunity the divisions between patriot and loyalist offered. Some supported an American victory, in hopes that the confiscation of their Loyalist master's estate might make their emancipation possible. But Loyalism was more often the best choice. The British had courted black support from the beginning of the war, promising freedom to all slaves who deserted rebel masters and benefits to black men willing to enlist with the British Army. With conscious irony, black Loyalist troops had marched to battle under the banner "Liberty to Slaves." Thus, when the British evacuated Loyalists from New York City at the end of the war, 3,000 African Americans boarded the transport ships headed for Canada. Over 900 were women, usually accompanied by children. Most of these former servants or slaves did not think of their departure as an exile but as a chance for a new beginning. Yet for many the costs were high: permanent separation from family members who had not won their freedom, who had been captured or seized as booty by Revolutionary forces, or whose Loyalist masters took them to another location. When Phillis Halstead, for example, boarded a transport in New York Harbor, she carried with her a two-year-old daughter born free behind British lines, but if this thirty-five-year-old woman had a husband or older children they did not make the journey with her.

Native American women of the coastal regions also participated in a struggle to retain their independence that intersected with but was not joined to the colonists' struggle for nationhood. The conflict between Crown and colonies left the Indians few and limited choices: American independence meant certain and immediate white expansion into tribal territories, while a British victory promised only a delay, a pause in the struggle to preserve their own autonomy. Most tribes chose to support the British, although some, like the Cherokee and two tribes of the Iroquois Confederation, cast their lot with the colonists. Thus, Indian women became Loyalists through diplomacy rather than direct commitment to the Crown.

The defeat of the British drove both white and black Loyalist women from their homes in the newly independent nation. War veterans of both races were given land grants in Canada, and British transports carried the refugees to Newfoundland and Nova Scotia. Here, African Americans experienced such intense racism, including physical violence and abuse of their legal rights, that a contingent left their land behind and relocated in Liberia. Other African Americans were less fortunate; viewed as captured booty by the officers and crew of the transport ships they boarded, these men and women were frequently resold into slavery in the Caribbean.

For white Loyalists, Canada was not refuge but exile. Leaving behind family, friends, neighbors, and familiar landscape and climate, they started new lives in the sparsely populated, forbidding land they called "Nova Scarcity." Their despair was captured in the words of one woman, who wrote: "I climbed to the top of Chipman's Hill and watched the sails disappear in the distance, and such a feeling of loneliness came over me that though I had not shed a tear through all the war, I sat down on the damp moss with my baby on my lap and cried bitterly."

The women who took refuge in England fared no better. Even the wealthiest and most prominent Loyalist men and women who began their exiles in England soon found themselves struggling to make ends meet. As their money or credit ran out, families moved frequently, each time to smaller, shabbier quarters. Husbands and fathers grew melancholy or morose, for they realized that their exile was permanent and their careers disrupted forever. Like Grace Galloway, these Loyalists had lost their place in society.

Loyalist widows in both England and Canada faced the complex and confusing task of filing claims with the British government for their pensions and for compensations for their husbands' loyalty or service and often for their own. These claims are riddled with worries of poverty and isolation, and the same anxiety over their children's futures that Grace Galloway felt. If widowhood left one Boston woman unhappy, she was certain that "what adds to my affliction is, my fears for my Daughter, who may soon be left a Stranger and friendless." And begging assistance from the British treasury, a New Jersey woman wrote of "the inexpressible mortification of seeing my children in want." For these women, and for all those like them, the struggle continued long after peace was declared.

Had the war ended for patriot women? In the decades after the Peace Treaty of 1783, the answer appeared to be this: The war was over, but the impact of the Revolution upon the roles, behaviors, expectations, and identity of American women was just beginning.

FAIR DAUGHTERS OF COLUMBIA:
WHITE WOMEN IN THE NEW REPUBLIC

THE AMERICAN REVOLUTION ENDED in 1783. But
for most ordinary Americans, war did not segue smoothly
into peace. Economic crises, both regional and national, marred
the first decades of the new republic. In New England, wartime
markets for local farm products contracted and farm families found
themselves struggling to meet mortgage payments. British restrictions on the American carrying trade brought New England ship-
building to a standstill, leaving whole communities without
livelihoods. In the nearby middle states, urban artisans and laborers
were out of work and merchants struggled to collect the debts
owed to them. In the Southern states, the devastation brought by
two British campaigns and local civil war was evident everywhere—crops had been ruined, barns and stables burned, and
many white families suffered from the loss of their most valuable
asset: slaves. Backcountry settlers remained braced for warfare
despite the peace treaty with England, for they knew Indian resistance to American sovereignty was likely. These regional problems led one historian to call the postwar decades the "critical
period in American history." But many groups within American
society had other crises to grapple with. For example, African

Americans who had won their freedom through service to the military or in the emancipation programs that followed the Revolution in Northern states sought to establish their own community services and institutions and find employment in still-hostile environments. And in the West, Native Americans prepared for the inevitable encroachment upon their lands by white settlers. For some tribes this meant migration; for others, new warfare.

There can be little doubt that the immediate concerns of family survival, of rebuilding, restoration, and creation of communities preoccupied most women and men in postwar America. Under these circumstances, did anyone stop to consider the impact of the war on women's roles in the family or in society at large? There were, of course, Americans who did. For if the postwar decades were a critical period in reconstructing the everyday life of Americans, they were also an era of sustained debate over many critical political and social issues, among them the structure of the national government, the definition of citizenship, the role of slavery in the new nation—and the role women could and should play in a republic.

The women and men who took up the question of women's place in the new republic subjected customary assumptions about women's "nature" and women's role in the family and society to careful scrutiny. In speeches, sermons, novels, and essays, they reflected on the lessons of the Revolution for women of the next generation and argued the need for a new definition of womanhood suitable to a republic. This public discussion on women was intense, but it was relatively brief, and its impact is difficult to measure. Nevertheless, the arguments given voice by critics such as Susannah Rowson, Judith Sergeant Murray, Charles Brockden Brown, and Dr. Benjamin Rush tell us much about the legacy of the war. For if these critics did not speak for the majority, they addressed issues and analyzed ideas that were current and compelling in their society.

The women and men who chose to scrutinize gender roles and gender ideals came, not surprisingly, from the privileged classes. Educated, with time to devote to intellectual issues, they spoke for and of a "womanhood" they believed to be universal, although that womanhood was more often a reflection of their own social class. The social authorities to whom they addressed their arguments and with whom they debated or allied themselves were also members of the nation's elite. This fact influenced, in subtle but evident ways, the problems they defined, the solutions they proffered, and the scope of the changes they envisioned. Nevertheless, their demand for reforms in the laws restricting married women's rights, their insistence on the rational capacities and intellectual potential of women, and their effort to create a political space for women in the new republic went beyond the boundaries of their own social position. When, for example, Abigail Adams pressed her husband and his colleagues in Congress to ameliorate the dependency of married women by extending their property rights, she may have been thinking of problems facing a woman of her own circle—a "lady." But had such reforms been implemented, their impact would have reached every level of the American social hierarchy.

These reformers began with the assumption that women, no less than men, were capable of reasoned, moral behavior and thought. In this, they were the daughters and sons of the Enlightenment, with its emphasis on human beings' capacity to learn, to develop their intellect, and to refine their moral sense through nurturing instruction. From this assumption came an insistence that women's apparent intellectual inferiority and the frivolity or irrationality that opponents claimed to be innate were in fact the products of educational neglect. As Judith Sergeant Murray, a leading advocate of women's education, crisply put it: "Will it be said that the judgment of a male of two years old, is more sage than that of a female of the same age? But . . . as their years increased, the sister must be wholly domesticated, while the brother is led by the hand through all the flowering paths of science."

But if Enlightenment theory helped dispel the notion of women's natural limitations, experience proved an equally compelling basis for their arguments. During the Revolution, women had shown themselves capable of political commitment, of patriotic action, and, in the nonconsumption of British goods, of political morality in eschewing luxury and abandoning frivolity. Thus, reformers' arguments about women's capacities were made that much more convincing in light of their generation's recent experiences.

Reformers drew heavily upon what they believed to be the lessons of the Revolution: the need for both sexes to be resilient, flexible, and equipped with the skills to survive in times of crisis. They did not stress, however, what many ordinary women frequently stressed in their wartime recollections: that the Revolution had proved women could rise to the occasion in crises and tap hidden resources and abilities. Instead, the reformers read the Revolution as a warning that women must be carefully prepared for a crisis before it occurred. As the novelist Charles Brockden Brown put it, the desire to prepare for the future reflected "the common sense of a revolutionary era in which the unexpected was very likely to happen, in which large numbers of people had lived through reversals of fortune, encounters with strangers and physical dislocation."

How did Brown and his colleagues suggest that the survivors of one crisis prepare for the next? By nurturing personal independence. Yet if the reformers all agreed that independence was crucial, they did not always define it in the same manner. In her influential essays, collected in 1789 under the title *The Gleaner*, Judith Sergeant Murray defined independence in economic terms. "I would give my daughters every accomplishment which I thought proper," she wrote, "and to crown all, I would early accustom them to habits of industry and order. They should be taught with precision the art economical; they should be able to procure for themselves the necessaries of life; independence should be placed within their grasp." But others seemed to place less emphasis on practical preparation and more on the molding of a character that could withstand adversity. The dangers, they believed, lay in an upbringing that encouraged, or allowed, the development of a feminine character defined by frivolity, vanity, love of luxury, and reliance on charm and beauty. The antidote was a regimen encouraging such virtues as intelligence, good judgment, competence, economy, and modesty. Sometimes the formula called for both the practical and the moral. In works of fiction such as Charles Brockden Brown's 1799 novel *Ormond*, for instance, the heroine survived the unexpected loss of her father's fortune by an easy renunciation of "every superfluous garb and trinket," coupled with a skill at needlework that allowed her to earn a meager but honest living.

In the end, the balance tipped in favor of molding women's moral character rather than promoting their economic self-sufficiency. The ability of women to earn their livelihood faded from the discussion and independence became an issue of character. Thus, programmatic suggestions quickly narrowed. Reformers made few demands for changes in the law that might allow women greater control over property in their married years and in widowhood. They made few calls for expanded vocational opportunities. And on the issue of direct exercise of political independence, they were largely silent. Instead, the institutional *deus ex machina* of women's independence they endorsed was formal education. Murray, Brown, Rush, Timothy Dwight—all were staunch supporters of schooling for young women.

The emphasis on education and the refinement of moral character developed in the context of a broader but sometimes less clearly articulated debate over the nature of women's citizenship in a republic. That women had acted with political consciousness and as patriots in their own right was a fact of the Revolution few could ignore. But what political role was appropriate for women in peacetime? The question was not simply one of women's entitlement, although that surely was important. It was also a question of what contribution they could make to the survival of what many believed was a great, and potentially fragile, political experiment: a republic.

The parameters of this debate are important to consider: full political participation was never an option. Why this is so is less clear than it might seem. To argue that woman suffrage ran counter to tradition or custom, threatened viable gender-based divisions of labor, or challenged male dominance is only to say that it was a radical proposition. But, in fact, this radical reform was put into effect in one state with little opposition. In 1790 New Jersey adopted an election law that explicitly referred to voters as "he or she." By 1800, suffrage was the right of every "maid or widow, black or white" in the state. And some women exercised that right. In 1797, women played a critical role in a closely contested election in Elizabeth, New Jersey. Ironically, this activism led to the rescinding of voting privileges, for the loser in this election took his revenge in 1807, when he mounted a successful campaign to disenfranchise both women and African Americans. The grounds given for limiting suffrage on the basis of sex and race are instructive. As dependent groups within the society, both women and blacks were considered too easily manipulated by more powerful members of the community. Although New Jersey legislators thus reverted to older notions that dependent groups could not be full citizens, the question remains: why was one state's initial willingness to permit women's suffrage not replicated in any other state?

And if no other government was willing to grant women formal political rights, how was women's citizenship to be defined? Here, the connection to reformers' emphasis on moral character and education clearly emerges. For in the new republic women were to be assigned civic duties rather than accorded formal political rights. They would be named guardians of the virtues essential to the republic and socializing agents of the next generation. Women were to embody and to impart to husbands and children what the rhetoric of the day called "republican virtues" —simplicity, honesty, and a willingness to sacrifice for the sake of the nation. They were to nurture in their children, and most particularly in their sons, a patriotic devotion to representative government and a keen sensitivity to signs of tyranny or decadence in the nation's leadership.

Assigning to women the role of guardians of and instructors

in virtue resolved several troubling ambiguities. First, it allowed the nation to acknowledge women's contributions during the war without intentionally disrupting long-standing gender relations. Second, it enlisted the family in the service of a young and underdeveloped state. In addition, it diminished any potential opposition to women's formal education by providing that education with a clear purpose. Many critics of formal educational institutions for women voiced concern that intellectual pursuits would have a defeminizing effect on women. As one Boston minister bluntly put it: "Women of masculine minds have generally masculine manners." Opponents drew a vivid picture of the dire consequences of a curriculum that included geography, rhetoric, and English composition. The woman pictured was a mirror image of the emerging republican ideal, for she was "disgustingly slovenly in her person, indecent in her habits, imperious to her husband, and negligent of her children." With well-defined ends for women's education, however, the means were justified: if a good education prepared a woman to be a good mother and wife, an exemplar and conveyor of moral character, then it was an asset to the republic.

Who had elaborated this new civic role for women? What individuals or groups were the source of what came to be called "republican womanhood"? On this, historians disagree. Some see this new gender ideology as the handiwork of political leaders, and thus a role constructed for rather than by women. Others insist that republican womanhood was the creation of women themselves; a creation to be admired, considering the lack of political traditions women had to guide them. Neither Enlightenment philosophers nor the seventeenth-century English commonwealth men upon whom American male patriots so heavily and eagerly leaned outlined a political role for women. Indeed, these English thinkers most often used the *feminine* in apposition to the *virtuous*, arguing that political manliness led one to support a republic and to defend it, while effeminacy, with its love of luxury and its vulnerability to corruption and vice, led one to tolerate tyranny and accept political dependence. It was the task—

and the achievement—of postwar women in America to confront this identification of virtue with the masculine and corruption with the feminine and deprive it of its powers. Women, or a group of women speaking for their sex, molded a revolutionary role for themselves by placing "the mother, not the masses . . . as the custodian of civic morality." Perhaps the simplest, and best, explanation of the origins of republican womanhood is that it emerged out of a multitude of interactions between women and men and among members of the same gender, that it was the handiwork of political leaders and social critics, and that it bore the marks of self-interest, self-justification, and a postwar effort to understand the experiences of the Revolution.

It is also critical to remember that the broad social changes which predated the Revolution contributed powerfully to the issues raised and the solutions devised in republican womanhood. The rise of gentility by mid-century had already diminished the emphasis on housewifery in most prosperous households. Greater reliance on the purchase of household goods had given the wives and daughters of merchants, shippers, lawyers, planters, and gentlemen more leisure time. How this time should be spent was a subject of some controversy in the decades before the Revolution. Women's leisure hours could be spent socializing and refining the home environment. Or they could be spent attending to children and to the development of their character and values. Long before Judith Sergeant Murray wrote her *Gleaner* essays, Eliza Lucas Pinckney was applying Mr. Locke's theories of child-rearing to her oldest son. Or women could, with or without conscious articulation or consideration of the implications, use leisure to advance their own individual growth and satisfaction. An incipient credo of individualism was already evident among men of the new genteel classes. The clearest evidence of its entry into women's lives was the craze for reading novels. Before the Revolution, the allocation of women's leisure time and of their energies was a *private* matter. Genteel women were indeed often criticized and satirized as frivolous, extravagant, and selfish before the Revolution. But their sins were against their own good reputations or the reputations of their husbands. They were not sins against the body politic.

The Revolution altered this. It politicized leisure time and women's activities within it. And in the postwar years, Americans debated this issue in a vocabulary highly charged with morality and patriotism. A political crisis had transformed the question of women's leisure time into a matter of civic concern. Women's capacity for and inclination toward extravagance could no longer be viewed as simply the failure of personal restraint. It now "raised questions about the continued independence and survival of the nation." "Mothers," proclaimed a minister in 1802, "do in a sense, hold the reins of government and sway the ensigns of national prosperity and glory." If this demonstrates the compelling nature of the Revolution and the creation of a republic, it also makes clear that the material out of which republican womanhood was constructed already existed in American society.

Measuring the impact of this new ideology is as critical as discovering its origins, and as difficult. Certainly, it was not internalized by the wives and mothers of the largest minority population in the new nation—African Americans—or among the oldest residents of what was now the United States—Indian women. The issues raised by republican womanhood had no context in the lives of enslaved women. And among the Northern and urban free black communities formed by private manumission, by state-mandated plans for abolition, and by escaped Southern slaves seeking refuge in Northern cities, very different issues of identity confronted both women and men. Their preoccupation lay in testing the limitations and opportunities of freedom, in shaping institutions such as the family and the church to their own needs and desires, and in negotiating relationships with the larger white community. Republican womanhood was based upon the assumption that a wife and mother operated within a secured family circle, unthreatened by the separation of a wife from her husband or a mother from her children. It depended as well on the notion that the sons of a republican woman, once carefully educated, would take their place as full citizens in the new society.

These were not the circumstances in the free black communities of Philadelphia or New York.

Native American women might find, in their fierce loyalty to clan or tribe, a spirit analogous to the patriotism that underlay republican womanhood. But in any form it took, the ideology of the victors would have been rejected by Indian women whose families, homes, and cultures were imperiled by American independence. After the last British forts vanished from the Ohio Valley, the remaining tribes had no ally to support their claims on Western lands. Even among the few tribes who had supported the Revolution, the price of survival was often the steady erosion of traditional gendered divisions of labor and family power. Among the Catawba, for example, women were slowly squeezed into English gender molds. For Catawba women, struggling to retain their own family names and pass them on to their sons and daughters and to remain active agents of commerce and land management within their community, the opportunity to be lauded as self-sacrificing mothers and wives—the hallmarks of republican womanhood—would be more ironic than rewarding.

Republican womanhood was, therefore, a set of gender roles and ideals that could evoke a positive response only within white communities. But even there, questions remain about the extent of its reception and the consequences of its adoption. If the tenets of republican womanhood were actually incorporated into the daily lives of the white families of America, did they reorder the hierarchy of women's domestic roles? Was mothering valorized at the expense of what colonial society called "notable housewifery"? Did women acquire greater self-esteem from their role as educators and guardians of patriotism than they once had from their duties as household producers and frugal household managers? Were there hidden costs to this new civic role? It is possible, for example, to read the didactic literature of republican womanhood as a literature of restraint, by which women are exhorted to curtail passion and to renounce the sensuality of the material world for a reasoned and simple life of virtue. It has also been suggested by some historians that republican womanhood de-

manded that women sacrifice individualism on the altar of patriotism, just as a new ideology of healthy self-interest and individualism was gaining strength among white middle-class and
elite males. If these men began to endorse self-interest as a more
effective means of ensuring the republic than communal loyalties
and self-sacrifice—and, by the nineteenth century, they did—
then what civic value could republican womanhood continue to
claim?

The extent to which republican womanhood was actually embraced or adopted by white Americans is the last of many uncer-
tainties. Women without leisure time and without the resources
to acquire formal education could not meet the demands of the
ideology. The thousands of war widows whose petitions for relief,
compensation, or pensions went unanswered by state and national
governments were keenly aware of the fact that they had "don
much to Carrey on this war." However, their political consciousness did not translate into a contentment with raising patriotic
sons and daughters. Even among the privileged classes, diaries and
letters indicate that the definition of "virtue" heeded by many
women did not arise from republican womanhood but from a
religious ethic that long predated the war. Christian morality
rather than civic morality lay at the core of the education these
well-to-do mothers provided their children.

Perhaps the most telling fact is that republican womanhood—
which kept alive women's right to follow political developments
and form political judgments—did not appear to outlive the Revolutionary generation. In the early decades of the nineteenth century, a Boston matron looked back on her childhood in the
earliest days of the new republic. In particular, she recalled the
odd fact that the women in her family—her mother and aunts—
had been interested in politics. She could remember their frequent
political discussions, although the content had long ago faded from
memory. Political discussion was a tradition, she quickly added,
that she had not fostered in her own household. For this woman,
and for others of her generation, the Revolution had been relegated to a historical event that no longer influenced their personal

lives. Whatever exigencies had prompted their grandmothers to become "great politicians" no longer seemed relevant in their own lives. "In my opinion," wrote one young woman in 1801, "[political subjects] are altogether out of a lady's sphere." It remained for the daughters of these women to rediscover and expand women's place in the civic and political realms of American society later in the nineteenth century.

BIBLIOGRAPHICAL ESSAY

CHAPTER 1: IMMIGRANTS TO PARADISE: WHITE WOMEN IN THE SEVENTEENTH-CENTURY CHESAPEAKE

In the late 1970s a new scholarship on the colonial South emerged. By the end of the 1980s, that scholarship had succeeded in ending the "New Englandization" of colonial history. Through demographic studies and the examination of court records, wills, and material culture, this new group of scholars overcame the absence of more traditional sources such as diaries, letters, sermons, and political tracts in drawing their portraits of the region's people, economy, and culture. Their work reflected the techniques and focus of the new social history, for in the resulting articles and books they reconstructed birth and death cycles, traced inheritance patterns, and looked closely at the division of labor in daily work life. This attention to issues such as community building, family structure and formation, and the establishment and transmission of culture made women central rather than marginal figures. Two collections of articles, published some nine years apart, are a good measure of the field's development. The first is Thad Tate and David Ammerman, eds., *The Chesapeake in the 17th Century: Essays in Anglo-American Society* (Chapel Hill: University of North Car-

olina Press, 1979); the second is Lois G. Carr, Philip Morgan, and
Jean B. Russo, eds., *Colonial Chesapeake Society* (Chapel Hill: Uni-
versity of North Carolina Press, 1988). The former contains path-
breaking articles on women, including Lorena Walsh's " 'Till
Death Us Do Part': Marriage and Family in Seventeenth Century
Maryland," and Darrett B. and Anita H. Rutman's "Now-Wives
and Sons-in-Law: Parental Death in a Seventeenth Century Virginia County." The more recent of the two volumes has James
Horn's "Adapting to a New World: A Comparative Study of
Local Society in England and Maryland, 1650–1700," and Lorena
Walsh's "Community Networks in the Early Chesapeake." The
authors in these two collections form the core of a highly productive group of scholars who work collaboratively and individ-
ually on the history of the Chesapeake.

Demographic studies are the basic building blocks in seventeenth-century Chesapeake women's history. Among the most
important articles are: Russell Menard, "Immigration to the Chesapeake Colonies in the Seventeenth Century: A Review Essay,"
Maryland History Magazine LXVIII (1973); Lorena Walsh and Russell R. Menard, "Death in the Chesapeake: Two Life Tables for
Men in Early Colonial Maryland," *Maryland Historical Magazine*
LXIX (1974); Darrett B. and Anita H. Rutman, "Of Agues and
Fevers: Malaria in the Early Chesapeake," *William and Mary Quar-
terly*, 3d Series, XXXIII (1976); and on black immigrants, Rus-
sell R. Menard, "The Maryland Slave Population, 1658 to 1730:
A Demographic Profile of Blacks in Four Counties," *William and
Mary Quarterly*, 3d Series, XXXIII (1976), and Allan Kulikoff,
*Tobacco and Slaves: The Development of Southern Cultures in the Ches-
apeake, 1680–1800* (Chapel Hill: University of North Carolina
Press, 1986).

On the lives and experiences of seventeenth-century Southern
white women, see the overview article by Mary Beth Norton,
"The Evolution of White Women's Experience in Early America," which appeared in the *American Historical Review* 89 (1984).
Norton has just completed a large-scale research project on
seventeenth-century women entitled *Founding Mothers & Fathers:*

Gendered Power and the Forming of American Society (New York: Knopf, 1996). In addition, see the most often reprinted articles in the field of seventeenth-century women's history: Lorena Walsh and Lois G. Carr, "The Planter's Wife: The Experience of White Women in 17th Century Maryland," which originally appeared in the *William and Mary Quarterly*, 3d series, XXXIV (1977); Carole Shammas, "The Domestic Environment in Early Modern England and America," in *Journal of Social History* 14 (1980–81); Lorena Walsh, "The Experience and Status of Women in the Chesapeake, 1750–1775," in Walter J. Fraser, Jr., R. Frank Saunders, Jr., and Jon L. Wakelyn, eds., *The Web of Southern Social Relations: Women, Family, and Education* (Athens: University of Georgia Press, 1985). See also Lois G. Carr, Russell R. Menard, and Lorena S. Walsh, *Robert Cole's World: Agriculture and Society in Early Maryland* (Chapel Hill: University of North Carolina Press, 1991), from which the information on Mary Cole was gleaned. For a critique of the literature on Southern colonial women, see Carol Berkin, "Clio's Daughters: Southern Colonial Women and their Historians," in Catherine Clinton and Michelle Gillespie, eds., *The Devil's Lane: Sex and Race in the Early South* (Oxford University Press, forthcoming).

Women's legal status and inheritance rights have been the subject of several important studies in the last decade. The work is often daunting, since it requires competence in both women's history and legal history and because the variation from colony to colony, region to region, and sometimes decade to decade are so great that few generalizations can be made from the case study of one colony or one court. Nevertheless, a reader interested in the subject can profit from reading Lois G. Carr, "Inheritance in the Chesapeake," and Carole Shammas, "Early American Women and Control over Capital," both in Ronald Hoffman and Peter J. Albert, eds., *Women in the Age of the American Revolution* (Charlottesville: University Press of Virginia, 1989). They can also read Marylynn Salmon, "The Legal Status of Women in Early America: A Reappraisal," *Law and History Review*, vol. 1 (1983).

On gossip and reputation, see Mary Beth Norton's insightful

article "Gender and Defamation in 17th Century Maryland," *William and Mary Quarterly*, 3d Series, XLIV (January 1987). See also Clara Ann Bowler, "Carted Whores and White Shrouded Apologies: Slander in the County Courts of 17th Century Virginia," *Virginia Magazine of History and Biography* LXXXV (1977).

CHAPTER 2: GOODWIVES AND BAD: NEW ENGLAND WOMEN IN THE SEVENTEENTH CENTURY

New England provides historians with more traditional sources than any other region. Letters, diaries, sermons, newspapers, and books abound, allowing scholars the opportunity to explore the mental and affective world of their subjects as well as the institutions, political and military developments, and economies that constitute the external setting for these New Englanders. Nevertheless, the most fully drawn portraits of seventeenth-century New England women come from scholars who took advantage of court records, both civil and criminal, and who employed available material culture sources to reconstruct the daily life of colonial wives, daughters, and widows. The most ambitious reconstructions are Laurel Ulrich, *Good Wives: Image and Reality in the Lives of Women in Northern New England, 1650–1750* (New York: Alfred A. Knopf, 1982) and Lyle Koehler, *A Search for Power: The "Weaker Sex" in Seventeenth Century New England* (Urbana: University of Illinois Press, 1980). Working with some of the same sources, Ulrich and Koehler arrive at strikingly different conclusions about the quality of women's lives in early New England.

Women's roles in the great theological and institutional debates within New England Puritanism have been the subject of many studies. The Anne Hutchinson controversy has been covered in classic works such as Emory Battis, *Saints and Sectaries: Anne Hutchinson and the Antinomian Controversy in the Massachusetts Bay Colony* (Chapel Hill: University of North Carolina, 1962) and in Edmund Morgan, *The Puritan Dilemma: The Story of John Winthrop* (Boston: Little, Brown and Company, 1958), but more recent works have focused more fully on the gender aspects. See, for example, M. J. Lewis, "Anne Hutchinson, 1591–1643," in Catherine Clinton and G. J. Barker-Benfield, eds., *Portraits of American Women: From Settlement to the Civil War* (New York: St. Martin's Press, 1991); G. J. Barker-Benfield, "Anne Hutchinson and the Puritan Attitude Toward Women," *Feminist Studies* I (1973); Lyle Koehler, "The Case of the American Jezebels: Anne Hutchinson and Female Agitation During the Years of the Antinomian Turmoil, 1636–1640," *William and Mary Quarterly*, 3d Series, XXXI (January 1974); Margaret W. Masson, "The Typology of the Female as a Model for Regenerate Puritan Preaching, 1690–1730," *Signs* 2 (Winter 1976); Laurel Ulrich, "Vertuous Women Found: New England Ministerial Literature, 1668–1735," *American Quarterly* 28 (Spring 1976); and Stephen Grossbart, "Seeking the Divine Favor: Conversion and Church Admission in Eastern Connecticut, 1711–1832," *William and Mary Quarterly*, 3d Series, XLVI (October 1989). For a comparison of roles for women in the Quaker and Puritan sects, see Mary Maples Dunn, "Saints and Sisters: Congregational and Quaker Women in the Early Colonial Period," in Janet W. James, ed., *Women in American Religion* (Philadelphia: University of Pennsylvania Press, 1989).

Witchcraft and the witchcraft trials of 1692 have attracted the interest of scholars for many decades and prompted a variety of interpretations of the causes of the 1692 episode, the motives of both the accusers and the judges, the extent of witchcraft practice in colonial New England and its social meaning within the communities, not to mention some conflicting profiles of the typical "witch" within this society. See Marion Starkey, *The Devil in Massachusetts: A Modern Inquiry into the Salem Witch Trials* (New York: Doubleday & Company, 1949); Paul Boyer and Stephen Nissenbaum, *Salem Possessed: The Social Origins of Witchcraft* (Cambridge: Harvard University Press, 1974); Chadwick Hansen, *Witchcraft at Salem* (New York: G. Braziller, 1969); Carol Karlsen, *The Devil in the Shape of a Woman: Witchcraft in Colonial New England* (New York: Vintage, 1989); Kai Erikson, *Wayward Puritans: A Study in the Sociology of Deviance* (New York: Macmillan, 1966), and John Demos, *Entertaining Satan: Witchcraft and the Culture of Early New England* (New York: Oxford University Press, 1982).

A small but significant body of work exists on the legal and economic status of women in the region. Two studies of widowhood and its economic consequences are William F. Ricketson, "To Be Young, Poor and Alone: The Experience of Widowhood in the Massachusetts Bay Colony, 1675–1676," *New England Quarterly* 64 (1991); and Kim Lacy Rogers, "Relicts of the New World: Conditions of Widowhood in Seventeenth Century New England," in Mary Kelley, ed., *Woman's Place: Female Identity and Vocation in American History* (Boston: G. K. Hall, 1979). Two works that explore gender-based differences in criminal prosecution are C. Dallet Hemphill, "Women in Court: Sex-Role Differentiation in Salem Massachusetts, 1636 to 1683," *William and Mary Quarterly*, 3d Series, XXXIX (January 1982) and Henry B. Parkes, "Morals and Law Enforcement in Colonial New England," *New England Quarterly* V (1932).

While demography has been central to the portraits drawn of Chesapeake women, New England scholars are just beginning to work in this field. For a look at the potential of this approach, see Richard Archer, "New England Mosaic: A Demographic Analysis for the Seventeenth Century," *William and Mary Quarterly*, 3d Series, XLVII (October 1990). In a different vein, Karin Calvert's *Children in the House: The Material Culture of Early Childhood, 1600–1900* (Boston: Northeastern University Press, 1992) suggests the potential for understanding women's domestic life through the examination of material culture.

CHAPTER 3: THE SISTERS OF POCAHONTAS: NATIVE AMERICAN WOMEN IN THE CENTURIES OF COLONIZATION

The reconstruction of Native American women's experiences is a challenge to scholars trained in a discipline that relies on written sources. We have turned to anthropologists and ethnographers to gain a better understanding of the gender structures of Indian society and an appreciation of the role religion and ritual played in gender ideals for Native Americans and how that role has been conveyed to us as their historians. Thus, a reader interested in pursuing the subject ought to turn to such works as Robert S. Grumet, "Sunsquaws, Shamans, and Tradeswomen: Middle Atlantic Coastal Algonkian Women during the 17th and 18th Centuries," in Mona Etienne and Eleaner Leacock, eds., *Women and Colonization: Anthropological Perspectives* (New York: Praeger, 1980); Eleanor Leacock and N. Lurie, eds., *North American Indians in Historical Perspective* (New York: Random House, 1971); Judith Brown, "Economic Organization and the Position of Women among the Iroquois," in *Ethnohistory* 17 (Summer/Fall, 1970); A. A. Goldenweiser, "Functions of Women in Iroquois Society," *American Anthropologist* 17 (1915); and Bruce Trigger, "Iroquoian Matriliny," *Pennsylvania Archaeologist* 48 (1978).

The most useful written sources from the seventeenth and eighteenth centuries remain the reports, journals, and observations of Europeans, many of whom were priests and missionaries. Historians have learned to approach these sources with caution, for they are the products of a largely unexamined European and Christian cultural bias. Nevertheless, when used with care, these observations and commentaries are rich with information about everything from child-rearing practices to marital customs to the gendered division of labor within Indian cultures. The best collection of such sources, complete with annotations and introductions that place the document in cultural and historical context is James Axtell's excellent *The Indian Peoples of Eastern America: A Documentary History of the Sexes* (New York: Oxford University Press, 1981). Peter Nabokov's *Native American Testimony* (New York: Thomas Y. Crowell, 1978) is also a useful primary source collection. In addition, see Charles T. Gehring and Robert S. Grumet, "Observations of the Indians from Jasper Danckaert's Journal, 1679–1680, *William and Mary Quarterly,* 3d Series, XLIV (January 1987), and John Lawson's "A New Voyage to Carolina" (1709), reprinted in Hugh Lefler, ed., *North Carolina History Told by Contemporaries* (Chapel Hill: University of North Carolina Press, 1956). Historians have begun to analyze changes in the European stereotypes of Native American women and to attempt to reconstruct Indian women's roles within their communities without the European bias of early commentators. Two of the best of these new efforts are Theda Perdue's excellent "Indian Women: Old World Perspectives, New World Realities" (paper presented at the OAH Conference, April 1982) and E. McClung Fleming, "From Indian Princess to Greek Goddess: The American Image, 1783–1815," *Winterthur Portfolio* III (1967).

Interestingly, the focus of several of the most recent studies has been on white or black women assimilated into Indian societies. These include women who entered Indian culture voluntarily as runaway slaves or, initially, involuntarily, as captives taken during raids or in warfare. The most powerful attempt to understand the motives of captives who refused to be "redeemed," or ransomed back into white society is John Demos's remarkable study, *The Unredeemed Captive: A Family Story from Early America* (New York: Alfred A. Knopf, 1994). But see also James Axtell, "The White Indians of Colonial America," *William and Mary Quarterly*, 3d Series, XXXII (January 1975); Alexander Medlicott, Jr., "Return to This Land of Light: A Plea to an Unredeemed Captive," *New England Quarterly*, 38 (June 1965); and Norman J. Heard, *White into Red: A Study of the Assimilation of White Persons Captured by Indians* (Metuchen, N.J.: Scarecrow Press, 1973). For studies that include African-American assimilation into Indian culture, see Irving Hallowell, "American Indians, White and Black: The Phenomenon of Transculturation," *Current Anthropology*, 4 (December 1963); K. Porter, "Relations between Negroes and Indians Within the Present Limits of the United States," *Journal of Negro History* XVII (1932); and Pauline Strong, "Captives, White and Red, in Seventeenth Century New England" (paper presented at the Sixth Berkshire Conference on the History of Women, Smith College, Northampton, Massachusetts, June 1984). For an analysis of the captivity tradition in literature and in history, see Kathryn Zabelle Derounian-Stodola and James Arthur Levernier, *The Indian Captivity Narrative, 1550–1900* (New York: Twayne Publishers, 1993).

Many major studies of Indian tribes or of critical events in the history of Indian societies still have no entries under "women" in their indexes. However, there is a growing scholarship that effectively integrates women into the narrative and considers women's roles in the political and economic life of Indian societies. See especially Anthony F.C. Wallace's pathbreaking study, *The Death and Rebirth of the Seneca* (New York: Alfred A. Knopf, 1970); Daniel K. Richter, *The Ordeal of the Longhouse: The Peoples of the Iroquois League in the Era of European Colonization* (Chapel Hill: University of North Carolina Press, 1992); James H. Merrell, *The Indians' New World: Catawbas and Their Neighbors from European Contact through the Era of Removal* (Chapel Hill: University of North Carolina Press, 1989); Neal Salisbury, *Manitou and Providence: Indians, Europeans, and the Making of New England, 1500–1643* (New York: Oxford University Press, 1982); and J. Leitch Wright, Jr., *Creeks and Seminoles: The Destruction and Regeneration of the Muscogulge People* (Lincoln: University of Nebraska Press, 1986).

CHAPTER 4: IN A "BABEL OF CONFUSION": WOMEN IN THE MIDDLE COLONIES

As Jean Soderlund points out in her essay "Women in Eighteenth-Century Pennsylvania: Toward a Model of Diversity" (*Pennsylvania Magazine of History and Biography* CXV, 1991), women in the middle colonies have been caught between two regional female stereotypes: the New England housewife and the Chesapeake planter's wife. Nevertheless, recent work on New York, Pennsylvania, New Jersey, and Delaware women has gone far to help the emergence of a distinctive regional identity. For family and demographic patterns, see Robert V. Wells, "Quaker Marriage Patterns in a Colonial Perspective," *William and Mary Quarterly*, 3d Series, XXIX (July 1972); Stephanie Wolf, *Urban Village: Population, Community, and Family Structure in Germantown, Pennsylvania, 1683–1800* (Princeton: Princeton University Press, 1976); Daniel Snydacker, "Kinship and Community in Rural Pennsyl-

vania, 1749–1820," *Interdisciplinary History* XIII (Summer 1982);
Robert V. Wells, "Family Size and Fertility Control in Eighteenth
Century America: A Study of Quaker Families," *Population Studies*
XXV (1971); Joan Jensen, *Loosening the Bonds: Midatlantic Farm
Women, 1750–1850* (New Haven: Yale University Press, 1986);
and Barry Levy, *Quakers and the American Family: British Settlement
in the Delaware Valley* (New York: Oxford University Press, 1988).

The uniquely activist role women played within the Quaker
faith has been a subject of interest to several historians. See Mary
M. Dunn, "Women of Light," in Carol Berkin and Mary Beth
Norton, eds. *Women of America: A History* (Boston: Houghton
Mifflin, 1979); Mary M. Dunn, "Saints and Sisters: Congregational and Quaker Women in the Early Colonial Period," in Janet
W. James, ed., *Women in American Religion* (Philadelphia: University of Pennsylvania Press, 1989); and Jean Solderlund, "Women's
Authority in Pennsylvania and New Jersey Quaker Meetings,
1680–1760," *William and Mary Quarterly*, 3d Series, XLIV (Oc-
tober 1987).

The discussion of women's property rights, inheritance patterns, and economic strategies in widowhood in the middle colonies reflects the multicultural and highly commercialized character of the region. Dutch inheritance patterns are traced in David
E. Narrett, "Dutch Customs of Inheritance, Women, and the Law
in Colonial New York City," in William Pencak and Conrad E.
Wright, eds., *Authority and Resistance in Early New York* (New
York: New-York Historical Society, 1988) and in Linda Biemer,
*Women and Property in Colonial New York: The Transition from Dutch
to English Law, 1643–1727* (Ann Arbor: University of Michigan
Press, 1983). For Pennsylvania, see Marylynn Salmon, "Equality
or Submersion? Feme Covert Status in Early Pennsylvania," in
Berkin and Norton, eds., *Women of America: A History* and Mary-
lynn Salmon, *Women and the Law of Property in Early America*
(Chapel Hill: University of North Carolina Press, 1986). On widows, see the debate that emerges in Lisa Wilson (Waciega), "A
'Man of Business': The Widow of Means in Southeastern Pennsylvania, 1750–1850," *William and Mary Quarterly*, 3d Series,

XLIV (January 1987) and Deborah Gough, "A Further Look at Widows in Early Southeastern Pennsylvania," *William and Mary Quarterly*, 3d Series, XLIV (October 1987). Wilson develops her arguments more fully in *Life After Death: Widows in Pennsylvania, 1750–1850* (Philadelphia: Temple University Press, 1992).

Women's work roles, particularly among the poorer classes, are examined in Paul G.E. Clemens and Lucy Simler, "Rural Labor and the Farm Household in Chester County, Pennsylvania, 1750–1820," in Stephen Innes, ed., *Work and Labor in Early America* (Chapel Hill: University of North Carolina Press, 1988); in Sharon Salinger, " 'Send No More Women': Female Servants in Eighteenth Century Philadelphia," *Pennsylvania Magazine of History and Biography* CVII (1983); and in Carole Shammas, "The Female Social Structure of Philadelphia in 1775," *Pennsylvania Magazine of History and Biography* CVII (1983).

CHAPTER 5: THE RHYTHMS OF LABOR: AFRICAN-AMERICAN WOMEN IN COLONIAL SOCIETY

Historians of African-American women have done little work on the colonial era. Much of what we do know about black women in the seventeenth and eighteenth centuries comes from scholars interested in the demographic conditions that led to the development of relatively stable slave communities and slave families. While women are central to these interdependent institutions, they are often presented as instrumental figures rather than as the direct subjects of the narrative. Few of the articles that deal with African-American work patterns or with the free black populations of the North and South are directly focused on women. Much of the work done on the seventeenth century focuses on the origins of a clearly defined slave system and on the debate over when this system was set in place. For historians of women, therefore, the challenge lies in extrapolating information about their subjects.

For example, the lives of free black women and their families can be explored in works that argue for the existence of viable free black communities in the early decades of settlement in the Chesapeake region. See Warren Billings, "The Cases of Fernando and Elizabeth Key: A Note on the Status of Blacks in Seventeenth Century Virginia," *William and Mary Quarterly*, 3d Series, XXX (July 1973); Timothy Breen and Stephen Innes, *'Myne Owne Ground': Race and Freedom on Virginia's Eastern Shore, 1640–1676* (Chapel Hill: University of North Carolina Press, 1980); Douglas Deal, "A Constricted World: Free Blacks on Virginia's Eastern Shore, 1680–1750," in Lois G. Carr, Philip Morgan, and Jean Russo, eds., *Colonial Chesapeake Society* (Chapel Hill: University of North Carolina Press, 1988); Michael Nicholls, "Passing Through This Troublesome World: Free Blacks in the Early Southside," *Virginia Magazine of History and Biography* XCII (1984); Ross M. Kimmel, "Free Blacks in Seventeenth Century Maryland," *Maryland Historical Magazine* LXXI, no. 1 (Spring 1976); Robert Twombly and Robert Moore, "Black Puritan: The Negro in Seventeenth Century Massachusetts," *William and Mary Quarterly*, 3d Series, XXIV (April 1967); James Brewer, "Negro Property Owners in 17th Century Virginia," *William and Mary Quarterly*, 3d Series, XII (October 1955); and John Russell, "Colored Freemen as Slave Owners in Virginia," *The Journal of Negro History* I (July 1916).

The most important works of demography that help us understand women's life-cycle experiences and their role in the community are Russell R. Menard, "The Maryland Slave Population, 1658 to 1730: A Demographic Profile of Blacks in Four Counties," *William and Mary Quarterly*, 3d Series, XXXII (January 1975); Allan Kulikoff, "The Beginnings of the Afro-American Family in Maryland," in Aubrey C. Land, Lois G. Carr, and Edward C. Papenfuse, eds., *Law, Society and Politics in Early Maryland* (Baltimore: Johns Hopkins University Press, 1977); and Kulikoff's major synthesis of Southern African-American demography, *Tobacco and Slaves: The Development of Southern Cultures in the Chesapeake, 1680–1800* (Chapel Hill: University of North Carolina Press, 1986). Kulikoff's argument that slave communities were well established before the American Revolution is challenged by

Jean B. Lee in a provocative article, "The Problem of Slave Community in the 18th Century Chesapeake," *William and Mary Quarterly*, 3d Series, XLIII (July 1986). However, Philip Morgan's "Slave Life in Piedmont Virginia, 1720–1800," in Carr, Morgan, and Russo, *Colonial Chesapeake Society*, appears to corroborate Kulikoff's position.

Women's family life is also explored by other historians. Particularly useful are Darrett Rutman, Charles Wetherell, and Anita Rutman, "Rhythms of Life: Black and White Seasonality in the Early Chesapeake," *Journal of Interdisciplinary History* XI (Summer 1980); Herbert Foster, "African Patterns in the Afro-American Family," *Journal of Black Studies* XIV (December 1983); Merle G. Brouwen, "Marriage and Family Life: American Blacks in Colonial Pennsylvania," *Pennsylvania Magazine of History and Biography* XCIX (July 1975); Joan Gundersen, "The Double Bonds of Race and Sex: Black and White Women in a Colonial Virginia Parish," *Journal of Southern History* LII (August 1986); Cheryll Cody, "Naming, Kinship and Estate Dispersal: Notes on Slave Family Life on a South Carolina Plantation, 1786–1833," *William and Mary Quarterly*, 3d Series, XXXIX (January 1982); and Herbert Gutman, "Marital and Sexual Norms among Slave Women," in Nancy Cott and Elizabeth H. Pleck, eds., *A Heritage of Her Own: Toward a New Social History of American Women* (New York:.Simon and Schuster, 1979).

Work patterns and the gendered distribution of tasks have been examined by several historians. Their scholarship has allowed us to identify the distinctive organization of labor on tobacco plantations and rice plantations and to trace the shift in women's work roles between the seventeenth and eighteenth centuries. They have also allowed us to consider the impact of an internal slave economy, independent of the work performed for the slave masters. The best sources are: John T. Schlotterbeck, "The Internal Economy of Slavery in Rural Piedmont Virginia," in Ira Berlin and Philip D. Morgan, eds., *The Slaves' Economy: Independent Production by Slaves in the Americas* (London: Frank Cass & Co., 1991); Carole Shammas, "Black Women's Work and the

Evolution of Plantation Society in Virginia," *Labor History* XXVI (Winter 1985); Sarah S. Hughes, "Slaves for Hire: The Allocation of Black Labor in Elizabeth City County, Virginia, 1782 to 1810," *William and Mary Quarterly*, 3d Series, XXXV (April 1978); Philip Morgan, "Work and Culture: The Task System and the World of Lowcountry Blacks, 1700 to 1880," *William and Mary Quarterly*, 3d Series, XXXIX (October 1982); Philip Morgan, "Task and Gang Systems: The Organization of Labor on New World Plantations" and Lorena Walsh, "Economic Diversification and Labor Organization in the Chesapeake, 1650–1820," both in Innes, *Work and Labor in Early America.*

The publication of Ira Berlin and Ronald Hoffman's collection of articles, *Slavery and Freedom in the Age of the American Revolution* (Evanston: University of Illinois Press, 1983) was a major step in reconstructing the lives of African Americans in the last half of the eighteenth century and the early years of the republic. In that volume Gary Nash explored the impact of emancipation on Northern blacks in "Forging Freedom: The Emancipation Experience in the Northern Seaport Cities, 1775–1820"; Allan Kulikoff looked at black migration in "Uprooted Peoples: Black Migrants in the Age of the American Revolution, 1790–1820"; and Richard Dunn offered a portrait of "Black Society in the Chesapeake, 1776–1810." Other scholars have also focused on the impact of the war on African-American life and a few have looked explicitly at the experiences of black women during this era. See, for example, Debra L. Newman, "Black Women in the Era of the American Revolution in Pennsylvania," *Journal of Negro History* LXI (July 1976); Jean Soderlund, "Black Women in Colonial Pennsylvania," *Pennsylvania Magazine of History and Biography* CVII (January 1983), and Suzanne Lebsock, "Free Black Woman and the Question of Matriarchy: Petersburg, Virginia, 1784–1820," *Feminist Studies* VIII (1982).

Little work has been done on women's resistance to slavery in the mainland colonies. Gerald Mullin, *Flight and Rebellion: Slave Resistance in Eighteenth Century Virginia* (New York: Oxford University Press, 1974) examines male and female runaways and rebels, but the best source on women remains Betty Wood, "Some Aspects of Female Resistance to Chattel Slavery in Low Country Georgia, 1763–1815," *Georgia Historical Journal* XXX (September 1987).

CHAPTER 6: THE RISE OF GENTILITY: CLASS AND REGIONAL DIFFERENCES IN THE EIGHTEENTH CENTURY

Historians have documented the distinctive differences based on social class and region in the lives of eighteenth-century colonial white women. The most inclusive discussions of these differences can be found in Mary Beth Norton, *Liberty's Daughters: The Revolutionary Experience of American Women, 1750–1800* (Glenview, Ill.: Scott Foresman, 1980) and Cary Carson, Ron Hoffman, and Peter Albert, eds., *Of Consuming Interests: The Style of Life in the Eighteenth Century* (Charlottesville: University of Virginia Press, 1994). The reader should also look at Carole Shammas, "How Self Sufficient Was Early America?" *Journal of Interdisciplinary History* XIII (Autumn 1982) and at Lois G. Carr, "Diversification in the Colonial Chesapeake: Somerset County, Maryland, in Comparative Perspective," in Carr, Morgan, and Russo, eds., *Colonial Chesapeake Society*.

On the development of genteel family relations, Jan Lewis has written most extensively. See her full-length study, *The Pursuit of Happiness: Family Values in Jefferson's Virginia* (New York: Cambridge University Press, 1983), but see also her "Domestic Tranquillity and the Management of Emotion Among the Gentry of Prerevolutionary Virginia," *William and Mary Quarterly*, 3d Series, XXXIX (January 1982) and her joint study with Kenneth Lockridge, " 'Sally Has Been Sick': Pregnancy and Family Limitation Among Virginia Gentry Women, 1780–1830," *Journal of Society History* XXII (Fall 1988). Genteel child-rearing methods are central to Philip Greven's excellent study, *The Protestant Temperament: Patterns of Child-Rearing, Religious Experience, and the Self in Early America* (Chicago: University of Chicago Press, 1977) and to Ross W. Beales, Jr., "Nursing and Weaning in an Eighteenth Century

New England Household," The Dublin Seminar for New England Folklife, *Annual Proceedings*, 1985 (Boston: Boston University Press, 1987).

Changes in inheritance patterns and in the laws regulating women's right to own or manage property are the subject of numerous studies. For the best overview of the laws governing women's relationship to property, see Salmon, *Women and the Law of Property in Early America* and her review article, "The Legal Status of Women in Early America: A Reappraisal," *Law and History Review*. But see also the several fine studies of particular regions or localities, including: Lois G. Carr, "Inheritance in the Colonial Chesapeake," in Hoffman and Albert, eds., *Women in the Age of the American Revolution*; Jean B. Lee, "Land and Labor: Parental Bequest Practices in Charles County, Maryland, 1732–1783," in Carr, Morgan, and Russo, eds., *Colonial Chesapeake Society*; Linda Speth, "More than Her 'Thirds': Wives and Widows in Colonial Virginia," *Women and History* 4 (1982); Lisa Wilson, *Life After Death: Widows in Pennsylvania, 1750–1850*; Carole Shammas, "Early American Women and Control Over Capital," in Hoffman and Albert; and Lorena Walsh, "The Experiences and Status of Women in the Chesapeake, 1750–1775," in Walter J. Fraser, Jr., R. Frank Saunders, Jr., and Jon L. Wakelyn, eds., *The Web of Southern Social Relations: Women, Family and Education* (Athens: University of Georgia Press, 1985).

Historians have begun to look more closely at poverty, widowhood, and the opportunities for work available to women in economic need. See, for example, Alfred Young, "The Women of Boston: 'Persons of Consequence' in the Making of the American Revolution, 1765–1776," in Harriet Applewhite and Darlene Levy, eds., *Women and Politics in the Age of the Democratic Revolution* (Ann Arbor: University of Michigan Press, 1993); Carole Shammas, "The Female Social Structure of Philadelphia in 1775," *Pennsylvania Magazine of History and Biography* CVII (1983); Gary B. Nash, "The Failure of Female Factory Labor in Colonial Boston," *Labor History* XX (Spring 1979); Gloria Main, "Gender, Work and Wages in Colonial New England," *William and Mary*

Quarterly, 3d Series, LI (January 1994); and Gloria Main, "Widows in Rural Massachusetts on the Eve of the Revolution," in Hoffman and Albert.

CHAPTER 7: "BEAT OF DRUM AND RINGING OF BELL": WOMEN IN THE AMERICAN REVOLUTION

Women's participation in the decade of protest that preceded the Revolutionary War has been richly covered in the many books, both scholarly and popular, that began to appear as the bicentennial of the American Revolution approached. This intense interest in eighteenth-century women culminated in the publication of two major studies, Mary Beth Norton's *Liberty's Daughters* and Linda Kerber's *Women of the Republic: Intellect and Ideology in Revolutionary America* (Chapel Hill: University of North Carolina Press, 1980), works that set the parameters of discussion and debate about the topic for over a decade. Even before the bicentennial celebration spurred these modern authors, however, a nineteenth-century writer, Elizabeth Ellet, produced three volumes of biographical sketches entitled *Women of the American Revolution* (1848–1850). Ellet's work was a paean to the white, primarily elite women, like Martha Washington, who she believed inspired patriotic actions in their husbands and sons. The first scholarly examination of women's role in pre-Revolutionary activity also preceded the bicentennial by some three decades. In 1947, Elizabeth Cometti published an article that described the arenas of women's patriotic activity and the forms that activity took. Her "Women in the American Revolution," *New England Quarterly* XX (September 1947) remains the starting point for anyone interested in the topic. The best modern treatment can be found in Norton's *Liberty's Daughters.* Among the dozens of popular studies that have been published, the best are Elizabeth Evans, *Weathering the Storm: Women of the American Revolution* (New York: Charles Scribner's Sons, 1975) and Sally Smith Booth, *The Women of '76* (New York: Hastings House, 1973).

Few scholars since Cometti have analyzed the significance of

how women's Revolutionary participation sharpened their political consciousness or have traced the traditions women drew upon
when they protested and demonstrated, although Mary Beth Norton and I address these issues in our introductions to the essays in
Women of America. Two recent articles have focused our attention
on these issues: Alfred Young, "The Women of Boston: 'Persons
of Consequence' in the Making of the American Revolution,
1765–1776," in Applewhite and Levy, eds., *Women and Politics in
the Age of the Democratic Revolution*; and Laurel Ulrich, "Daughters
of Liberty: Religious Women in Revolutionary New England,"
in Hoffman and Albert, eds., *Women in the Age of the American
Revolution.* For an earlier analysis of women's participation in a
comparative perspective, see Carol Berkin and Clara Lovett, eds.,
Women, War and Revolution (New York: Holmes & Meier, 1980).

The best study of women camp followers remains Walter H.
Blumenthal, *Women Camp Followers of the American Revolution*
(New York, Arno Press, 1952). For the best discussion of the
problems engendered by a home-front war—scarcity and rape, in
particular—a reader can turn to Kerber's *Women of the Republic*
and to Mary Beth Norton, " 'What an Alarming Crisis Is This':
Southern Women and the American Revolution," in Jeffrey
Crow and Larry Tise, eds., *The Southern Experience in the American
Revolution* (Chapel Hill: University of North Carolina Press,
1978). A fuller sense of the impact of the war, particularly on
Loyalist exiles, can also be acquired from Mary Beth Norton,
"Eighteenth Century American Women in Peace and War: The
Case of the Loyalists," *William and Mary Quarterly*, 3d Series,
XXXIII (July 1976). For a discussion of the impact of the war
on African-American Loyalist refugees, see Vivian Kruger, "Born
to Run: The Slave Family in Early New York, 1626–1827" (1985
dissertation, Columbia University).

EPILOGUE: FAIR DAUGHTERS OF COLUMBIA: WHITE WOMEN IN THE
NEW REPUBLIC

The search for the significance of the Revolution in women's lives
has been as intense as the search for the significance of women in
the Revolutionary struggle. In the early 1970s, Linda Kerber published two important articles on a postwar shift in gender roles
and ideals to what she called "republican motherhood." Since the
publication of these essays, "Daughters of Columbia: Educating
Women for the Republic, 1787–1805," in Stanley Elkins and Eric
McKitrick, eds., *The Hofstadter Aegis* (New York: Alfred A. Knopf,
1974) and "The Republican Mother: Women and the Enlightenment—An American Perspective," *American Quarterly* XXVII
(Summer 1976), the debate over an ideological and functional
transition in women's lives during the Revolutionary era has continued unabated. The question of the nature, origins, and extent
of change has been linked to questions of a change in status for
women in the new republic. To explore this debate, the reader
can turn to the following: Joan Hoff Wilson, "The Illusion of
Change: Women and the American Revolution," in Alfred
Young, ed., *The American Revolution: Explorations in the History of
American Radicalism* (DeKalb: Northern Illinois University Press,
1976); Nancy Cott, *The Bonds of Womanhood: "Women's Sphere"
in New England, 1780–1835* (New Haven: Yale University Press,
1977); Norton, "Eighteenth-Century American Women in Peace
and War: The Case of the Loyalists"; Nancy Cott, "Divorce and
the Changing Status of Women in Eighteenth-Century Massachusetts," *William and Mary Quarterly*, 3d Series, XXXIII (October
1976); Mary Beth Norton, "The Paradox of Women's Sphere,"
in Berkin and Norton, eds., *Women of America*; and, finally, to the
two full-scale treatments of these issues, Norton's *Liberty's Daughters* and Kerber's *Women of the Republic*. For an analysis of the
historiography up to this point, the reader can turn to my
"Remembering the Ladies: Historians and the Women of the
American Revolution," in William Fowler, Jr., and Wallace
Coyle, eds., *The American Revolution: Changing Perspectives* (Boston:

Northeastern University Press, 1979). In 1987, Jan Lewis revived and altered this debate by challenging the centrality of motherhood to the new ideology for American women. In her provocative article, "The Republican Wife: Virtue and Seduction in the Early Republic," *William and Mary Quarterly*, 3d Series, XXXXIV (October 1987), Lewis argued that a woman's role as virtuous wife was the critical element in her new civic identity. Ruth Bloch argues for the same emphasis on a virtuous wife in two important articles, "American Feminine Ideals in Transition: The Rise of the Moral Mother, 1785–1815," *Feminist Studies* IV (1978) and "The Gendered Meanings of Virtue in Revolutionary America," *Sign: Journal of Women in Culture and Society* XV (Spring 1990).

Several historians have focused their attention on the material rather than the ideological impact of the Revolution on women of the new republic, framing the issue in terms of "gains" or "losses." This question of progress is central to Joan Hoff Wilson's article "The Illusion of Change," as it is to the meticulous and important work of Marylynn Salmon on women's legal rights and restrictions. The reader should turn to Salmon's " 'Life, Liberty, and Dower': The Legal Status of Women after the American Revolution," in Berkin and Lovett, eds., *Women, War and Revolution* and to her *Women and the Law of Property in Early America*. Carole Shammas picks up the question of women's economic and legal power after the Revolution in her article "Early American Women and Control over Capital," in Hoffman and Albert, eds., *Women in the Age of the American Revolution*. Other scholars have looked at the impact of the Revolution on women's educational opportunities. The best work on this subject is Ann D. Gordon, "The Young Ladies' Academy of Philadelphia," in Berkin and Norton, eds., *Women of America*, but readers should also turn to Kerber and Norton's 1980 studies for coverage of this important reform.

Recently, historians have turned their attention to the existence of a dichotomy between "public" and "private" spheres and its significance for women in shaping a civic or political identity. For an introduction to this aspect of the discussion, see Linda

Kerber, " 'I have Don . . . much to Carrey on the Warr': Women and the Shaping of Republican Ideology after the American Revolution," in Applewhite and Levy, eds., *Women and Politics in the Age of the Democratic Revolution*; "Beyond Roles, Beyond Spheres: Thinking about Gender in the Early Republic," a Forum in *William and Mary Quarterly*, 3d Series, XLVI (October 1989); and Cynthia S. Jordan, " 'Old Words' in 'New Circumstances': Language and Leadership in Post-Revolutionary America," *American Quarterly* XL no. 4 (December 1988).

INDEX

Adams, Abigail, 181, 197
Adams, John, 171, 184–85
African Americans: African traditions of, 104, 116; black life cycle of, 113–14; in Chesapeake colony, 103–19, 124; childbearing among, 110, 113; child-rearing among, 104, 114; creole (native-born) vs. immigrant slave experience of, 110, 112–13; family and kinship among, 110, 112, 113, 114–15, 118, 119, 125; free blacks, 104, 105–6, 109, 127–28, 137, 195–96; internal economy of slaves, 117–18; laws and, 109, 116; life expectancy of, 108; marriage among, 104, 109; midwives among, 113, 118; mortality of, 110; population of, 108–9; racial discrimination and, 107, 109; records of, 106–7; religion of, 104, 112, 117; after Revolution, 195–96, 203; in Revolution, 185, 186, 192; runaway slaves, 126–27; sex ratios of, 110, 112, 113;
slave culture of, 112–13, 118; slave quarters of, 113, 116–17; slave trade and, 103–4, 108, 109; slavery in North of, 124–28, 137, 140; slavery in South of, 138; on tobacco plantations, 103–11, 114; women's work of, 104, 111–12
Algonquin peoples, 55, 58, 61, 63–64, 69, 70, 75, 77
American Revolution, see Revolution, American
Andros, Edmund, 80
Anglican Church, 24, 27, 35–36

Bates, Ann, 190
Boston, 27, 38, 45, 47, 137, 138, 151, 153, 205; in Revolution, 174, 177, 178, 181, 193; slavery in, 124, 125
Brant, Sally, 100–1
Brown, Charles Brockden, 196, 198, 199

Canada, 43, 44, 75, 170, 171, 192, 193